UNSETTLING SIGHTS

UNSETTLING SIGHTS
The Fourth World on Film

Corinn Columpar

Southern Illinois University Press
Carbondale and Edwardsville

Printed in the United States of America
A portion of chapter 3 was originally published in "'Taking Care of Her Green Stone Wall': The Experience of Space in *Once Were Warriors*," *Quarterly Review of Film and Video* 24, no. 5 (October 2007). Lyrics of songs from the soundtrack of the film *Stryker* are reprinted with permission from Arbor Records.

13 12 11 10   4 3 2 1

Library of Congress Cataloging-in-Publication Data
Columpar, Corinn, 1970–
Unsettling sights : the fourth world on film /
Corinn Columpar.
     p. cm.
Includes bibliographical references and index.
ISBN-13: 978-0-8093-2962-5 (pbk. : alk. paper)
ISBN-10: 0-8093-2962-X (pbk. : alk. paper)
ISBN-13: 978-0-8093-8573-7 (ebook)
ISBN-10: 0-8093-8573-2 (ebook)
1. Indigenous films—History and criticism.
2. Indigenous peoples in motion pictures. I. Title.
PN1995.9.I49C65 2010
791.43'63529—dc22   2009023079

For Frederick

CONTENTS

Illustrations

PREFACE

In a talk delivered at the University of Auckland in 2002, pioneering Maori filmmaker Barry Barclay developed his notion of a Fourth Cinema by defining it against its First, Second, and Third counterparts, all of which he designates "invader Cinemas." An Indigenous phenomenon—"that's Indigenous with a capital 'I,'" notes Barclay—Fourth Cinema derives its potency from "ancient remnant cultures" that persist within, yet separate from, modern nation-states and thus offers up an outlook that is markedly distinct from that which informs the institutions that typically lend it financial and/or infrastructural support.[1] Given the scarcity of films that qualify as such, Barclay is the first to admit that Fourth Cinema is more of an ideal than an actuality, yet he puts stock in its eventual viability, concluding his talk with a vision for the future: "It seems to me that some Indigenous film artists will be interested in shaping films that sit with confidence within the First, Second, and Third cinema framework. While not closing the door on that option, others may seek to rework the ancient core values to shape a growing Indigenous cinema outside the national orthodoxy. I hope that, in the not too distant future, some practitioner or academic will be able to stand up in a lecture room like this and begin a talk on Fourth Cinema which begins at this very point, rather than ends on it."[2]

In light of Barclay's stated hope, the 2006 Toronto International Film Festival (TIFF) was an extremely encouraging event. With its opening night gala, a screening of Zacharias Kunuk and Norman Cohn's *The Journals of Knud Rasmussen*, and the Canadian premiere of Rolf de Heer's *Ten Canoes*, the festival featured prominently two films that capture incisively at their outset the imperative behind Fourth Cinema: to foreground the perspectives, experiences, storytelling traditions, and thus "core values" of the Indigenous characters at their center and thereby to divest those characters from a representational logic in which they can only ever function as two-dimensional savage (be it noble or not), ethnographic specimen, or absolute other.[3] In the case of *Ten Canoes*, iconic Australian Aboriginal actor David Gulpilil announces the film's agenda in its first minutes in his capacity as "the storyteller." Via voice-over narration that accompanies aerial shots of the wetlands of Arnhem Land, home to Gulpilil as well as the rest of the film's cast, he begins (in English), "Once upon a time, in a land far, far away . . ." At this point he bursts into boisterous laughter and changes his tack: "No, not like that. I'm only joking. But I am going to tell you a story. It's not your story. It's my story, a story like you've never seen before. But you want a proper story, huh? Then I must tell you something of my people and my land. Then you can see the story and know it." Like *Ten Canoes*, *The Journals of Knud Rasmussen* also begins with a representational form familiar to non-Indigenous viewers—in this case, an ethnographic artifact rather than the invocation of a time and place outside of history—only to undercut it from and with an Aboriginal perspective. In its opening scene, a group of Inuit congregate in front of the camera, alternately meeting its gaze, engaging with one another, and readying their surroundings for the photo about to be taken. Once their images are drained of both animation and color, assuming photographic form, one of the film's protagonists begins her voice-over narration (in Inuktitut): "I am called Usarak, though I was named Apak as a young woman, during the time of the story I am telling you now."

Yet as much as these films—and, by extension, TIFF in 2006—seem to realize Barclay's vision, they also complicate it, for neither *The Journals of Knud Rasmussen* nor *Ten Canoes* is as fully Indigenous as Barclay would like. First, despite the fact that Rolf de Heer collaborated extensively with the Yolngu community in the process of completing *Ten Canoes* (especially with Gulpilil, who was integral to its development, and with Peter Djigirr, who is credited as "co-director"), he is nonetheless named as the film's screenwriter, co-producer, and "director," which suggests that his was the last word during multiple stages of the film's production. Second, *The Journals of Knud Rasmussen* qualified for the much-coveted position of the festival's opening night feature by virtue of its status as a Canadian film, a designation that implicitly undermines the very sovereignty toward

- I am called Usarak,

Undercutting the ethnographic artifact in *The Journals of Knud Rasmussen*.
(Igloolik Isuma Productions/www.isuma.tv)

which Barclay's vision gestures. As a result, it necessarily ends up complicit in the same nationalist project that Monika Siebert associates with Kunuk and Cohn's prior feature, *Atanarjuat* (2001): the construction of Canada as "a multicultural democracy fully delivering on its claims of being a nation of distinct yet equal societies."[4]

As a result of mitigating factors such as these, Houston Wood prefers to speak of Indigenous filmmaking in terms of a continuum, with Indigenous film and non-Indigenous film constituting the poles that most productions fall between, rather than as a self-contained category. As he notes in his recent book *Native Features: Indigenous Films from around the World*, the capital-intensive, collaborative, intercultural, and transnational nature of cinema makes for a situation in which it is nearly impossible to conceive of a film that is shaped by Indigenous protocols or personnel on all relevant counts, from content to aesthetics, funding to cast and crew, mode of production to means of distribution. As a result, he employs a language of degrees when discussing the approximately fifty feature-length, narrative films that qualify for inclusion in his survey. While many of the films that make Wood's less rigorous cut would likely find a place within Barclay's categoric ideal as well, others—for example, *Whale Rider* (2002), which was directed by the white New Zealander Niki Caro, and *Rabbit-Proof Fence* (2002), made by white Australian Phillip Noyce—would not, since creative control did not ultimately rest with their Aboriginal participants. With his inclusive analytical approach, Wood throws into fresh relief both the potency and the limitations of Barclay's more stringent paradigm. As the linchpin of a polemic, Fourth Cinema, like the most politically uncompromising definitions of Third Cinema,[5] speaks persuasively to the ideological and aesthetic stakes of Indigenous cinema. As an actual taxonomic category, however, it inherits a problem fundamental to the three-cinema model from which it derives: the failure "to account for, let alone address . . . the interactions between varying forms of cinema within national industries diverse enough to sustain co-existing forms of First, Second, and Third Cinema."[6] Indeed, it is not only the first group of Indigenous filmmakers invoked by Barclay—those who choose to work within other cinematic modes—who demand a consideration of said "interactions." Necessarily engaged in a dialogic, even interdependent, interaction with a national cinema that may contain First, Second, and/or Third cinematic strains, Fourth Cinema inevitably does so as well.

Insofar as this book is dedicated, in the broadest of terms, to the construction and transnational circulation of Aboriginality as sign in contemporary narrative cinema, it is fundamentally concerned with interactions between Indigenous and non-Indigenous. Specifically, I take as my starting point Marcia Langton's incisive definition of Aboriginality as "a field of intersubjectivity in that it is remade over and over again in a process of dialogue, of imagination, of representation and interpretation," and I take as my object of examination the specific role that cinema plays within that field by way of the multiple intersubjective interactions it fosters: those that condition film production at any point along Wood's continuum; those that occur when heterogeneous audiences watch films that represent Aboriginal peoples and cultures (or, for that matter, that rely on them as a signifying absence); and those that emerge across an entire body of filmic work, be that body delimited in national or transnational terms.[7] The result is an identification of the conventions by which Aboriginality is represented and, in turn, an exploration of their legibility and resonance outside as well as inside the specific national contexts in which they are employed. In the process, Aboriginality emerges as a concept with (potentially) universal currency, as grounds for not only a stereotyped and broad notion of "the native" but also the political identity of capital-*I* Indigenous that Barclay invokes, which has the capacity to recast local phenomena resulting from settler colonialism as global in dimension and systemic in nature.[8]

Due to its frequent employment and deployment by non-Indigenous and Indigenous filmmakers alike, Aboriginality has historically accrued through convention multiple layers of meaning, from a historically sedimented association with prehistory, primitivity, and savagery that endures, thereby proving that "the episteme of the Ethnographic is still alive and well," to its recent fashioning as a site of resistance to all those geopolitical excesses that have led to a "life out of balance," to invoke the English translation of the Hopi title of Godfrey Reggio's *Koyaanisqatsi* (1982).[9] In order to get at those many layers, I not only embrace Wood's notion of a representational continuum but traverse continually over the entirety of that continuum rather than focusing my attention exclusively on the array of films that are closer to the Indigenous end than not. In other words, this project takes up contemporary films that are informed to some degree by an ethos of manifest destiny and a Manichean logic that regards Aboriginality as one half of a binary opposition, as well as films that pointedly resist, refute, and/or forge alternatives to the pernicious stereotypes that emerge from such logic. In doing so, it broaches the very issues that Barclay responds to and, in turn, raises: chiefly, the historical imbrication of imperialism and cinema, the ongoing negotiation of Aboriginal identity in and through cultural production, and the initiative to produce countercinematic traditions predicated on representational, if not political, sovereignty. Yet at the same time, it complicates an "invader Cinema"/Fourth Cinema schema as well as the reductive antinomies that such a critical paradigm can invoke: white versus Aboriginal filmmaker, stereotypical versus authentic representation, dominant versus marginal cinema, illusionist versus self-reflexive form, maintenance of the ideological status quo versus political subversion, fiction versus documentary. In short, all the films I engage with share one fundamental trait—they produce Aboriginality as a sign within their discursive economy—but they do so by a plurality of means and to a variety of ends.

By taking up a diverse array of representational practices over the course of this project, I build on the work of not only Langton, Barclay, and Wood but also visual anthropologist Faye Ginsburg. Speaking in 1994 to the benefits of an inclusive approach to her field of study, she charted the course for an anthropological practice that would be responsive to the myriad ways visual representations mediate cultural and social relations in our contemporary world. Explaining her desire to employ a comparative framework that could accommodate a consideration of both ethnographic cinema and Indigenous media in "Culture/Media: A (Mild) Polemic," she writes, "I borrow the term 'parallax effect,' used to describe the illusory perception of displacement of an object observed due to a change in the position of the observer. My argument is that looking at media made by people occupying a range of cultural positions, from insider to outsider, can provide a kind of parallax effect, offering us a fuller sense of the complexity of perspectives on what we have come to call culture."[10]

Given her goal, a more fulsome understanding of culture, the kind of approach that Ginsburg advocates when studying any form of media is one that foregrounds questions related to the circumstances surrounding its production, consumption, and social function. In a project such as this one, however, which creates a parallax effect vis-à-vis the textual production of Aboriginality rather than culture, the general province of the anthropologist, another methodology recommends itself: one that is concerned first and foremost with the formal and narrative operations that structure film—in this case, that of the narrative, fictional variety—as a signifying system. While such an approach relies heavily on textual analysis, it does not preclude a consideration of various interdependent contextual, extratextual, and intertextual factors surrounding a film, such as its production and circulation history, its resonances with other texts and historical events, its manner of exhibition, and the way viewers (be they critics, scholars, bloggers, programmers, politicians, or spectators of some other stripe) incorporate it into public discourse. Such factors are integral to the production of meaning(s).

In conceiving of this book project in such an inclusive manner—that is, with an interest in the parallax effect and on a global stage, to boot—I run certain risks of which I am acutely aware. First of all, to emphasize Aboriginality as a transnational phenomenon brings with it the danger of emptying a representation thereof of its specific historical and political significance by ignoring the circumstances that have produced a particular group of people as Aboriginal and the particular contexts—ideological and cultural, iconographic and narrative—in which that identity has been negotiated in an ongoing manner through the present. Yet I hope to prove that a consideration of intertextual echoes need not come at the expense of those elements that distinguish one film, one community, and one history from another, since the potential rewards of thinking about a cinema of Aboriginality outside of the national cinemas framework that often prevails in film studies are great, as I discuss in my introduction. Nonetheless, in order to put some checks on this endeavor, I limit it by focusing on films made in and about Canada, the United States, New Zealand, and Australia, four predominantly Anglophone settler societies bound by many significant ties, both historic and cinematic. Second, in taking up works like *beDevil* (Tracey Moffatt, 1993) and *The Business of Fancydancing* (Sherman Alexie, 2002) alongside such mainstream fare as *Dances with Wolves* (Kevin Costner, 1990) and *The Piano* (Jane Campion, 1993), both of which have circulated far more widely as films for general audiences and fodder for critics and scholars, I risk positioning the former in the shadow of the latter. Again, however, I am mindful of the productive possibilities of this approach, which is engaged with the varying scales of commercial cinema. Indeed, insofar as they are informed by the conventions of a classical and colonialist cinema as well the auto-ethnographic mode of filmmaking typically privileged in anthropological accounts of Indigenous media, narrative features by Aboriginal filmmakers lend themselves well to a discussion structured along dialectical lines. In an effort to shore up this claim, I begin my introduction by shifting my attention from a contemporary instantiation of transnational film culture (TIFF) to one from cinema's infancy.

Prior to doing so, though, I want to acknowledge and thank sincerely the following for the contributions they have made to this project: The American Association of University Women as well as the Cinema Studies Institute, Innis College, the English department, and the Connaught Fund at the University of Toronto, all of which provided considerable institutional and/or financial support; Matthew Bernstein, Gaylyn Studlar, David Cook, and Pam Hall, who gave me invaluable guidance while this project was in its earliest stages; Charlie Keil, Kay Armatage, Kass Banning, Nic Sammond, and Sophie Mayer, who have been generous with both advice and feedback over the years; everyone at Southern Illinois University Press, especially Karl Kageff, Barb Martin, Wayne Larsen, and Julie Bush, who have made this publishing experience a very smooth one; JP Larocque, Kelly Anne Downes, and Marc Saint-Cyr, my extremely reliable research assistants; and, finally, those many filmmakers who feature here, whose inspiring work commands my greatest respect.

UNSETTLING SIGHTS

INTRODUCTION
The Cinema of Aboriginality as Transnational Phenomenon

Among the films that Auguste and Louis Lumière screened for rapt audiences at the Paris World's Fair of 1900 was one titled *Indochina: Namo Village, Panorama Taken from a Rickshaw.* Shot by Gabriel Veyre from the back of a rickshaw as it makes its way through an Indochinese village, the film captures that which the vehicle leaves in its wake: a dirt road, thatched structures of varying sizes, and a crowd of gleeful children who, in their erratic pursuit of the rickshaw, run in and out of frame repeatedly. As an advertisement for the technology of light and shadows that the Lumière brothers had first made public over four years earlier, *Indochina* could not be more effective. By representing its dynamic subject matter in a likewise dynamic manner, the film does more than just depict movement; it embodies movement, thereby allowing the spectator to participate in as well as to witness the seemingly spontaneous yet perfectly choreographed activity represented. For this reason, it showcases the full kinesthetic potential of the medium, as opposed to most films of this era, which were characterized by static framing. Yet the pleasure this film offered French audiences of the time was not just a visceral one, for in addition to delivering the thrill of the (playful) chase, it also presented a slice of life from a culture markedly different in appearance from their own. In fact, *Indochina* allowed its viewers to come into contact with a distant land that most French citizens knew only by reputation and thereby to assume the role of colonial adventurers without ever losing their bearings.

That same year, anthropologist Alfred Cort Haddon staged a similar encounter when he used a talk he was giving at the Royal Geographical Society in London to screen footage that he had taken during his Torres Strait expedition of 1898. While the featured films lacked the technical polish of Veyre's *Indochina* due to Haddon's relative inexperience with his cinematograph, damages incurred by the apparatus while in transit, and the difficult conditions in which he was shooting, they nonetheless also showcased the enormous potential of cinema as both a technology and a means of virtual travel. With their images of Mer Islanders engaging in a variety of activities, from the salvaged and traditional (a Malu-Bomia ceremony) to the mundane and commonplace (dancing and starting a fire), they served as a most persuasive pictorial accompaniment to Haddon's talk while also delivering the additional pleasure of transporting the viewing audience to a remote corner of the world in which they, as members of the British Empire, had a stake.

On the one hand, these two examples of early film exhibition differ greatly, demonstrating the variety of guises that cinema assumed in its infancy. The first is indicative of the Lumière brothers' initial foray into the movie business whereby they would hire a battery of camera operators and send them out into the world in order to make films in the Lumière name; the second reveals what was possible as of 1897, when the cinematograph became available for purchase by anyone with a vision. The first is a typical travelogue, a self-contained glimpse of a foreign land with the capacity to entertain and educate in equal measure; the second is part and parcel of Haddon's fieldwork, which included a range of data collection methods, including sound recordings, interviews, participant observation, and still photography. Finally, the first involves viewers choosing among any number of visually pleasurable spectacles, from a Loïe Fuller dance performance to the "human zoo" to a tour of the newly constructed Grand Palais; the second addresses a specialized audience for whom visual aids were a surprising supplement to the day's main event.

On the other hand, the examples are also strikingly similar not only as texts characterized by the presentational mode that Tom Gunning associates with the cinema of attractions but also as social artifacts lying at the intersection of multiple histories: those of colonialism and cinema, anthropology and visuality, popular culture and scientific discourse.[1] It is precisely the dovetailing of these various histories that has intrigued a substantial number of scholars over the past twenty years. The sum of their efforts has shown early cinema to be, among other things, extremely transnational as a direct result of the fact that film was invented during the height of the age of imperialism, when over half of the world's land mass was under the control of a handful of European powers and a complex network of trade and travel routes traversing the globe had already been established in order to ensure the flow of populations, capital, raw materials, and consumer goods. As a result of this existing infrastructure, the equipment needed to make and view films moved fairly freely between the European metropoles and various colonial outposts from the inception of the medium, thereby allowing cinema, in turn, to assume an important role in the further expansion and consolidation of individual empires. While films like those made in Indochina and the Torres Strait islands produced, in the words of Robert

Stam and Louise Spence, "armchair conquistadors" by providing viewers in Europe with an opportunity to visit virtually those territories captured first by annexation and then on celluloid, screenings of European films at public venues in the colonies were occasions for settlers to convene and thereby affirm ties with one another as well as the distant homeland on-screen.[2]

At the same time that colonialism helped foster a transnational film culture by facilitating various material flows—that is, the movement of people, films, and equipment across the boundaries of the nation-state—the disciplinary field of anthropology, which provided colonialism with its alleged rationale, was integral in the production of a transnational aesthetic. Given a long-established practice of classifying people according to their physical attributes, be it in the name of a nonhierarchical catalog of racial types or a natural order in which Caucasian people ranked superior to all others, anthropologists greeted the invention of film with enthusiasm.[3] Based on assumptions about its transparency and objectivity, they considered cinema to be, like its predecessor still photography, a perfect means by which to capture and save for posterity documentation of races regarded as always, already vanishing. Thus, early cinema institutionalized looking relations forged in world fairs, laboratories, museums, and "the field" and thereby conventionalized certain objects of sight: namely, to paraphrase Fatimah Tobing Rony, those "dark-skinned people known as 'savages' or 'primitives'" whose consistent subjection to scientific scrutiny has provided anthropology with its historical unity.[4] The result was a set of representational tropes shared across the Western world that served to shore up a general Eurocentrism, which Robert Stam and Ella Shohat associate with both Europe and the various settler societies it produced and define as "the procrustean forcing of cultural heterogeneity into a single paradigmatic perspective in which Europe is seen as the unique source of meaning, as the world's center of gravity, as ontological 'reality' to the rest of the world's shadow."[5]

It was not just anthropologists, however, who turned the apparatus on "savages" and "primitives" during the first decade of cinema. Rather, as demonstrated with aplomb by select contemporary scholars, such subject matter was to be found in work from a wide array of filmmakers; in order to reflect this fact, these scholars have taken liberties both small and large with the term "ethnographic cinema." For example, Alison Griffiths, author of *Wondrous Difference: Cinema, Anthropology, and Turn-of-the-Century Visual Culture*, argues that ethnographic cinema "should be seen as a generalized and dispersed set of practices, a way of using the cinematic medium to express ideas about racial and cultural difference, rather than as an autonomous and institutionalized film genre."[6] Moreover, she asserts that when assessing a film's status as ethnographic, the identity of a filmmaker and, more specifically, whether he or she is an anthropologist is typically far less important than a range of extratextual factors, with exhibition context being chief among them. Based on this more lenient definition, she, for example, devotes chapters of her book to not only the pioneering film work of Alfred Cort Haddon and Walter Baldwin Spencer but also the popular travelogues of Lyman H. Howe and E. Burton Holmes.

Rony goes a couple of steps further by specifying those "ideas about racial and cultural difference," positioning them at the very heart of her (re-) definition, and moreover expanding the concept of ethnographic cinema to accommodate narrative films, be they documentary or fiction, as well as scientific films and, for that matter, travelogues. In *The Third Eye: Race, Cinema, and Ethnographic Spectacle*, she organizes her polemic around three case studies that collectively exemplify the process of racialization at the center of the ethnographic enterprise: the (pre-)cinematic work of anthropologist Félix-Louis Regnault, who produced a variety of chrono-photographic studies of West African performers at the Paris Ethnographic Exposition of 1895; Robert Flaherty's *Nanook of the North* (1922), considered by many to be the first documentary film; and, finally, Merian Cooper and Ernest Schoedsack's *King Kong* (1933), a carnivalesque version of the racial films with which its directors got their start in the 1920s.[7] In denying their anthropological subjects historical agency, individual voice, and psychological complexity, these works reduce them to a racial type that is reassuringly distinct from, yet utterly legible to, the typically white spectator. In the process, they are constructed as "ethnographiable"—that is, as existing outside of or, more accurately, prior to history—and thus relegated to what Anne McClintock calls anachronistic space: "a permanently anterior time within the geographic space of the modern empire."[8] Yet such iconographic conventions not only fix nonwhite bodies as an immediately recognizable sign of the primitive and a flesh and blood example of the remote prehistory of humanity; they also position the filmmaker and film viewer as the norm against which those bodies are measured. As a result, whiteness comes to be defined retroactively in terms of everything that the native is not: civilized, progressive, and "historifiable." In short, ethnographic cinema, according to Rony, explicitly or implicitly narrativizes evolution, mapping difference onto a diachronic axis whose teleology posits the white male as the crowning achievement of historical progress and the racialized native as the embodiment of his evolutionary past.

I begin *Unsettling Sights: The Fourth World on Film* with mention of recent work on the relationship between colonialism and early cinema as well as on the foundations of ethnographic film for a couple of reasons. The first, simply enough, is that this scholarship has shed much light on the central concern of this book, the cinematic representation of Aboriginal cultures, and thus will prove germane to issues broached in subsequent chapters. The second is that it also exists in an interdependent fashion with another body of work that is experiencing a growth spurt of late and reflects the profound impact that postcolonial theory has had on film studies: that which is dedicated to the exploration of contemporary transnational cinema, that which has, in fact, consolidated "transnational cinema" into a category of both classification and analysis. In many ways, this latter work is the obverse of that dedicated to the relationship between colonialism and cinema's beginnings insofar as it asks similar questions about the construction (or destabilization) of identity, the consolidation (or disruption) of various imagined communities, and the fortification (or undermining) of certain ideological assumptions, but in relation to film culture created on the other side of the historical era that began in 1947 and witnessed the dissolution of European empires in piecemeal fashion thereafter. One of the most noteworthy differences between scholarship on the colonial and postcolonial eras concerns the way that present or formerly colonized people get implicated in the transnational flows of their particular historical moment. For Griffiths and Rony, for example, they are by and large a spoken subject insofar as it is across the body of the ethnographiable, the cinematically produced native, that a transnational film aesthetic was inscribed and a sense of racial solidarity (over and above any particular national allegiance) was cultivated. In work on the contemporary era, however, they are speaking subjects and, moreover, key contributors to a cinema that both results from and attests to a global economy in which the autonomy of the nation is eroding and a static geography of (First World) center and (Third World) margin has given way to something far more dynamic, syncretic, and dispersed.

The Emergence of Transnational Cinema/Studies

The year 2006 marked the publication of Elizabeth Ezra and Terry Rowden's anthology *Transnational Cinema: A Film Reader*, the first volume to market itself explicitly and specifically as an overview of the phenomenon to which so many film studies scholars are presently turning their attention. As dictated by the subject at hand, the essays included in the volume cover a lot of territory both conceptually and geographically. Authors discuss Hollywood's global reach and universalizing discourse as well as the counterhegemonic output of filmmakers and industries associated with formerly colonized locales such as India, Africa, Latin America, and Hong

Kong. Additionally, their fodder for case studies ranges from mainstream fare like *The Matrix* and *Lord of the Rings* trilogies to crossover stars such as Bruce Lee, Jet Li, and Jackie Chan to, finally, the more marginalized arenas of transnational documentary filmmaking and *beur* film aesthetics.[9] Providing a thread of continuity among these diverse topics, however, is an image that takes shape for the reader both verbally and visually. In their introduction, Ezra and Rowden write, "As a figure within cinematic productions, the image of the displaced person grounds the transnational both thematically and in terms of global awareness. In such works, loss and deterritorialization are often represented not as transitional states on the transnational subject's path to either transcendence or tragedy, but instead as more or less permanent conditions—as, for example, in the film *Blackboards* (Samira Makhmalbaf, 2000), which depicts a group of nomads forced to travel ceaselessly throughout Kurdistan on the Iran-Iraq border. In much transnational cinema, identities are necessarily deconstructed and reconstructed along the lines of a powering dynamic based on mobility."[10] Shoring up the poignancy and potency of this passage is the book's cover, which features an image from *Blackboards* in which a woman and man engage in the very travel described. Prominently positioned thus, the transient couple comes to embody not only the hypothetical figure invoked at the start of the above quotation but also the postindustrial and postnational forces that are generally at issue in the volume as a whole.

In their choice of representative trope for the subject at hand, Ezra and Rowden follow in the footsteps of Hamid Naficy, who was among the first cinema studies scholars to mount a systematic and sustained examination of certain transnational flows in contemporary film culture. For this reason, a consideration of Naficy's work, particularly *An Accented Cinema: Exilic and Diasporic Filmmaking*, reveals precisely what kinds of mobility and, by extension, which deconstructed and reconstructed identities tend to be of interest to Ezra and Rowden as well as to other scholars for whom Naficy's work is a touchstone. Over the past decade, Naficy has consistently devoted his critical attention to the way those events that radically changed our global landscape in the second half of the twentieth century—for example, Third World decolonization, the disintegration of the Eastern Bloc, and the consolidation of economic power in the hands of multinational corporations—have fostered a uniquely transnational film style and mode of production. In *An Accented Cinema*, he focuses on the work of filmmakers who have been dislocated as a result of these events and whom he therefore identifies as "the products of this dual postcolonial displacement and postmodern or late modern scattering."[11] Specifically, he argues that the experience of deterritorialization and a consequent ambivalence about the notion of "home" exert a structuring influence on such work, and the result is a cinema that speaks, both literally and metaphorically, in a voice different from a dominant cinema that communicates in the manner considered to be standard and normative in Western society. As a comment upon the experience of deterritorialization, these so-called accented films incorporate themes, perspectives, and formal techniques normally excluded from mainstream cinema; as a result of it, they employ an interstitial mode of production, which "operate[s] both within and astride the cracks and fissures of the system, benefiting from its contradictions, anomalies, and heterogeneity."[12]

Given this broad focus, Naficy's project encompasses an extremely wide range of filmmakers, including those who have been displaced due to exile, diasporic movement, and immigration. Moreover, many of the filmmakers he discusses hail, at least originally, from former European colonies and confront, through the material they produce and/or their role behind the camera, the ethnographic legacy as well as assumptions regarding racial difference that prevail therein. Yet there is one group of filmmakers that falls outside of his analytical purview: those Aboriginal peoples whose deterritorialization follows from their "staying put," to borrow Avtar Brah's phrase, rather than taking flight. While Naficy's decision to delimit his project is certainly understandable given the sprawling nature of his subject, this omission is quite striking. Insofar as "the dispossession of territory is the hallmark of aboriginal minorities," to quote David Pearson, one could argue that Aboriginal peoples are exemplars of the deterritorialization that Naficy cites as criterion for accented speech.[13] Nonetheless, Naficy, like so many contemporary scholars across the humanities and social sciences, forestalls any discussion of Indigeneity under the rubric of the transnational by privileging routes over roots and thereby foregrounding social processes, artifacts, and texts that fracture rather than consolidate a coherent sense of home and, in turn, self.

Naficy starts his study by distinguishing between three varieties of accented filmmaker and, by extension, film—exilic, diasporic, and ethnic—based on two related factors: the specific experience of dislocation that informs his or her work and the way that he or she consequently defines home (that is, in terms of the past and/or present, as a cultural insider and/or outsider, through the lens of nostalgia and/or resignation). The result is a continuum of accented work with exilic and ethnic occupying opposite poles and diasporic forging a middle ground. As Naficy explains, "Exilic cinema is dominated by its focus on there and then in the homeland, diasporic cinema by its vertical relationship to the homeland and its lateral relationship to the diaspora communities and experiences, and postcolonial ethnic and identity cinema by the exigencies of life here and now in the country in which the filmmakers reside."[14] Given his discussion of what each type of cinema accomplishes stylistically, thematically, and affectively, films by Aboriginal directors could quite readily qualify as any one (or more) of them, but ultimately Naficy defines these categories so as to preclude a consideration of such work. For example, although Naficy acknowledges the existence of internal exiles who wage "the good fight at home—a fight that often defines not only their film style but also their identity as oppositional figures of some stature," he turns his attention almost exclusively to external exiles, those who, by either force or choice, leave their country of origin for a foreign destination.[15] Likewise, his working definition of diaspora, which builds from that of exile—a "necessarily collective" experience thereof—is also limited to the international ilk.[16] As a result, failing to figure in Naficy's analysis is the specific variety of banishment experienced by those communities that historically were rounded up, sent away, run off, and shuttled about in the wake of European settlement and, in turn, presently occupy marginalized spaces that are both part of and distinct from the nations in which they are located.

Finally, he defines ethnic cinema not only as that which foregrounds those who are racially and/or ethnically distinct from the majority in a given community but also as the output of recent immigrants who are engaged in negotiating the "politics of the hyphen." Thus, Aboriginal peoples, whom mass European settlement has constituted as ethnic minorities and who produce cultural texts that speak to their status as such, do not qualify for inclusion in this third category either. Not only are they native to the land encompassed by the modern nation-states in which they live, but their exceptional position makes their politics less of the hyphen than of the space within. Since Naficy offers up the hyphenated identities of Asian-American, African-American, and Latino-American in order to illustrate the dual allegiances that attend the politics of the hyphen, it is instructive to consider how the controversial term "Native American" speaks to the specificity of an Aboriginal social (dis)location.[17] In the case of Naficy's examples, both constitutive elements of the compound term modify the person being named as such: for example, an Asian-American person is both Asian and American simultaneously. In the case of Native American, however, Native modifies American, simultaneously intensifying it (American in origin and thus as American as one can get) and excepting it (not actually American at all). As with those marginalized spaces just invoked, sites of internal exile such as reservations, the Native American moniker locates difference at the heart of America instead of at its edges.[18]

As already mentioned, Naficy's decision to privilege mobility and, moreover, that of an international variety over and above other means of deterritorialization may have been a purely pragmatic response to the overwhelming abundance and variety of accented films. Yet based on the direction in which he takes a number of his textual analyses, another impetus for making such a move recommends itself as well: the interdependent relationship that exists at both the literal and metaphorical levels between the politics of location on the one hand and the politics of identity on the other. On this count, a short passage from Naficy's discussion of exilic filmmakers is revealing: "As partial, fragmented, and multiple subjects, these filmmakers are capable of producing ambiguity and doubt about the taken-for-granted values of their home and host societies. They can also transcend and transform themselves to produce hybridized, syncretic, performed, and virtual identities."[19] Brimming with the language of poststructuralism, these two sentences make clear the types of identity that movement, particularly that across borders, engenders in both practice and theory and thus the reason that, to quote John Durham Peters, "nothing is more dispersed in intellectual life today than the concept of diaspora, nothing more nomadic than the concept of nomadism."[20] In short, the literal transgression of physical borders both enables and makes performative the destabilization of those figurative borders that contain and delimit discrete identities; as such, it has the potential to facilitate the deconstruction of identity, a central critical project within poststructuralist thought as well as within the various discourses that have taken shape in its shadow, including postcolonial theory, critical race theory, and queer theory.

Given this dual interest in mobility and the destabilization of identity, which can be traced from Naficy to Ezra and Rowden and beyond, it is no surprise that Aboriginal identity proves an unpopular topic of conversation. After all, dominant culture has so often constructed the figure of the native as the radically different yet utterly knowable other who never changes, even in the face of (intranational) geographical mobility, cross-cultural exchange, or technological development. Perhaps even more important, however, Aboriginal communities themselves have often pragmatically seized upon an identity defined in terms of the bonds of blood and specificity of place as, in the words of Brah, "the privileged space of legitimate claims of belonging."[21] In *Cartographies of Diaspora: Contesting Identities*, Brah sets herself apart from many contemporary critics by confronting rather than sidelining the unique situation of Aboriginality within the context of a much broader field of inquiry, one dedicated to the ways difference is made meaningful in a world where societies are irrefutably multicultural, migration is utterly routine, and identity is necessarily complex and contingent. At the center of Brah's project is an understanding of contemporary social landscapes in terms of diaspora, a notion that, to her mind, offers an alternative to essentialist conceptions of place and self on the one hand and postmodern fantasies of limitless mobility and endless shape-shifting on the other. As she notes, "The *concept* of diaspora places the discourse of home and dispersion in creative tension, inscribing a homing desire while simultaneously critiquing discourses of fixed origins."[22] It is the Indigene subject position in particular that lends itself to a discourse of fixed origins wherein the relationship between people and place, identity and home is assumed to be natural and unchanging rather than socially constructed and historically determined. As a result, she concludes, it is always in danger of reifying and, moreover, naturalizing extant stereotypes, be it imposed by a colonizing culture with an investment in notions of primitivity or appropriated by a colonized culture staking a claim on land from which it has been displaced. Committed to an anti-essentialist vision that is all-inclusive, she attempts to sidestep such dangers by mapping the contours of what she calls diaspora space: "a conceptual category [that] is 'inhabited,' not only by those who have migrated and their descendents, but equally by those who are constructed and represented as indigenous" and "the site where the native is as much a diasporian as the diasporian is the native."[23]

In a certain respect, Brah's association between Indigeneity and diaspora is potentially quite productive. In allowing for recognition of the fact that Aboriginal populations have actually experienced profound displacement, she addresses a concern that Ward Churchill, for one, has with the critical paradigms used to analyze Aboriginal experience. In the chapter "Like Sand in the Wind: The Making of an American Indian Diaspora in the United States," Churchill protests the neglect of American Indian history by those working in the nascent field of diaspora studies, noting with typical incision, "To say that a Cherokee remains essentially 'at home' so long as s/he resides within the continental territory claimed by the U.S. is equivalent to arguing that a Swede displaced to Italy, or a Vietnamese refugee in Korea, would be at home simply because they remained in Europe or Asia."[24] At the same time, however, Brah's use of italics in the above quotation ("the *concept* of diaspora") is telling, for she is far more interested in making a theoretical argument than a historical one, in dismantling a contemporary subject position than a misapprehension of past events and their repercussions. Her reservations notwithstanding, however, it is in terms of origins that many Aboriginal activists and cultural producers identify themselves. To wit, Churchill follows the sentence quoted above with one that would likely trouble Brah due to its blatant investment in roots: "Native Americans, no less than other peoples, can and should be understood as identified with the specific geographical settings by which we came to identify ourselves as people."[25] Indeed, an attachment to specific geographical settings and the consequent imperative to define oneself in local terms is one of the primary grounds on which Aboriginal peoples from around the world have cultivated a transnational alliance, which has, in turn, allowed them to assume a political presence in global forums. In sum, an investment in roots does not preclude Aboriginal peoples from the transnational; rather, it is precisely what qualifies them as members of a movement that is international in composition, supranational in structure, and worldly—Fourth Worldly, to be exact—in outlook.

The Fourth World Takes Root

The term "Fourth World" was first coined in 1974 when George Manuel, a Shuswap Indian and president of Canada's National Indian Brotherhood, published *The Fourth World: An Indian Reality*, which he co-wrote with Michael Posluns. Yet Manuel began to recognize that which it indicates—a shared history and status among Indigenous peoples around the world—in the early 1970s, when he supplemented his knowledge of existing policies in both Canada and the United States by traveling overseas to research the laws and protocols dictating the treatment of Aboriginal populations in New Zealand, Australia, and Sweden. Based on those experiences, he came to the conclusions articulated at the outset of his book, which presents the history of Canada's First Nations as a microcosmic example of a global phenomenon. Specifically, he asserts that Aboriginal peoples throughout the world are united by, first, a shared history of subjection to and survival of settler colonialism and, second, "a common understanding of the universe," which encompasses a reverence for the land and an emphasis on those communal networks through which individuals are defined.[26] Reconciling the seemingly contradictory call for an identity that both acknowledges the specificity of place and proves universally applicable, he writes, "The Fourth World emerges as each people develops customs and practices that wed it to the land as the forest is to the soil, and as people stop expecting that there is some unnamed thing that grows equally well from sea to sea. As each of our underdeveloped nations begins to mature, we may learn to share this common bed without persisting in a relationship of violence and abduction. Such mutuality can come only as each respects the wholeness of the other, and also acknowledges his own roots."[27] To be sure, the category Fourth World subordinates the vast cultural and historical differences between various Indigenous groups to their similarities, just as the designations of Maori, American Indian, First Nation, and Australian Aborigine level those differences between individual tribes that are so salient in the construction of identity at the individual and local levels. Indeed, the point made by Toon Van Meijl about the definition of Maoritanga, or a Maori way of being, within the New Zealand context—that it "is not a product of primordial ties, but a strategic concept"—is applicable to the Fourth World as well. In the case of the latter, however, the coalition at hand, which gives rise to a political identity around which large numbers can rally, is international in nature.[28] In 1975, the Fourth World gained an institutional backbone with the founding of the World Council of Indigenous Peoples under Manuel's leadership; the subsequent establishment of additional organizations with an international profile, including the Working Group on Indigenous Populations in 1981 and the UN Permanent Forum on Indigenous Issues in 2002, have only continued to realize the political vision put forth by this landmark collective.

Over the course of three decades of mobilization, some individuals have insisted on redefining the Fourth World so as to exclude any reference to a privileged relationship to the land, be it spiritual or proprietary in nature; in so doing, they have followed in the footsteps of Lieuwe Pietersen, who produced one of the earliest competing definitions of the term when he, in a publication from 1976, applied it to any group constituting a linguistic and cultural minority within its nation-state.[29] For example, Richard Griggs writes of the Fourth World as "nations forcefully incorporated into states which maintain a distinct political culture but are internationally unrecognized."[30] In so doing, he identifies it as a product of the European state system, with its propensity for centralizing power, as opposed to settler colonialism and thereby creates a more inclusive category that can take into account the struggles for sovereignty taking place in the heart of Europe (for example, in Spain over Catalonia) as well as throughout its periphery. In general, however, the Fourth World is most readily associated with an international movement on behalf of Aboriginal rights that has remained firmly rooted in a land-based discourse, as demonstrated by the term under which most self-defined Fourth World individuals and collectives currently organize: Indigeneity or Indigenism. Granted, the precise meaning of these labels has also been the subject of extensive discussion and debate, with constituencies disagreeing most frequently over the level of self-consciousness and/or political engagement they suppose, but the common denominator to all the definitions proffered is an acknowledgment of those relations of descent that tie certain communities to the original inhabitants of a given land. As Roger Maaka and Augie Fleras summarize well in their examination of the relationship between Aboriginal peoples and the nation-state in Canada and New Zealand, "Indigeneity as discourse (principle) and transformation (practice) embraces the foundational premise of ancestral occupation as moral justification for reward and recognition."[31]

While such principles and practices may have gone international only in the 1970s and 1980s in tandem with a newly emergent infrastructure, many Aboriginal spokespeople working within an exclusively local context had been honing them for many years prior. In *Blood Narrative: Indigenous Identity in American Indian and Maori Literary and Activist Texts*, Chadwick Allen advances the following argument after surveying a plurality of writings produced between 1945 and 1980: "Indigenous minority writers and activists in the early contemporary period developed a range of narrative tactics that enabled them to define an enduring Indigenous identity ('blood') in terms of narratives of connection to specific lands ('memory'), and to use narratives of connection to specific lands ('memory') to assert an enduring identity ('blood')."[32] According to Allen, the tautological logic of this endeavor is proof of the extent to which Indigenous specificity has historically been conceived of in relation to a "blood/land/memory complex," in which each of the three entities named is defined in and through the others. Based on these observations, Allen concludes that it is a willingness, eagerness even, to take the risk of essentialism that most distinguishes Indigenous work from that produced by a postcolonial critic like Brah. Of course, it is not the case that essentialist conceptions of identity have no place within postcolonial theory or criticism; to wit, Stuart Hall and Gayatri Chakravorty Spivak both acknowledge that essentialism can be a politically expedient, if theoretically impure, strategy when starting to mount counterhegemonic resistance to a former or extant colonial presence. Nonetheless, they regard it as the means to an anti-essentialist end, the first step in a protracted process that culminates in an embrace of that which Naficy cites explicitly in the above quotation: the partial, fragmented, multiple, hybridized, syncretic, performed, and virtual.

Given this teleology, Allen is reluctant to read the work of Indigenous writers through the lens of postcolonial theory. While a suspicion of essentialist rhetoric is certainly warranted, especially when those employing it are in the position to benefit from a colonialism that is not quite "post," to his mind there is nothing inevitable or automatically progressive about anti-essentialism. In fact, as suggested by much of the material he examines throughout his study, the specific situation of Indigenous minorities, who are continually at risk of "total engulfment by powerful settler nations," frequently recommends a contrary political program.[33] Ojibwa scholar Joanne R. DiNova shares Allen's skepticism about the politics of anti-essentialism. In her book *Spiraling Webs of Relation: Movements toward an Indigenist Criticism*, she begins to create a space for the dynamic activity of her subtitle by demoting poststructuralism, as well as the Western tradition of which it is representative, from its assumed position as "the pinnacle of epistemological achievement" to the status of one among many theoretical paradigms (a particularly aberrant one, at that).[34] Echoing Allen, DiNova explains why such a move has implications that extend far beyond the field of literary criticism, in which DiNova is making an intervention: "In order to argue that Indians have sovereignty over land, resource, or culture (including literature), one must maintain that there is something more tangible than an idea socially construed that makes an Indian an Indian. Since abandoning essence, then, entails abandoning claims to sovereignty, it is not hard to see why Indian scholars have, when pressed to choose, favored essentialism. It is also not hard to see that if social constructionist arguments did somehow manage to move beyond academic walls, they would more quickly eradicate Indian claims to sovereignty than eradicate racism."[35]

While Allen's observations are based on a literary survey that is limited in scope both geographically and historically, they nonetheless have resonance within discussions of contemporary Aboriginal visual media as well, be they produced before or after the year 1980 and by Maori and American Indian filmmakers or other members of the Fourth World. Indeed, scholars examining cinematic forms of Aboriginal self-representation have also identified the types of connections for which the term "blood/land/memory complex" is shorthand. Exemplary in this regard are two landmark studies of the inaugural use of film and video technologies among Aboriginal communities. The first is Sol Worth and John Adair's *Through Navajo Eyes: An Exploration in Film Communication and Anthropology*, which analyzes the results of an experiment the two men conducted in 1966 with seven local residents of the Navajo reservation in Palm Springs, Arizona. After instructing the recruits in the fundamentals of cinematography and editing, Worth and Adair provided them with the materials and support needed to make a series of shorts, ranging from two to twenty minutes in length. Prior to doing so, they assumed that the resulting representations would reveal something about the Navajo culture in general as well as about the possibilities of cinema as a form of intercultural communication, and the results of their experiment bore out this assumption. Among the numerous thematic and technical proclivities that distinguished the films made by the

Navajo from those of filmmakers schooled and practiced in the conventions of Western filmmaking was the repeated use of, first, shots of people walking and, second, a circular story structure that eschewed suspense in favor of symmetry. In combination, these two attributes led Worth and Adair to ascribe to the filmmakers not only a strong affinity with nature (that is, the earth and the cycles of life) but also a compulsion to return to one's origins via a restaging of the journey that propels the Navajo origin myth.

The second is the series of essays that Eric Michaels wrote about the three years he spent with the Warlpiri in Central Australia between 1982 and 1986 in order to study their introduction to media technologies in the capacity of consumers of Western television and then as producers of their own video recordings for local broadcast. Throughout the essays, which are collected in the volume *Bad Aboriginal Art: Tradition, Media, and Technological Horizons*, he, unlike Worth and Adair, focuses less on textual factors than on contextual ones, repeatedly illustrating the extent to which kinship structures and landscape shape the Warlpiri community's viewing practices and production processes. In the chapter "For a Cultural Future: Francis Jupurrurla Makes TV at Yuendumu," in particular, he illustrates one fundamental way that media made by the Warlpiri defines the self in relation to land and memory when he describes the shooting of a video called *Conistan Story*. Based on a historical massacre wherein a hundred members of the Warlpiri community were killed in retribution for the earlier slaying of a white trapper and dingo hunter, *Conistan Story* presents ample footage of the site where the massacre occurred. When describing the decision on the part of the filmmaker, Jupurrurla, to bring almost thirty people with him when he visited the site for the purposes of filming, Michaels notes, "Everyone has rights to both the story and the land on which—of which—it speaks. The credibility of the resulting tape for the Warlpiri audience is dependent upon knowing that these people were all participating in the event, even though the taped record provides no direct evidence of their presence."[36]

Since both the Warlpiri and Navajo communities featured in these studies had extremely limited experience as consumers, never mind as producers, of film, video, and television prior to the period of time discussed, their creative and organizational decisions lend themselves to a particular kind of interpretation: one that positions the media makers as conduits for the inevitable expression of those social values, cultural norms, and locally specific ways of knowing shared by the community at large rather than as individual agents engaged in deliberate representational practices.[37] Yet other examples of anthropological work in the same vein as that of Michaels, Worth, and Adair demonstrate clearly that the terms of discussion must be revised once a community has become familiar with a medium and, moreover, with the effects its mass circulation can have. On this count, Terence Turner's work with the Kayapo of Brazil is instructive. During a talk that he gave at the Royal Anthropological Institute's Third International Festival of Ethnographic Film in 1992, thirty years after his first research trip to Amazonia and seven years after the Kayapo started experimenting with video production in order to document events such as local rituals and political meetings, he described the Kayapo as capable of representing themselves with profound savvy. Having witnessed the kind of attention their work attracts both nationally and internationally, they were by 1992 fully aware that "a prerequisite of cultural and political survival is the ability of a group to objectify its own culture as an 'ethnic' identity, in a form in which it can serve to mobilize collective action in opposition to the dominant national society and Western world system."[38] As a result, Turner argues, connections between blood, land, and memory did not simply inform the textual operations of their work as well as the conditions of its production but were strategically performed in order to galvanize support for political goals related to the preservation of Kayapo land and culture. In making these claims, however, Turner suggests neither that such performances were contrived nor that they depended on the maintenance of an "authentic" culture impervious to historical change or what he calls "inter-cultural adulteration."[39] On the contrary, he contends that the Kayapo have proven themselves both able and willing to adapt to the exigencies of life in a multicultural and industrialized context, so long as they are able to do so on their own terms and without forsaking their cultural specificity. In fact, as soon as they realized how frequently images of them with camcorders in hand were reprinted in the popular press, they found more occasions to present themselves thus publicly, thereby capitalizing on the currency of their appearance and engaging in what might best be called a strategic anti-essentialism, the obverse of Spivak's much-touted construction.

When considered in tandem, Allen's work on American Indian and Maori literature and Turner's work on Kayapo media, both of which present case studies that lay bare the political stakes of self-representation for Aboriginal peoples, raise a number of pressing questions, especially now that film festivals, satellite television, and the Internet facilitate the international circulation of Indigenous work. For example, how does one assert a community's connection to a homeland or ancestral line without reducing it to that connection? How can one emphasize the bonds of blood or specificity of place without reifying existing stereotypes as well as the assumptions about the authenticity of culture and the biology of race that sustain them? How does one maintain a boundary between self and other without presenting one's community as homogeneous or one's culture as hermetic? While these questions may bespeak concerns that are particularly pertinent to Aboriginal media makers (and their critics), they can also be asked both by and of those contemporary non-Aboriginal artists who represent Aboriginal people, from those who conceive of their projects as acts of social advocacy and political agitation to those who are simply a product of these postmodern, postcolonial times in which the destructive effects of colonialism cannot be denied. When they are, a host of other, equally pressing questions emerge. Does a particular representational strategy have different effects depending on who employs it? How do the risks of essentialism differ for Aboriginal and non-Aboriginal artists? And, finally, what are the risks of anti-essentialism? That is, what is to be gained and/or lost aesthetically and politically from an approach that divests itself of the blood/land/memory complex and realizes the diaspora space that Brah maps only in theory?

By pursuing this line of inquiry in relation to contemporary films from the United States, Canada, Australia, and New Zealand, I carve out a space in between the two existing bodies of English-language work in which scholars have heretofore addressed issues related to Aboriginality and cinematic representation. Comprising the first are those works that address representations of and/or by a particular Aboriginal community and thus make an intervention in a national cinemas discourse that assumes a unified nation-state or a homogenous film culture. Such texts have often made groundbreaking contributions to the field of cinema studies, whether by examining the politics of representing a particular group, as indicated by telling titles like *Naming the Other: Images of the Maori in New Zealand Film and Television* (Martin Blythe) and *Celluloid Indians: Native Americans and Film* (Jacquelyn Kilpatrick); cataloging the major themes of texts that address Aboriginal experience, as do Christopher E. Gittings, Tom O'Regan, and Robert Stam in their surveys of Canadian, Australian, and Brazilian national cinema, respectively; or highlighting those unsung figures, usually documentarians, who have contributed to the development of an Indigenous film culture (see Randolph Lewis's *Alanis Obomsawin: The Vision of a Native Filmmaker* and Beverly Singer's *Wiping the War Paint off the Lens: Native American Film and Video*). Exemplifying the second body of writing wherein the cinema of Aboriginality has been broached consistently are certain surveys driven by a general concern with the relationship between cinema, colonial discourse, and postcolonial theory. John King, Ana M. López, and Manuel Alvarado's edited volume *Mediating Two Worlds: Cinematic Encounters in the Americas* and Robert Stam and Ella Shohat's foundational *Unthinking*

Eurocentricism: Multiculturalism and the Media are two such texts, which demonstrate clearly that this approach is more likely to generate work of impressive breadth rather than sustained engagement with any particular group of texts, filmmakers, or political concerns. Widening the scope of discussion beyond the national, yet remaining shy of the global, *Unsettling Sights* occupies a middle ground between these two bodies of work. In so doing, it remains sensitive to the nuances of both text and context and posits the transnational nature of representation, both artistic and political, while simultaneously respecting the exceedingly local terms in which Aboriginal cultures often define themselves.

The Ties That Bind

Daiva Stasiulis and Nira Yuval-Davis provide a useful working definition of "settler societies" when they describe them as "societies Europeans have settled, where their descendents have remained politically dominant over indigenous peoples, and where a heterogeneous society has developed in class, ethnic, and racial terms."[40] While much of the literature on settler societies assumes there is sufficient similitude between even the most far-flung of such nations to warrant a comparative approach, the United States, Canada, Australia, and New Zealand have even more in common insofar as they all trace the roots of their dominant culture back to the British empire. Of these four countries, the one that might seem least at home in such a grouping is the United States. As Pearson explains, the other three, as dominion nations that continue to recognize the queen of England as an (albeit ceremonial) figurehead, assume a similar position on the world stage; susceptible to influence, and even control, by more powerful entities, yet exempt from the status of "underdeveloped" regularly associated with the Third World, they constitute a "semi-periphery" and, as such, are distinct from the United States. Elaborating upon this point, Pearson writes, "If Australia, Canada, and New Zealand's semi-peripherality hinged on their 'special relationship' with Britain and its Empire, and its peculiar condition of privileged dependence, the United States swiftly moved to core status, cementing autonomy in economic and political terms, and acquiring its own imperial sway along the way. Ultimately, such dominance, particularly with respect to Canada, but hardly unimportant in Australia and New Zealand, saw one Northern American offspring of Britannia replacing its parent in its sphere of hegemonic influence over other siblings around the Pacific Rim. The United States, therefore, diverged in important respects from the 'dominions' and relatively swiftly attained an exceptional position among post-settler states."[41]

While certainly this exceptional status, as well as the particular relationship to Britain from which it is derived, is significant, it does not invalidate the move to discuss the United States alongside its fellow former British colonies, especially when the topic at hand is Aboriginal-settler relations. As Dolores Janiewski demonstrates in "Gendering, Racializing and Classifying: Settler Colonization in the United States, 1590–1990," ethnic and racial relations in the contemporary United States cannot be fully grasped without reference to the history of colonial expansion in which they are rooted and by which they are profoundly informed. Besides, Australia, New Zealand, and Canada could each lay claim to exceptional status as well for various reasons. For instance, setting Canada apart from the pack is its history of French colonialism, which preceded British rule and continues to inspire a vital separatist movement. Compounded by those social divisions common to all settler societies, the French-English divide so fundamental to the Canadian state has led Scott MacKenzie, for one, to identify Canada as "the first postmodern and perhaps first postnational state" in the world.[42] New Zealand's singularity derives from not only its relatively small size but also an unparalleled tradition of integration that has prevailed over the last century and a half. Evidence of such integration can be found in the politico-legal sphere (in 1867, four Maori seats were established in the nascent New Zealand parliament), social customs (intermarriage has been prevalent and widely accepted since the beginning of European settlement), and public policy (under the Labour government of the 1980s, New Zealand began pursuing a series of initiatives with the explicit goal of institutionalizing biculturalism).[43] Finally, its start as a penal colony and the high percentage of Irish (and to a lesser extent Scottish, Welsh, and Cornish) immigrants render Australia exceptional, for such beginnings, among other things, tempered early settlers' attachment to England as "motherland." The resulting ambivalence bred a fervent desire on the part of many settlers to construct Australian character as a rugged and roguish counterpoint to British restraint and propriety, especially from 1901, the year of federation, onward.

In an article on Australia, Argentina, New Zealand, Uruguay, South Africa, and Chile, Donald Denoon, one of the more pioneering and influential scholars to write on settler societies, declares, "The fact that settler societies resemble one another in several respects, is not a consequence of conscious imitation, but of separate efforts to resolve very similar problems."[44] While the problems that are of particular interest to Denoon are economic ones and the resolution, that of rapid adaptation to capitalist relations of production, his statement has more general applicability as well. Indeed, another similar problem stems from the very elements that define a settler society as such and dictate that the following is true in nations born of settler colonialism: "The contradictions between the ideal image of the nation-state and the reality of contemporary nation-states are especially striking."[45] As concise as is Stasiulis and Yuval-Davis's definition of settler societies (cited at the start of this section), it indicates clearly certain endemic fault lines. In *The Politics of Ethnicity in Settler Societies*, Pearson takes these fault lines as his subject, arguing that there are three historical factors that not only distinguish the settler society from other colonial enterprises but also make nation-statehood difficult to achieve, thereby contributing to the contradictions that Stasiulis and Yuval-Davis identify: the Aboriginal presence; the bonds between the first contingent of settlers, especially the elite, and a homeland from which they have been displaced; and subsequent waves of immigration that make for a multicultural society with likewise divided allegiances.

In the face of the problem that these three factors generate, that of a fragmented populace, settler societies must work extra hard to build community and define the nation as a unified entity with both political and social dimensions. An integral part of this effort, as Pearson notes, is the generation of myths of origin. Given the circumstances of settler societies, these myths must not only define the nation in terms of its dominant culture, narrating the founding of those institutional structures and cultural practices that serve its interests and reflect its worldviews, respectively; they must also designate the moment of European arrival as the start of historical time and thereby preempt claims to land or sovereignty on the part of those Indigenous peoples who populate the nation's prehistory accordingly. Traditionally, there have been two primary, and oftentimes intertwined, ways of accomplishing this, each of which can be summed up with a loaded phrase: *terra nullius* on the one hand and "white man's burden" on the other. While Australia is the only one of the settler societies under consideration in this project to adopt the former as a founding doctrine (at least until it was overturned with the Mabo decision in 1992), it can be argued that any country that employs the rhetoric of "discovery" to describe European arrival in an already populated land is tacitly designating that land as "of no one" as well. Derived from the same episteme, the latter, used to refer to the imperative to civilize "savages," similarly denies something fundamental about Aboriginal peoples: in this case, however, it is not their proprietorship but rather their very humanity.

Ideally suited for the mass circulation of spectacles with tremendous affective and persuasive power, cinema has proven, over the course of its history, an extremely effective tool for the creation, perpetuation, and/or dissemination of various myths of origin as well as the assumptions about race on which they depend. To wit, Aboriginal populations have typically been treated in one of two ways in the cinema of settler societies: they have either been evacuated from the mise-en-scène of a burgeoning nation altogether, or they have been presented within the context of a contact scenario, which dictates that their narrative function is circumscribed by their difference from (and often their consequent conflict with) white settler-invaders. While the former convention does not provide much fodder for analysis, the latter is an important site for critical intervention since it is the primary means by which Aboriginal peoples have been envisioned in popular culture throughout the First World. As heir to the ethnographic cinema of people like Félix-Louis Regnault and Alfred Cort Haddon, films featuring a contact scenario have much in common with films produced within the anthropological tradition; indeed, it is these commonalities that compel Rony to expand the category of the ethnographic, as discussed at the beginning of this chapter. Yet in addition to facilitating (mediated) contact between the native, as de-individualized scientific specimen, and a typically white audience, such films also narrativize contact. In other words, nationalism, like sadism, demands a story: specifically, one in which those traits that define the ethnographiable serve as motivation for conquest, assimilation, and/or extermination on the part of white colonizers who are at the center of the dramatic action.[46]

Undoubtedly, the *content* of a myth of origin—the exact time and place of contact, the precise parties involved—differs from one settler society to another. Yet filmmakers from disparate parts are likely nonetheless to convey that content with a common cinematic vocabulary (for example, formal conventions, narrative trajectories, and visual tropes). The lack of variability in this regard is in large part explained by the fact that the contact scenarios contained within/by origin myths are responding to the same set of conditions (a fragmented populace) and incorporating the very racialized bodies across which a transnational film aesthetic was initially inscribed. Yet one final factor is also at issue: the widespread circulation of certain exemplars, which have consequently become iconic, throughout the better part of the twentieth century. The most significant of these exemplars is the Hollywood Western, the genre with which the United States created a national(ist) mythology bound up with "cowboys and Indians," manifest destiny, and the rule of the gun and simultaneously ensured captive audiences internationally. "Among the most coveted American cultural imports" in the wake of World War I, when the United States gained dominance of the global film market, the many Westerns produced from the 1920s through the end of the studio era traveled far and wide, inspiring appropriation by past and present filmmakers from countries as diverse as Italy and Algeria, Japan and Germany.[47] Of course, New Zealand, Australia, and Canada were a substantial part of that global market. In fact, their largely Anglophone public, their lack of stringent quotas and import taxes like those in place intermittently in Britain, and the relative impotence of their own national industries, especially when it came to the production of feature-length narrative films, qualified them as particularly fertile markets for the export of classical Hollywood films. As a result, the claim Glen Lewis makes regarding Australia can be extended to New Zealand and Canada (and beyond) as well: American cinema has "created the language and genre conventions that audiences recognize and expect."[48] At the same time, studio-era Hollywood was not the only industry creating contact narratives that gained international exposure. During the heyday of the Western, British colonial epics also circulated widely, especially throughout the dominion nations. Prominent examples include three films that were released at the very end of a particularly productive period in British film history: *The Drum* (1938) and *The Four Feathers* (1939), both directed by Zoltan Korda and produced by his brother Alexander, as well as *King Solomon's Mines* (Robert Stevenson, 1937). These films are noteworthy not only for the enthusiasm they generated at home and abroad upon their release; each one also constitutes a single iteration of a tale so compelling to Western audiences as to merit numerous retellings (upwards of six in the case of the latter two) by British and American directors alike.

It would be foolhardy to suggest that all contact narratives of any variety that were produced in serial form prior to the 1960s are identical in their textual or ideological operations; this goes not only for Westerns and colonial epics but also for those films they were coincident with and often influenced: the bushranger tales of Australia, the nationalist documentaries sponsored by various Canadian public institutions, and the frontier films of Rudall Hayward in New Zealand. Of course, there is much variation in these representations, and any given text can be read in multiple ways. Nonetheless, as has been demonstrated by scholars working on said bodies of work, the classic contact narrative, a highly conventionalized way of representing Aboriginal peoples in itself, has often served to animate any number of pernicious stereotypes. Within the last thirty years, however, the period in which I am interested, historical developments in the film industries and social landscapes of the United States, Canada, New Zealand, and Australia have effected changes in the cultural and discursive contexts in which Aboriginality is understood and in the ways that Aboriginal peoples are depicted.

First of all, those nationalist narratives with transnational resonance—that is, myths of origin that displace Aboriginal peoples both figuratively and literally—have been contested and complicated due to a series of events. Chief among these are the myriad decolonization struggles that took place throughout the latter half of the twentieth century; the wide range of national and international social movements that gained momentum in the 1960s and 1970s and ushered in a subsequent era of history wars, culture wars, and identity politics; and the introduction and, in turn, popularization of critical paradigms associated with poststructuralism and postmodernism. Consequently, as John Mowitt notes, "The narrateme of the 'white man's burden' . . . is now widely decried if not actually retired," while the underbelly of settler colonialism—that is, the systematic dispossession and ongoing devastation of extant Aboriginal communities—is a matter of public knowledge, if not necessarily public concern.[49] Within this larger cultural context, a cinema of Aboriginality possesses yet another attribute that Ezra and Rowden ascribe to the films and filmmaking practices addressed in their volume: the capacity to "[transcend] the national as autonomous cultural particularity while respecting it as a powerful symbolic force."[50] That is, insofar as it acknowledges Aboriginality, at the very least, it evokes the history of force and exclusion that has conditioned acts of imagining community in an ongoing fashion since the start of European settlement and thereby foregrounds the constructed nature of the nation-state.

Second, as a greater diversity of filmmakers have assumed positions behind the camera, the types of Aboriginal people seen on-screen have proliferated. In recent decades—the 1970s in Canada and Australia and the 1980s in New Zealand—these three countries gained a foothold in the international marketplace of feature-length fiction films due largely to a commitment, both financial and otherwise, on the part of their respective governments. Additionally, in the same period of time, the United States witnessed the emergence of its own shadow industry as a self-proclaimed "independent" film culture defined itself against Hollywood, even while, at times, drawing on the same resources and courting the same audience as its counterpart. While Aboriginal people still constitute a very small percentage of the filmmakers, actors, and technicians working in these industries, they nonetheless constitute a presence that is only growing in visibility. With respect to all of these cinemas, output has been quite varied. While certain filmmakers have produced high-concept entertainment made in the Hollywood mold so as to ensure commercial viability, others have aspired for a distinctly local sensibility so as to differentiate themselves from the lingua franca of contemporary film culture.[51] Insofar as the latter approach (even when married with the former) requires that filmmakers divest themselves of some, if not all, of the most conventionalized of representational paradigms, it constitutes a site of potential transformation for Aboriginal and non-Aboriginal filmmakers alike.

The Organization of *Unsettling Sights*

Parallel histories of both colonial relations and postcolonial discourse as well as a common cinematic vocabulary due to certain Eurocentric generic precedents with widespread circulation (for example, ethnographic film and the Western) have created a situation in which even the most provincial of film productions partakes of representational conventions that have currency throughout the Anglophone world (and potentially beyond). In recent years, transnational flows within film culture have only intensified—hence, the emergence of transnational cinema/studies—and the result has been the consolidation and continued development of a cinema of Aboriginality that lies at the intersection of the local and global, the national and transnational. Indeed, the production histories of many of the films that I analyze attest to the frequency with which collaboration occurs across the national boundaries of those settler societies under consideration in this book. While my interest in Aboriginality as sign dictates that the following chapters of *Unsettling Sights* focus on those occasions of textual resonance across a wide array of films, it is important to note how such occasions contribute to a transnational aesthetic that both feeds and feeds off of the transnational mobility of funds, texts, and industry personnel.

In some cases, a single figure, such as a director, can exemplify the ties between different national contexts and thus the ease with which one can move between them in order to make work that has widespread recognizability and relevance. Two particularly instructive figures in this regard are Australian Bruce Beresford and New Zealander Vincent Ward, both of whom have not only traveled between their homeland and Hollywood (a fairly commonplace occurrence for directors from the Antipodes once they prove themselves) but also worked in Canada. In fact, in the case of both these directors, it is their Canadian co-productions, which take place in Canada, engage with Canadian history, and feature prominently a range of characters from Canada's Aboriginal populations, that I discuss in the greatest detail. Specifically, Beresford's *Black Robe* (1991) figures prominently in chapter 1, and Ward's *Map of the Human Heart* (1993) is taken up in chapter 2. At the same time, each has also contributed to a cinema of Aboriginality through a film that takes his homeland as both setting and subject: Beresford directed *The Fringe Dwellers* in 1986, prior to not only *Black Robe* but also his most celebrated Hollywood venture, *Driving Miss Daisy* (1989), while Vincent Ward's historical epic *River Queen*, which takes place during the New Zealand land wars of the 1860s, was released (in a limited capacity) in 2005.

In other cases, it is a single film that speaks to a film culture that transcends the national insofar as it is financed by funds from a diversity of sources and/or assembles cast and crew that are international in composition. *The Piano* (1993), broached in chapter 1, is a particularly prominent case in point. While there has been much debate over whether the film can be claimed by New Zealand, where Campion was born and raised through age sixteen, or Australia, where she was trained and started her film career, the assumption that Campion's national identity dictates that of her film ignores all the other factors that qualify it as an international co-production involving (at least) four countries: an Australian producer, an American distributor, French and Australian financial backing, and two Hollywood stars in the leading roles. Another salient example is *Dead Man* (1995) from chapter 2, a film whose director (Jim Jarmusch) and genre (the Western) are decidedly American in origin but whose financing came from Japan and Germany as well as the United States. Perhaps even more interesting, however, is the fact that it has been claimed by yet another national tradition with its recent inclusion in an anthology dedicated to Canadian cinema. According to the volume's editor, Jerry White, the film qualifies as in part Canadian due to the involvement of actor Gary Farmer, a director in his own right, who both worked closely with Jarmusch in the development of the story and gave a scene-stealing performance as the affable Nobody. Employing the language of the transnational skillfully (and, moreover, in a manner that anticipates the project of *Unsettling Sights*), White names the following goal as his motivation for making *Dead Man* a part of *The Cinema of Canada*: to "identify a continental understanding of Aboriginal culture—one that seeks to transcend the borders of colonially-imposed nation-states."[52]

In addition to attesting to the transnational face of a contemporary cinema of Aboriginality, the four films just singled out for future discussion—*Black Robe, Map of the Human Heart, The Piano,* and *Dead Man*—are all exemplary of the type of film to which I dedicate my attention in the first of the two parts that make up the remainder of *Unsettling Sights*. Specifically, they are contact narratives, which remain the most popular vehicle for the representation of Aboriginal peoples. A primal scene bearing witness to the conception (if not birth) of a nation as well as that which must be suppressed in the process of imagining its constitutive community, the contact narrative is a most intriguing text. As has already been demonstrated by scholars writing on, for example, the Western in a North American context or on the bushranger tale in an Australian one, contact narratives have frequently forged a pernicious association between Aboriginal people and savagery; moreover, the legacy of such representational conventions is evident in many contemporary iterations of the first encounter tale. At the same time, however, especially in their most recent postcolonial variety, they frequently play with and at the very limits of those identity categories upon which their contact scenarios depend by either dramatizing the process of cross-cultural identification and, in turn, producing hybridized characters that have the potential to lay bare the performativity of identity or approaching contact from the perspective of an Aboriginal character. By examining the visual figuration and narrative function of these two character types in light of the theoretical work of various postcolonial and Indigenous critics, I assess the capacity of contemporary contact narratives to problematize those assumptions about both racial and gender difference that animate colonial discourse and to represent Aboriginal subjectivity. After engaging in textual analysis of a number of films from the last three decades, ranging from Geoff Murphy's *Utu*, released in 1983, to *The New World* (Terrence Malick) and *The Proposition* (John Hillcoat), both from 2005, I conclude that the second of these tasks does not necessarily follow from the first.

The majority of the films I foreground in the second part of *Unsettling Sights* differ from those featured in part 1 by their setting (present rather than past) and creators (Indigenous themselves). Yet what actually qualifies them for consideration is the fact that they, unlike contact narratives, feature Indigenous characters whose dramatic roles are not circumscribed by their cultural difference from white settlers and thus whose identities are not simply negotiated in reactive response to a colonizing presence. Certainly, some of the material covered in this part also partakes of the types of transnational flows discussed above, as evinced by, for example, the career of New Zealand filmmaker Lee Tamahori, who followed up his feature film debut *Once Were Warriors* (1994) with a quintessentially American neo-noir, *Mulholland Falls* (1996). Yet in general, the films in this section tend to be more local productions whose international currency is guaranteed by, first, their transnational circulation via various means, including theatrical distribution, film festivals, and Web sites devoted to Indigenous media, and, second, the fact that they foreground those priorities that George Manuel identifies as points of commonality throughout the Fourth World: land and community. Specifically, they construct a sense of self vis-à-vis the landscape and/or alternate practices of (hi)story-telling, including, most significantly, the oral tradition. While certain recent contact narratives may facilitate the deconstruction of identity, the films in this section are far more likely to engage in its reconstruction. As a result, they function as an intriguing counterpoint to many of the films featured in part 1, which offer up a postmodern vision of the self (or, at least, some selves) but lose in the process that "something" upon which political claims to land rights, tribal rule, and cultural distinction are predicated. By contextualizing my analysis of films such as *Once Were Warriors*, *beDevil* (Tracey Moffatt, 1993), *Smoke Signals* (Chris Eyre, 1998), and *Atanarjuat* (Zacharias Kunuk, 2001) in critical literature dedicated to Indigenous cultural practice and production, I explore the vicissitudes of representation, both artistic and political, in a Fourth World context.

PART ONE

Making Contact, Producing Difference

With his 1971 feature *Walkabout*, British director Nicolas Roeg followed in the footsteps of a number of his compatriots, including, most famously, Harry Watt of Ealing Studios, by taking advantage of the Australian landscape, in all its solemnity and augustness, for the elemental grandeur it was able to lend the narrative action set in its foreground. At the center of Roeg's film is a journey rich in allegorical resonance involving a British teenaged girl (Jenny Agutter) and her little brother (Roeg's son, Luc). Stranded in the outback after their father commits suicide during a family outing, they eventually make their way back home to Sydney with the help of an Aboriginal boy (David Gulpilil) whom they encounter en route. Stripped of its usual pretext—a historical epic involving dramatic "discoveries" or intrepid pioneers—the contact scenario staged by this film lays bare the source of narrative tension at work in all its various cinematic iterations: the many differences that distinguish that which the film denotes (white and black, settler and Native) and connotes (civilized and primitive, present and past) as well as the occasional ability of its characters to transcend such differences in order to communicate, establish rapport, and perhaps even identify with one another. Underscoring the points of connection and, more often, contention narrated is the film's form, specifically its frequent preference for associative over continuity editing and its manipulation of sound. For example, Roeg presents extremely dissimilar renditions of the same object or activity by crosscutting between the predictable patterning of a brick wall and the irregular cragginess of a rock face, or between the Aboriginal boy clubbing the head of a hunted kangaroo and a butcher chopping meat with a cleaver; and he produces an uncanny effect by pairing nondiegetic sounds of a didgeridoo with images of a Sydney cityscape full of tall buildings and bustling bodies or showing the girl listening to a radio broadcast about dining etiquette while in the middle of the outback.

In the film's conclusion, this narrative and formal play on the dual themes of sameness and difference comes to structure not only the text but also the interior world of the girl as nostalgia and projection fuel, in equal measure, a vision of the split (Western) subject. At the start of the final sequence, the girl assumes the very position that her mother occupied in the film's opening minutes: she stands in the kitchen of the same high-rise apartment, preparing food for her family just as her predecessor had. What distinguishes the two, however, are glimpses of a different sort of life, which interrupt the girl's actions and presumably haunt her as fleeting memories. First, as is the case throughout the film, meat becomes an occasion for crosscutting, this time between the liver the girl is slicing in the present and a leg that the Aboriginal boy tore from a freshly killed kangaroo in the past. Then, once her husband returns home from work and begins relaying details of his recent promotion, that brief flashback develops into a more extensive depiction of an idyllic time passed. That is, the film shows the girl lost in thought and then cuts to a series of shots wherein she swims naked in a remote watering hole with both her brother and the Aboriginal boy while the following poem by A. E. Housman is read via voice-over:

> Into my heart an air that kills
> From yon far country blows:
> What are those blue remembered hills,
> What spires, what farms are those?
> That is the land of lost content,
> I see it shining plain,
> The happy highways where I went
> And cannot come again.

When describing this scene on a DVD commentary track, Roeg echoes Housman's invocation of a "land of lost content," opining, "I think she's back [home], but she reflects. . . . It's a passing thought. It's a secret, isn't it? It's that we all have that sort of secret. . . . They're not our complete lives, but that's what makes us up. We're all made up of the sum total of our experiences, and that was a beautiful one."[1] What this explanation obscures, however, is the fact that the happy highways the girl is revisiting during her final moment of reverie are purely hypothetical: the experience she has in flashback is an idealized version of her actual interaction with the Aboriginal boy. When taken earlier in the film, her swim in the pictured pool was hers alone, for the Aboriginal boy was busy hunting for the night's food. Even more to the point, however, the swim she recollects is entirely out of keeping with her character, for she was modest and careful to clothe herself whenever in the boy's presence during their journey together; moreover, when faced with overtures of intimacy during a courtship dance, she hid, besieged by a fear born of incomprehension.

Insofar as her "memory" is an idealized version of what actually happened, it perfectly crystallizes the project of *Walkabout* as a whole and thus functions, perhaps despite Roeg's intentions, as a *mise-en-abyme*, revealing that for both the girl and Roeg, the Australian outback and the Aboriginal boy occupying it serve as repositories for fantasies about a primordial past, a paradise lost. For this reason, the film can be regarded as a limit text for a dominant cinema structured by what Rey Chow calls "primitive passions." Ignited during moments of profound cultural crisis, when "the predominant sign of traditional culture is being dislocated . . . amid vast changes in technologies of signification," primitive passions signal an interest in the primitive and a concomitant impulse to construct fantasies of origin to which everyone can lay claim.[2] Such origins are, Chow explains, "'democratically' (re)constructed as a common place and a commonplace, a point of common knowledge and reference that was there prior to our present existence. The primitive, as the figure for this irretrievable *common/place*, is thus always an invention after the fact—a fabrication of a *pre* that occurs in the time of the *post*."[3] In her discussion of contemporary Chinese cinema, Chow designates representations of the countryside and women as the sites where primitive passions cathect in the work of Fifth Generation filmmakers Chen Kaige and Zhang Yimou. Within dominant Western cinema, however, particularly that produced by settler societies, it is the dual subject of the countryside—in this case, the outback—and its Aboriginal inhabitant, male or female, that emerges as the privileged signifier of the primitive with whom the contemporary subject craves reassuring association in periods of profound social change. Crystallizing this is the trailer for *Walkabout*: declaring via voice-over, "The Aborigine and the girl—30,000 years apart—together. *Walkabout*. Just about the most different film you'll ever see," it baldly relegates the boy to the anachronistic space posited by Anne McClintock and then displaces onto the film itself ("the *most different* film") his radical otherness vis-à-vis a norm typified by his white companions and the mechanized and alienating urbanity to which they are accustomed.

Just as its aspirations to allegory are what allow *Walkabout* to lay bare the extent to which contact narratives simultaneously depend upon and perpetuate assumptions about difference, thereby ensuring that contact amounts to conflict both culturally and narratologically, they also qualify the film as atypical of its kind. In other words, in addition to being a particularly revealing example of the cinematic contact narrative, *Walkabout* is also anomalous insofar as the myth it generates about humanity's origins is not bound up with a myth of the nation's origins. Made by a British director, written by a British playwright, and featuring in the roles of the lost siblings British actors who make no effort to disguise their accents, the film demonstrates little concern for any of the historical events that have created the conditions of possibility for the meeting that the film narrates. Intent on creating the oddest couple conceivable, it reproduces a contact scenario typically seen in films set in the precolonial or early colonial era and thereby disavows a specifically Australian history of interaction, exchange, and adaptation on the part of both settlers and Indigenous peoples.

In contrast, in most contact narratives made over the last forty years, the primitive passions fueling the representation of Aboriginal peoples are as much a response to locally specific crises as they are to those widespread changes wrought by the technological innovations associated with modernity and/or postmodernity (including, but not limited to, the proliferation of visual media, with which Chow is most concerned). Set against the backdrop of ongoing decolonization efforts and the emergence of a relatively autonomous Third World subject, entreaties and activism at the hands of extant Aboriginal communities over the last forty years have created ruptures in the popular national consciousness of Australia, New Zealand, Canada, and the United States. Specifically, social and political movements, such as the American Indian Movement and the Maori Renaissance, as well as the events that have catalyzed or revivified such movements, including the occupation at Wounded Knee, the Mabo decision, and the Oka crisis, have demanded a reconsideration of the narratives of nation that prevailed previously and an acknowledgment of the devastation—physical, cultural, and environmental—exacted in the name of imperialist expansion. It is conceivable that in such a context, contact narratives would lose their appeal for non-Aboriginal filmmakers. On the contrary, however, they have proven persistently popular, remaining to this day the means by which dominant cinema most frequently represents Aboriginal peoples.

Clearly, despite—or perhaps because of—the ruptures mentioned above, there is an ongoing need to rehearse, in almost ritualistic fashion, the processes of exclusion and inclusion, expulsion and incorporation that are part and parcel of any nation-building, but especially operative in settler societies. What distinguishes contemporary contact narratives, produced in the wake of decolonization efforts in the Third World and bids for sovereignty on the part of the Fourth, from many of their predecessors is the manner in which they negotiate the boundaries of the national communities they envision and thus whom or what they include, exclude, incorporate, and expel. The most profound shift in this regard is a general tendency on the part of contemporary filmmakers to indigenize—or primitivize, to invoke Chow—the origins of the nation. In some cases, this process entails writing Indigenous people back into the narrative of nation formation, thereby conferring on them the status of cinematic subject, if not national citizen. More frequently, however, it involves the preservation of Indigenous culture in trace form through the imprint it makes on white (male) characters who function as founding fathers. While I will examine in chapter 2 a selection of films that perform the former operation, it is to representations employing the latter strategy that I turn my attention in chapter 1.

1. Birth Pangs

Constructing the Proto-national Hero

Approximately a quarter of the way into *Dances with Wolves* (1990), Union army lieutenant John Dunbar, played by director Kevin Costner, is sighted for the first time by various members of the Sioux tribe into which he will integrate himself over the course of the film. In response to his presence at the otherwise abandoned frontier post of Fort Sedgwick, the male members of the tribe engage in debate over whether they should regard Dunbar (and the white race in general) as a formidable threat to their community. In particular, Kicking Bird (Graham Greene) and Wind in His Hair (Rodney A. Grant) take contrary positions on the significance of Dunbar's presence.

> WIND IN HIS HAIR: I do not care for this talk of a white man. Whatever he is, he is not Sioux and that makes him less. When I hear that more whites are coming, I want to laugh. We took one hundred horses from these people. There was no honor in it. They don't ride well. They don't shoot well. They're dirty. Those soldiers could not even make it through one winter here. And these people are said to flourish? I think they will all be dead soon. I think this fool is probably lost.
>
> KICKING BIRD: Wind in His Hair's words are strong, and I have heard them. It's true the whites are a poor race and hard to understand. But make no mistake. The whites are coming. Even our enemies agree on that. So when I see one man alone without fear in our country, I do not think he is lost. I think he may have medicine. I see someone who might speak for all the white people who are coming. I think this is a person with which treaties might be struck.

Having established two possible ways of interpreting Dunbar's character—as one who is lost or as one who possesses some type of political and/or personal power—the film provides evidence for the former, yet ultimately endorses the latter. While Dunbar did choose the remote Fort Sedgwick when given his pick of posts as reward for inadvertently leading his unit to a victory, he is nonetheless both displaced and misplaced in this terrain, which has proven fatally inhospitable to others before him. Not only has he lost his bearings, which he attempts to regain through a strict adherence to proper army procedure, but he is lost in another sense as well: after the deaths of Major Fambrough (Maury Chaykin), the commander who rubberstamped his request to man the frontier, and Timmons (Robert Pastorelli), who provided transportation to Fort Sedgwick, there remains not a single person who knows of his whereabouts. As a result, Dunbar's connection to any larger community—be it the military, the East, or white culture in general—is severed. In short, not only is Dunbar more naive than fearless and more dislocated than empowered, but he is also completely lacking in the type of social power to which Kicking Bird alludes. Nevertheless, just as Wind in His Hair's perspective on the fate of white settlers is discredited given the privilege of hindsight, so is his evaluation of Dunbar, whose "medicine," the film ultimately suggests, is his ability to transgress cultural boundaries.

Arriving in theaters a year after Costner's drama of cross-cultural identification, *Black Robe* (1991), Bruce Beresford's contact narrative set in seventeenth-century Québec, could not escape comparison with its much celebrated predecessor, despite the fact that the Jesuit priest at its center never initiates such a transgression.[1] That the release date of *Black Robe* was almost coincident with the quintencenary of Columbus's landing in North America only provided critics with further incentive to contextualize reviews of Beresford's film within a broader discussion of other contemporary cinematic representations of American Indians. Contrary to what might be expected in light of the phenomenal success of *Dances with Wolves*, *Black Robe* fares extremely well in such discussions, particularly delighting those who have little patience with the sentimental excess and self-congratulatory posturing of Costner's epic. Singled out as marks of *Black Robe*'s distinction are its fierce realism, its defiance of New Age tendencies to romanticize Aboriginal cultures, and its refusal of a narrative arc befitting an "over-decorated, pumped-up boy's adventure yarn"[2] and featuring "a simple-minded conversion to Indian ways."[3] Terrence Rafferty's review in the *New Yorker* is representative of the lot insofar as it lauds the "anthropological detachment" with which *Black Robe* was filmed.[4] Although *Dances with Wolves* is never mentioned by name in this particular article, it is no doubt exemplary of the films against which *Black Robe* is favorably pitted: those that offer a facile understanding of cross-cultural communication, thereby "[treating] the features of complex, integrated cultures as if they were merely lifestyle choices," and, moreover, that present viewers with a character with whom white audiences can readily identify.[5]

One critic who bucks this trend by reserving his more damning comments for *Black Robe* rather than for *Dances with Wolves* is Ward Churchill,

whose extreme prolificacy and consistent engagement with topical texts allow his work to function as a running commentary on the representation of
American Indians in contemporary public culture. To be sure, Churchill's
assessment of *Dances with Wolves* is mixed. He credits the film with outpac-
ing all Hollywood films that came before it by presenting multidimensional
Aboriginal characters with tremendous respect and accuracy but takes issue
with the fact that such characters are nonetheless supporting players in a
white man's drama, which he facetiously dubs "Lawrence of South Dakota."
His response to *Black Robe*, however, is far more reproachful, culminating
in a comparison with propaganda produced by the Third Reich: "*Black Robe*
is thus the sort of 'sensitive' and 'mature' cinematic exposition we might
have expected of the Nazis, had they won their war."[6] Citing the film's depiction of its Native characters as savage and bestial in comparison to those
seeking to "civilize" them, a portrayal made all the more insidious by the
matter-of-fact manner in which it is presented, he argues that *Black Robe*
not only diverts attention from First Nations, both past and present, but
also justifies genocide.

In making this argument, Churchill gives voice to the outrage of many
American Indian audience members, including a collection of community
leaders who unanimously denounced *Black Robe* after a public screening in
Los Angeles for its purportedly unbalanced account of events.[7] Responding
to this occurrence, Beresford went on the record with the following explanation: "I think it boils down to the fact that a lot of Indians today don't like to
see themselves portrayed as being antagonist to one other [*sic*], intertribally,
before the arrival of the Europeans. I think they like to think of themselves
as living quite harmoniously with nature and with one another, and then
the Europeans came and everything got messed up." He continued, "I don't
know why Indians don't like to see themselves portrayed in that way. I think
it has to do with some kind of romantic, liberal notions of a sort of utopia.
It wasn't really like that."[8] Bracketing momentarily Beresford's arrogant assumption that he knows more about their history than American Indians
themselves, I want to entertain one of the implications of his comments:
that the misunderstanding at hand is over what constitutes a positive image.
As Diane Waldman discusses, "positive" has at least two different meanings, empirical and affirmative, and thus "positive image" is a necessarily
ambiguous concept that lays bare the competing criteria critical viewers
employ when evaluating representations of underrepresented subjects. Not
only does Beresford pride himself on embracing the former definition of
"positive" by producing a depiction of First Nations people that is truth-
ful, if not always flattering, he also concludes that an Aboriginal audience

would prefer something positive in the latter sense of the word, even if it is fallacious. While the terms he invokes—truth versus fantasy, harmony versus bellicosity—prohibit an analysis of any complexity, Beresford's more general impulse to consider his portrayal of Indigenous characters in isolation from other elements of the film is equally problematic. For not only does it ignore the film's status as text, but it also betrays the logic of contact narratives, which foreground relations of sameness and difference, affinity and indifference between constitutive elements; indeed, as I explore in the next section, the representational politics of *Black Robe*—and *Dance with Wolves*, for that matter—cannot be reduced to, simply, the manner in which Aboriginal characters are portrayed. Yet even if one does start an analysis with this issue, Beresford's claims to realism demand qualification.

With regard to representation of its Indian characters, *Dances with Wolves* and *Black Robe* are similar in a few fundamental ways and thus have been evaluated largely in terms of the same criteria. First, each reveals itself to be fueled at least in part by an archival imperative with a concluding statement that foretells the eventual disappearance of a particular tribe: the Sioux in the case of *Dances with Wolves* and the Huron in that of *Black Robe*. As a result, they explicitly engage in an act of reconstruction and locate themselves in a past that remains "regrettably, obviously, but comfortably out of reach."[9] Second, close scrutiny of both texts reveals them to be dedicated to the pursuit of historical accuracy and thus informed by considerable research but also willing to sacrifice such accuracy in the face of a dramaturgical imperative. For example, the costume and production design of *Black Robe* has proven convincing and thus worthy of praise down to the smallest detail, but the film has also been taken to task for its reliance on First Nations languages (Cree and Mohawk) that are not appropriate for the tribes featured in the film (Algonquin, Iroquois, and Huron). Conversely, many have lauded *Dances with Wolves* for its extensive and capable use of the Sioux language, while Costner's decision to have his characters wear what Cahuilla and Luiseño Indian critic Edward Castillo identifies as "their finest ceremonial regalia" in every scene makes for misleading, albeit captivating, imagery.[10]

Third, both films' representation of one tribe as multidimensional is realized at the expense of another tribe whose members come to resemble the stereotypical villains of the classical Western. *Dances with Wolves* humanizes the Sioux while vilifying the Pawnee as those who follow the lead of one particularly fierce warrior among them and consequently wage attacks on tribal enemies, defenseless white settlers, and various animals that cross their (war)path. Likewise, *Black Robe*'s presentation of the Algonquin as relatively sympathetic characters is conditioned by its dehumanization of the Iroquois; not only do the latter exact the cruelest of punishments on those they take prisoner, from the slaying of a young boy in front of his father to the amputation of an enemy's finger with the edge of a mussel shell, but they are also singly (dis)credited with exterminating the Huron tribe. As has been demonstrated by multiple scholars, characterization in terms of this particular dichotomy, "Noble Red Man" and "Savage,"[11] is nothing new, for it has long been the most effective way of "addressing white historical fear and guilt within the same narrative, providing a way in which a fiction can remain simultaneously true to contradictory responses to history."[12] Nonetheless, its persistence even in films that purport to be producing revisionist iconography demonstrates to what extent contemporary representations of Aboriginal people are frequently beholden to the very conventions they simultaneously critique.

Despite their similarities, there is one significant difference between the two films. Unlike *Black Robe*, *Dances with Wolves* (at least in its version for theatrical release[13]) presents its Noble Red Men—and Women—as unflaggingly righteous and wholesome. Not only are they exceedingly attractive, in part due to the costuming choices mentioned above, but their striking visage is matched by a profound integrity that is established both formally (in, for example, low angle shots that lend the tribe members grandeur) and narratively (through, for instance, the depiction of the Sioux engaged in warfare only when on the defense). Should any doubt as to its honorable nature remain, Dunbar/Costner uses voice-over narration to sing the praises of his adoptive community, testifying that he has never before met a people "so eager to laugh, so devoted to family, so dedicated to each other."

As Randall Lake demonstrates after engaging in a thorough analysis of the critical commentary that *Dances with Wolves* elicited until as late as 1996, Native and non-Native critics responded to this characterization in exceedingly different ways. While many non-Native critics attack the film for romanticizing the Sioux, thereby reifying rather than dismantling persistent, if not pernicious, stereotypes, Native writers rarely take issue with this aspect of the film, reserving their critique for other failings, including those noted above (that is, its historical anachronisms, relegation of American Indian characters to supporting roles, and lack of respect for other tribes). Yet rather than lending credence to the assumption implicit in Beresford's comments above—that contemporary American Indians are prone to deluding themselves so as to preserve an idyllic image of their past—this discrepancy, in Lake's estimation, serves to suggest a couple of different points. The first is that the resistance of so many Euro-American critics to the representation of the Sioux may reveal more about their own continued investment in the stereotype of the "Savage" than Costner's fascination with that of the "Noble Red Man." The second is that *Dances with Wolves* is engaged in a dual project in which contemporary American Indians have a profound personal stake: the provision of a dramatic "antidote to reliving the calamities of the 19th century, to being trapped in history," and the modeling of an identity that is capable of adaptation but rooted in Indigenous tradition.[14]

Medicine Men, Missionaries, and Degrees of Eurocentricism

To be sure, the person who models the identity just mentioned most persuasively is Dunbar. In fact, *Dances with Wolves* is irredeemably Eurocentric insofar as it places a white man who "goes native" at its center and thereby follows in the tradition of a number of other "sympathetic Westerns,"[15] including *Broken Arrow* (Delmer Daves, 1950), *A Man Called Horse* (Elliot Silverstein, 1970), and *Little Big Man* (Arthur Penn, 1970). This narrative focus determines the function of a variety of supporting players since the film establishes Dunbar's character largely though his interactions with others. For example, his relationship with Two Socks, a wolf whose trust he wins, and Cisco, his cavalry horse, testify to Dunbar's capacity for compassion and sensitivity, while his refusal to cooperate with other white soldiers positions him as the exception within a group that is defined cumulatively as arrogant, foul, ignorant, insane, and trigger-happy. Yet it is the Sioux that most consistently, to paraphrase Virginia Woolf, reflect Dunbar's figure back at twice its natural size.[16] Inextricably linking his hybridization to heroism, the film aligns Dunbar with the Sioux community through a series of brave and loyal acts that earn him both special status among the tribe and center stage within the story. As a result, the more he integrates himself into his adoptive culture, the more he is set apart from it.

For Donald Hoffman, the film's unwavering focus on Dunbar, which comes at the expense of the Sioux, is grounds for its complete dismissal. He writes, "[The Sioux] are not . . . so important as vital humans as they are as morphological actants, as the adjuvant which, in myths and folklore, has been filled as adequately by fairies, frogs, and elfin cobblers, or, in recent cinema, by a variety of extraterrestrial gnomes from E.T. to Ewoks. The Sioux then, despite considerable discussion, are essentially decoration. What the film is about (and really only about) is Dunbar's initiation into otherworldly rituals and rise into a spiritual ascendancy over both his Indian followers and his white inferiors."[17] Earlier in his essay, Hoffman accuses Jane Tompkins of overstating her case in *West of Everything: The Inner Life of Westerns* when she makes the claim that Indians scarcely figure in her titular genre; ironically, he is guilty of the same. Indeed, *Dances with Wolves* is primarily about Dunbar, who occupies the role of not only protagonist but also savior; yet through his story, the film accomplishes more than mere hero-worship, for the "other world" in which he immerses himself and, by extension, the viewer is not a sheer fabrication entirely lacking in gravity or relevance beyond the diegesis. Rather, it is a site of alterity that has dimensions cultural and linguistic, historical and political. Thus, at the very least, the shift in allegiances and identity that *Dances with Wolves* narrates facilitates a defamiliarization of not only certain iconographic conventions associated with the Western but also certain ideological currents that hold sway to this day. Interested more in exploring seemingly insurmountable differences than such scripted shifts, *Black Robe* is less successful at divesting itself of those assumptions that *Dances with Wolves* makes strange. Indeed, the *New Yorker*'s ascription of "anthropological detachment" to the film is quite telling in this regard. After all, as discussed in the introduction, anthropology's claim to objectivity has historically rested upon a raced variety of looking relations, which specularizes nonwhite bodies while (re)producing whiteness as norm. Heir to these looking relations, *Black Robe*'s detachment is questionable.

At select moments in *Black Robe*, there are attempts to expose the blind spots that fuel the zealotry of Father Laforgue (Lothaire Bluteau) and thereby to call into question his need to understand cultural difference as cultural deficiency. Beresford accomplishes this visually in a brief sequence that calls to mind *Walkabout* insofar as it employs crosscutting to culturally relativist ends. Occurring quite early in the film, it involves the preparations for a nocturnal meeting between Champlain (Jean Brousseau), commander of New France, and Chomina (August Shellenberg), the Algonquin chief whom he is enlisting to guide Laforgue and his translator, Daniel (Aden Young), to the Huron camp. As the two men dress for the evening, the film cuts between them as each puts on items of clothing and ornamentation that distinguish him within the context of his community, and the resulting comparison serves to establish a profound similarity in the face of superficial differences. Likewise, the film offers a critique of the assumptions fueling Laforgue's mission with a verbal exchange between Daniel and Laforgue that takes place after Daniel has fallen in love with Annuka (Sandrine Holt), Chomina's daughter, and begun to resemble the Algonquin in his dress and manner. Presented in a shot–reverse shot pattern, wherein Daniel consistently shares the frame with Annuka in the background while Laforgue appears isolated against the landscape, the two debate the validity of competing belief systems:

LAFORGUE: I'm afraid of this country. The devil rules here. It controls the hearts and minds of these poor people.

DANIEL: But they are true Christians. They live for each other. They forgive things we would never forgive.

LAFORGUE: The devil makes them resist the truth of our teachings.

DANIEL: Why should they believe them? They have an afterworld of their own.

LAFORGUE: They have no concept of one.

DANIEL: Annuka has told me. They believe that in the forest at night the dead can see. The souls of men hunt the souls of animals.

LAFORGUE: Is that what she told you? It is childish, Daniel.

DANIEL: Is it harder to believe in than a paradise where we all sit on clouds and look at God?

While each of the two moments recounted above constitutes a significant intervention in the ideology propelling Laforgue's mission, it makes a fleeting impression since it is not part of a larger coherent pattern, be it iconographic or discursive. The only other time the film engages in associative crosscutting is during an extremely brief three-shot sequence wherein forest treetops are associated with the soaring roof of a French cathedral in order to underscore their humbling grandeur; and the (after)worldview to which Daniel gives voice remains peripheral to the film, just as does Daniel himself, whose motives, beliefs, and allegiances are rarely stable or transparent. Throughout the rest of the film, a Eurocentric frame of reference prevails since Laforgue functions as the norm against which difference is measured. By no means is he the valiant lead befitting a Western, be it classical or revisionist. That is, within those First World contexts that are in part defined by a commitment to a secular public culture, Laforgue's single-minded determination to bring Christianity to the tribes he encounters qualifies him more as a presumptuous zealot than an inspired hero. Nonetheless, he has a depth of character that no one else in *Black Robe* shares. As a result, the film may divest itself of the Jesuit imperative to convert the "heathen," but it nonetheless perpetuates the very episteme that makes "heathen" a meaningful concept in the first place.

While the film is generally characterized by a commitment to photographic realism, objective narration, and chronological temporality, the use of two devices allows for occasional deviation from this general rule. Insofar as these deviations contribute to the story, particularly character development, in decidedly distinct ways, they are revealing. The first is a series of three flashbacks, which provide glimpses of Laforgue's life in France before he embarks on his journey to New France. In one, a priest who has recently returned from a mission during which his ear and hands were mutilated convinces him that there is no greater glory than that of converting savages; in the next one, he listens dutifully to a musical performance by a marriage prospect; and in the final one, he and his mother discuss his future travels and impending martyrdom. The second is a dream sequence ascribed to Chomina, which contains a seemingly unconnected assortment of images, including ones of Laforgue walking alone along a snowy bank, a raven plucking Chomina's eyeball out of his head, and a thin land bridge leading to a distant island. Although the dream fails to cohere into a legible narrative for the spectator, Chomina assumes that it foretells the future and finds within it a message that dictates his subsequent actions. While similar in their introduction of the subjective into the film, these inserted sequences function in exceedingly different ways. The dream sequence, which is explicitly ascribed to Chomina insofar as it is linked by editing to a shot of him waking up with a start, does very little to enhance the viewer's understanding of Chomina or, more generally, the Algonquin community. Compounding its status as specious information is that fact that the dream's logic is lost even on Chomina; moments before dying, he realizes that he has been misinterpreting it all along. The flashbacks providing a backstory for Laforgue, in contrast, make both more and less sense than Chomina's dream. Directly and clearly representing those events that motivated Laforgue to come to New France and, furthermore, to traverse 1,500 miles to assume his position in a mission among the Huron, they make Laforgue a comprehensible character and, at least potentially, a sympathetic one as well. At the same time, there is no diegetic motivation for their insertion into the film, for they are not preceded or followed by shots of Laforgue lost in thought or even events in the present that are evocative of those depicted in flashback. Rather, they are awkwardly positioned in the text, as if produced in response to an imperative that is more ideological than narrative.

Further proof of this ideological imperative lies in the film's final scene, which features the Huron agreeing to be baptized in the belief that doing so will enhance their chances of weathering the pestilence that is spreading throughout the community. In many ways, the scene is evocative of one from the beginning of the film, which serves to introduce many of the Algonquin who will subsequently come to play a significant role in the journey north. In it, they sit on the floor of a makeshift chapel, enraptured by "Captain Clock," whose chimes they mistake for divine directives, while the French clergy take advantage of the situation rather than explain the mechanism by which the clock works in order to ensure the initiates' compliance. The final scene features another chapel, another tribe, and another exercise in deliberate mystification; in this case, however, it is the film rather than its characters that misleads by omission. The final shot of the scene starts by depicting Father Laforgue engaged in the rites of baptism with a chapel full of new converts and then ends with a camera movement that brings the area outside the chapel into full view as the nondiegetic sound of a choir grows louder. There, looming against the sky, is a cross illuminated dramatically by the setting sun as the following words appear on-screen: "Fifteen years later, the Hurons, having accepted Christianity, were routed and killed by their enemies, the Iroquois. The Jesuit mission to the Hurons was abandoned and the Jesuits returned to Quebec." Not only does this resolution offer up the image of a mystical and triumphant Christianity, but it sums up the fate of the Huron so as to suggest that their conversion did indeed ensure their survival—until, that is, they were slaughtered at the hands of the Iroquois.

Frontier Culture and Its Outlaws

For Jane Freebury, a rare voice of dissent in the chorus of approval by non-Native critics, the most fundamental flaw of *Black Robe* is its utter lack of self-consciousness and thus its inability to reflect in any meaningful way on its indebtedness to, never mind contention with, certain generic conventions and iconographic traditions. As a result, she concludes, "this western of the Canadian wilderness is a film more concerned with its historical credentials, with the material details of its cultural and social specificities, than it is with the context of its own production, with how it resonates with the contemporary audience, with what it has to say about contemporary issues of ethnicity and its representations."[18] In this way also it emerges as a countertext to *Dances with Wolves*. Evidence of what Freebury identifies simply as "postmodern play" on the part of Costner's film lies most markedly in the incorporation of a distinctly 1990s perspective on the Civil War era. Dunbar gives voice to that perspective in a most pointed manner when he explains to an army major his request to be posted at Fort Sedgwick in prescient terms: "I want to see the frontier . . . before it's gone." By raising the specter of loss before such a loss had been realized or even foretold, the film reveals its modern sensibility, creates a slippage between director and character, and designates Dunbar as a time-traveler who, armed with knowledge no one else in the film has, is en route to a fleeting moment in the history of colonization. In speaking about the frontier in the way he does, Dunbar/Costner captures with incision the teleology in which it is implicated; as Julia Evans writes in the context of an article dedicated to

Edward John Eyre, an English explorer and colonial official who lived in South Australia during the mid-nineteenth century, "the idea of the frontier implicitly foreshadows the demise of one [group of people] to the forceful intent of the other."[19] She continues by contrasting the relationships that the frontier produces with the "intersubjectivity" that frequently prevails during historical moments when contact is not conditioned by contests for land, sovereignty, and/or cultural dominance. Defining the latter in terms of mutual understanding and/or syncretic ways of life that draw on two or more cultural paradigms, she explains the former thus: "Within the time and space of the frontier, despite continuing opportunities for mutuality, prior possibilities for reciprocity recede in favour of more unequal exchange. Occasions for intersubjectivity are overshadowed by the assumption of superiority and a will to ignorance of other ways of knowing that underscore the coloniser's claims to exclusive sovereignty."[20]

As a result of its blatantly contemporary take on a distant past, *Dances with Wolves* devotes itself to an occasion of intersubjectivity despite a framing narrative that concludes with the demise of its Aboriginal characters, either through assimilation (Pawnee) or extinction (Sioux). In doing so, it is able to broach issues of profound relevance to present-day audiences, including not only "ethnicity and its representations," to repeat Freebury's phrase, but also the possibilities of cross-cultural communication, cooperation, or coalescence in the context of settler societies, which are by definition multicultural in composition. On this count, *Dances with Wolves* is not alone; the departures from historical fact that such an anachronistic approach guarantees notwithstanding, the majority of contact narratives produced in North America and the Antipodes over the last twenty years are far more likely to resemble *Dances with Wolves* than *Black Robe*. Frequently identifying non-Aboriginal characters with Aboriginal culture, these films as a group provide a way of thinking through the vicissitudes of a contemporary social world in which both identity politics and coalition politics have an important role to play. To be sure, such texts may be products of the impulse to cannibalize that which is culturally other, to romanticize outlaw status, and/or to exempt certain white characters or even settler communities from a history of domination and dispossession. Yet they also, arguably, embody the transgressive potential that Evans ascribes to the intersubjective in their capacity to subvert colonial interests by laying bare the fallacy of Eurocentric narratives of progress as well as the notions of racial or ethnic superiority that they engender. Thus, I devote the rest of this chapter to the examination of three texts—*The Proposition* (John Hillcoat, 2005), *The Last of the Mohicans* (Michael Mann, 1992), and *The Piano* (Jane Campion, 1993)—all of which indigenize the nation by defining their white characters in and through their relationships with Aboriginality, be it simply by positing a circumstantial alliance, typically that related to a parallel experience of marginality, or by additionally foregrounding a personal transformation that includes some measure of "going native."

The Australian bushranger film is a particularly fitting place to start such an analysis, given its foundational role in the construction of a national industry reputed for its proclivity toward "challenging all that is best and finest in the culture of the Mother Country [i.e., England]" and "insist[ing] upon its own ordinary ugliness."[21] Dominating Australian film production during an extremely fertile period of its infancy—that is, between 1904 and 1914—these films engaged in three interrelated projects: the identification of Australia and, moreover, Australian cinema with the spatiotemporality of the outback in the nineteenth century; the occasional incorporation of Aboriginal characters into the cinematic landscape in the role of either sidekick or natural wonder; and the construction of white Australian identity in terms of outlaw status. While the bushranger film was a short-lived phenomenon due to, first, censorship laws and, later, the atrophy of the local film industry, its legacy endures in contemporary iterations of the tales it tells as well as, more generally, in the larrikin archetype, which has figured prominently in Australian cinema since its rebirth in the 1970s. Based on the sheer number of films (not to mention ballads and plays) dedicated to his life, Ned Kelly ranks as the most celebrated of Australia's bushrangers. Starting with Charles Tait's *The Story of the Kelly Gang* from 1906, which is often acknowledged as the first feature-length film ever made in the world, numerous films have revisited the life of this native Australian of Irish descent who spent much of 1878 and 1879 on the lam with his accomplices after committing a string of crimes, ranging from armed robbery to murder.[22] Among the most recent of such revisitations is Gregor Jordan's *Ned Kelly* (2003).

Despite its recent date of release, *Ned Kelly* is in keeping with its cinematic antecedents since its incorporation, albeit fleeting, of an Aboriginal character into the diegesis is a perfect example of the phenomenon William Routt describes when discussing the earliest bushranger films: "These are not films about committing crimes or acts of rebellion—that is, about what bushrangers do—but about what bushrangers are. The landscape, the history, the communities of outcasts that surround the bushrangers are variant displays of the bushranger, different ways of figuring the same thing."[23] In *Ned Kelly*, Ned's status as outlaw is figured with hyperbolic economy by inclusion of a single shot of an Aboriginal man at a pivotal moment in the narrative—that is, once Ned (Heath Ledger) has taken to hiding in the woods with his posse of three after being falsely accused of attempting to murder a police officer. In the relevant scene, the four men are engaging in target practice when a noise compels Ned to turn quickly. Upon doing so, he catches sight of an Aboriginal man walking through the woods. While nothing comes of the encounter in terms of plot, it marks a turning point in the story, for shortly thereafter Ned relays via voice-over the police's reply to his request that his mother be released from police custody provided he turn himself in: "We don't bargains with outlaws." When Ned shoots Officer Lonigan (Peter Phelps) dead shortly thereafter, thereby committing the crime for which he would eventually be hanged, he begins playing the role into which he has already been cast and thus lives up to the newfound status embodied by the stranger.

For a more interesting and self-conscious examination of the outlaw and his relationship to the Aboriginal community, another variation on Kelly's story recommends itself: John Hillcoat's *The Proposition*. In Jordan's film, an Aboriginal character figures as fleeting symbol and thus functions as little more than trace remains of a disavowal process that culminates in Ned Kelly's designation as the ultimate outsider to Australian society. *The Proposition*, in contrast, includes numerous Aboriginal characters in a wide variety of roles, the two most prominent of which are played by actors of iconic stature—namely, David Gulpilil and Tom E. Lewis—who bring to their parts a fascinating intertextual history. While Hillcoat's film is not, strictly speaking, another retelling of Kelly's story, its subject is similar enough to create profound reverberations. At the center of *The Proposition* is the Burns gang, which has gone into hiding after committing a heinous crime; Captain Stanley (Ray Winstone), a British police chief whose career depends upon capture of the gang's leader, Arthur Burns (Danny Huston); and Charlie (Guy Pearce), Arthur's brother to whom the police chief makes the proposition for which the film is named, one entailing the capture of Arthur in exchange for the life and freedom of their younger brother, Mikey (Richard Wilson). Lacking those things that define Australia's most enduring folk-hero—a motive, a conscience, and a local fan-base—Arthur is definitely not Ned. The fact that the Burns brothers are Irish, however, is significant, for it allows *The Proposition* to play on the underdog cachet that surrounds the Kelly gang without having to explore in any detail itself the history of British-Irish relations both in and outside Australia. Thus, *The Proposition* rides the coattails of the Ned Kelly legend at the same time that it refuses the narrative conventions that structure every one of its iterations, including a detailing of the injustices the outlaw suffers at the hands of corrupt and elitist authorities, a dramatization of the reluctance with which he fulfills his role initially, and the inclusion of numerous characters for whom he is a rebellious proxy.

The film starts with a credit sequence featuring a succession of black and white photographs, twenty in all, which cumulatively provide a sense of the various constituencies making up the small community that Captain Stanley oversees. The first seven of the series (those that precede the presentation of the film's title) are all posed portraits, and most of them feature white and Aboriginal characters side by side. The resulting effect is that of a community wherein integration has occurred, but exclusively on the terms of the settlers: the Aboriginal figures pictured are almost always either in uniform, be it that of a police officer or a cricket team member, or in conventional European dress, thereby exemplifying the colonized subject's status as "a reformed, recognizable Other, as *a subject of difference that is almost the same but not quite.*"[24] According to Homi Bhabha, it is on this interplay of sameness and difference that the colonizer's authority rests. Mimicking the colonizing culture, the Aboriginal people in the portraits ensure the survival and normalization of its ways; yet their failure to be completely absorbed into that culture despite their imitative acts—that is, mimicry's capacity to "continually produce its slippage, its excess, its difference"[25]—maintains the distinction between self and other on which the colonizer's claim to superiority rests.[26]

As the credit sequence proceeds, it comes to serve another purpose in addition to establishing the colonial mise-en-scène in all its ambivalence. Specifically, the final six images in the sequence introduce the crime that sets the film's plot in motion by presenting evidence of the Burns gang's recent murder of the Hopkins family, including images of the victims inert on a bed, the wife's casket covered in flowers, and three freshly dug burial plots with crosses for markers. In light of this shift in both subject matter (first the community at large, then signs of the Hopkins family's victimization) and form (first portraiture, then documentary), it is tempting to conceive of the credit sequence as engaged in two distinct endeavors: the introduction of a general community on the one hand and a specific crime on the other. Yet with one photograph that lies between the first seven and the last six, the film makes a connection between these two endeavors, thereby implicating the entire community, as well as the "civilizing" imperative on which it is founded, in a narrative of brutality and violence. In that image, a bloodied and beaten criminal is on display outside the jailhouse for the inspection of the local townspeople who crowd around him as well as for a professional photographer engaged in documenting the spectacle. With this single image, the film makes in summary form a point it expands upon over its duration: that violence, especially when part of a public display involving an engaged and thereby complicit audience, is an integral component of the process of civilization as it is carried out by custodians of colonial culture. In other words, this image functions as a hinge, implicating the people featured prominently and proudly in the images that come before it in the violence whose effects are on display in those that succeed it. (That the director of photography's name, Benoit Delhomme, appears over this image suggests that *The Proposition* is also interested in interrogating its own complicity in the specularization of violence. As I discuss later, this turns out to be only partially true.)

As foreshadowed by these opening credits, *The Proposition* dedicates itself to baldly examining each character's participation in the culture of violence that has taken root in and around the frontier town where Stanley lives, from his troops and Arthur's followers, both of whom kill certain groups of people indiscriminately for varying reasons, to Charlie, who ironically seeks to divest himself of that culture by committing fratricide, to, finally, Stanley's genteel wife, Martha (Emily Watson), who defies her husband by calling for and then watching the public lashing of Mikey Burns. As a result, the lines along which a film might, based on previous precedents, separate the good guys from the bad ones—settler/Aborigine, man/woman, law/outlaw—serve to make distinctions relative not to morality but rather to motive, means, and target. Yet even those distinctions prove provisional at best, as is demonstrated most pointedly by Jellon Lamb (John Hurt), an eccentric and verbose bounty hunter whom Charlie encounters while en route to his brother's hideout. Preoccupied with issues of identity and difference, Lamb dedicates himself in both speech and action to the task of forging alliances and erecting divisions. The inconsistency with which he does so,

The Proposition implicating spectators (and itself) in the brutality on display. (Surefire Films)

however, allows him not only to give voice to competing claims regarding the relationship between (him)self and others but also to demonstrate the extent to which such claims are often contingent and convenient responses to exigencies of the colonial (and, for that matter, postcolonial) context. For example, upon their first meeting, he convinces Charlie to lower his gun by appealing to a shared status and, moreover, a sense of racialized propriety when he says, "No need for that, sir. No need for that. We are white men, you and I." In the end, he betrays his own logic, proving himself a pragmatist by profession: not only does he capture Charlie, but he changes his definition of "white men" in the process, asking rhetorically, "What is an Irishman but a nigger turned inside out?" The comment of Lamb's that most provocatively frames the issues of similitude and difference, however, is one wherein he explains the work of Darwin to Charlie (who, in an act of dissimulation, has presented himself to Lamb as Charles Murphy): "Perhaps you've read *On the Origin of the Species by Means of Natural Selection* by Charles Darwin. Oh, don't be thrown by the title. He had some most fascinating things to say, chilling things. Mr. Darwin spent time studying Aboriginals. He claims we are at bottom one and the same. He infers, Mr. Murphy, that we share a common ancestry with monkeys. Monkeys!" In light of Lamb's uproarious laughter at the mention of monkeys, it is unclear where he himself stands on the issue of evolution. Nonetheless, in invoking Darwin, he raises the specter of both monogenesis and social Darwinism, two discourses that have inflected colonial discourse in myriad ways and to varying ends.

Just as Lamb raises without resolving multiple explanations of the ties that do or do not bind different groups of people, *The Proposition* represents a wide range of interracial and cross-cultural relations. In fact, one of the most fundamental factors that distinguishes the milieu of the Stanleys from that of the Burns gang is the extent to which each qualifies as a frontier with its attendant hierarchies or instead makes possible intersubjective relations like those discussed by Evans. Fully invested in the civilizing imperative that has brought them to Australia, Captain and Martha Stanley are representative of frontier culture. *The Proposition* captures this most summarily in the cultivation of their environs. Perfectly manicured, regularly irrigated, and separated from the expanse of surrounding desert by a white picket fence, the rose gardens flanking their home function as a British cocoon in the midst of the Australian outback. In arranging for the delivery of a small Christmas tree in preparation for the holidays, Martha further underscores both her family's displacement and its pursuit of conformity via control. Just as Martha devotes herself to refashioning the desert, against all odds, in the guise of an English garden, her husband dedicates himself to enforcing the law of the land and in the process producing an Australia in the likeness of the motherland whence he came. Within such a frontier context, Aboriginal survival depends upon assimilation, be it in accordance with the norms that prevail in the private sphere associated with Martha or in the public sphere associated with her husband. Cases in point are two Aboriginal men who dutifully act in service of those who employ them: Tobey (Rodney Boschman), a servant who works for the Stanleys, and Jacko (David Gulpilil), an officer who serves as tracker, interpreter, and helpmate to Captain Stanley's squadron.

Despite their integration into colonial culture, these two characters none-theless still manage to maintain a degree of autonomy and agency, as exem-plified by a scene wherein Tobey takes leave of the Stanleys after assisting in the setup of their imported Christmas tree. As he heads out into the heat, Captain Stanley wishes him a merry Christmas. Before replying in kind, Tobey removes the boots he has been wearing and leaves them sitting just inside the gate through which he subsequently makes his barefooted exit. While Tobey demonstrates his resistance to complete assimilation through a blatant renunciation of settler ways once out of settler company, Jacko does so when giving voice to Aboriginal perspectives, as in a scene wherein Stanley interrogates a group of Aboriginal men who were captured after the police killed one of their members. While Jacko's role in this scenario is technically that of interpreter, the staging of the interaction allows Jacko to display his insider knowledge of and investment in local culture. Specifi-cally, Jacko's translated answers to Stanley's questions come quickly and are typically spoken by him when isolated on-screen in close-up, suggesting that the answers he provides are as much his as those of the captured men. For example, when Stanley asks the men via Jacko how long they have been hiding in the ranges where they were captured, Jacko translates the men's response by correcting Stanley—"They don't hide in the ranges, they live in the ranges"—and then adding his own rejoinder: "They've always been living in the ranges." Additionally, later in the interrogation, when the men explain via Jacko that Arthur, according to local lore, turns into a dog at night, Jacko joins the men in howling repeatedly and raucously over the protests of an incredulous Stanley.

In providing Tobey and Jacko with opportunities to perform their alter-ity, these scenes also allow for disruption of the colonial order of things. In the first, for example, the film proves a point made repeatedly by Bhabha in his work on colonial discourse by mapping the distance between mimicry and mockery and demonstrating resemblance and menace to be two sides of the same coin. That is, in concluding this scene with a shot of the abandoned boots, the film calls attention to this element of British propriety, thereby defamiliarizing it at least momentarily and thus robbing it of its "representational authority."[27] In the second scene, Jacko disrupts colonial discourse by not only refuting its logic ("they *live* in the ranges") but also literally drowning it out by lending his voice to a collective bay, which even Stanley cannot quell. That Jacko is played by the most well-known Aboriginal actor both inside and outside Australia only lends further profundity to the performance. Having made a career of playing characters who serve as mediators between white and black culture—in films such as *Walkabout* and *Crocodile Dundee* (Peter Faiman, 1986), *Rabbit-Proof Fence* and *The Tracker* (Rolf de Heer, 2002)—his very presence captures the complexity of that social position and the potential for obsequiousness to give way to rebellion at any moment.

Yet a momentary disruption is not sustained resistance, and acts of autonomy and agency do not guarantee the coherence of an alternate discourse, episteme, or cultural paradigm. Indeed, Tobey's and Jacko's membership in colonial society, as employees and as subjects more generally, is conditioned by their assimilation; this point is made brutally clear to both them and the viewer by the fact that Stanley and those with whom he works consider any Aboriginal person suspected of being a rebel as utterly expendable. To wit, Eden Fletcher (David Wenham), the wealthy landowner from whom Captain Stanley begrudgingly takes occasional orders, responds to news that Stanley released the Aboriginal men brought in for interrogation with a demand for their extermination. He explains his reasoning to Stanley thus: "It's simple, Captain. It's called the law of reciprocity. Kill one of them, and they're going to kill one of ours. Do the job I brought you here to do. If you have to kill one, make sure you bloody well kill them all." Subsequently, Stanley sends his officers out to do just that. While their completion of that task takes place offscreen, the results of it are on full display in a shot surveying the mass of black bodies strewn on the ground in the wake of the massacre.

Given the extent to which colonial culture is associated with violence, the Burns gang's alterity vis-à-vis the Stanleys and all that they represent is evinced not by their brutality per se but rather by the way that brutality functions to configure an alternate paradigm of interracial and interethnic relations. That is, Arthur targets the British, a fact made perversely visual when he wraps Stanley's head in a British flag while giving him a thrashing toward the end of the film, and he serves as father figure to a makeshift family that allows for a measure of reciprocity and mutuality between Aboriginal and settler members. Included in the gang are two Aboriginal characters: Queenie (Leah Purcell), who does not participate in the gang's criminal ventures but is an integral part of their life in hiding, and Two Bob (Tom E. Lewis), who functions as Arthur's right-hand man in the absence of Charlie. While Queenie's role is limited by her exemption from the group's "professional" activities—she is the outlaw counterpart to Martha—Two Bob emerges as a key character who functions, among other things, as foil for Jacko; as he tells Sergeant Lawrence (Robert Morgan) when mistaken for his loyal tracker, "You got the wrong fuckin' black man." The difference that Two Bob evokes is a product of not only textual matters—that is, the fact that he and Jacko follow the lead of different white men and thus occupy parallel positions on different sides of the law—but also extratextual and, by extension, intertextual ones.

Like Gulpilil, Lewis has played characters who move between black and white culture, yet they do so for different reasons and to varying ends. While Gulpilil, whose dark skin serves so frequently to underscore his difference from the colonizer despite his compliance, serves as the ideal mimic ("almost the same but not quite"), Lewis embodies an interstitial racial identity due to his relatively lighter skin color and his personal and textual history as biracial. Indeed, it is difficult to view his character in *The Proposition* without reference to two things: first, his own status as a "yellow fella," which is explored in the recent documentary of that name by Ivan Sen (to be discussed in chapter 2); and, second, to the most (in)famous character Lewis has played in film—the titular "half-breed" whose inability to fit easily into white or Aboriginal culture leads to a rage-fueled killing spree in *The Chant of Jimmie Blacksmith* (Fred Schepisi, 1978), which was written by Thomas Keneally, based on his novel of the same name. Lewis himself makes a connection between *The Proposition* and the latter of these two texts when he describes his role of Two Bob thus: "I really enjoyed this character. I really find that he didn't have to promote himself, 'I'm here. I'm making an Aboriginal statement.' He was in there with his badge. And, yeah, a great piece of writing. It's been a long time since Thomas Keneally, but . . ."[28] Although Lewis does not clarify the nature of the connection, the manner in which he ends his comment—by trailing off and laughing—suggests that of the many characters he has played over the course of his career, these two, separated by more than twenty-five years, are among the most rich and resonant. Yet, unlike Jimmie, whose isolation plays an enormous role in his tragic fate, Two Bob is part of an outlaw community and an interracial one at that. As a result, through both his person and his position, he embodies a kind of intersubjectivity that calls into question the categories upon which racial hierarchies depend.

Despite his disruptive potential, however, the film's final word on race matters does not foreground the example of Two Bob, nor does it revive Jacko as a colonial archetype; rather, it draws attention to the many Aboriginal people who suffered fates similar to the group massacred by Stanley's men. With its closing credits, the film presents yet another succession of photographs, the first of which is similar to those seen at the start of the film insofar as it features a racially mixed group of police officers posing for the camera. The rest, however, bespeak an extreme and extremely racialized violence, featuring Aboriginal people standing in formation while bound by chains or huddling together in a seemingly defensive posture. The final image, the most blatantly brutal of the bunch, features a white man beating a black man, whose bared body is turned toward the camera. Like the photographs related to the Hopkins murders, these final four images are quite different and seemingly disconnected from those that precede them (namely, the single shot at the start of the closing credit sequence as well as the opening credit sequence in its entirety). Yet once again, there is a relationship of profound textual and historiographic significance. In this case, however, the hinge that brings together the seemingly unrelated material is the film as it plays itself out between the credit sequences, and the relationship at issue is one between an archetypal settler story and that which it disavows. In other words, the final credit sequence stages a return of that which is so commonly repressed in narratives of the frontier, be they concerned with the civic life or criminal activities of a particular community. The result is an ending that documents the violence that allows for white settler communities to take root and that thus has the potential to make painfully clear upon whose (bared and beaten) backs such communities have been built.

Despite its capacity to provoke, however, the ending does not fully realize that potential, since the five images just discussed only start to appear two and a half minutes into the credits, long after many spectators would have left the theater or stopped viewing the film in a home exhibition format. In fact, their delayed introduction calls into question the extent to which Hillcoat is trading on the violence they depict, especially when they are considered in conjunction with other aspects of the film: for example, the inclusion of certain images that are both visually graphic and narratively gratuitous (such as that of an Aboriginal man's head being shot off) and the film's relentless focus on the triangle created by Charlie, Arthur, and Stanley, which prevents it from fully excavating the buried history toward which the photographs at hand gesture. Despite the fact that its ambitions outrun its execution, however, *The Proposition* is still an exceptional genre film insofar as it grapples with issues that other texts of its kind rarely even acknowledge. In the process, it foregrounds the politics of location, both geographic and social, thereby confirming screenwriter and composer Nick Cave's description of it as a movie about "people struggling in a place where they really have no right to be."[29]

Going Native, Getting the Girl

At the conclusion of *The Proposition*, Charlie does finally shoot Arthur, but not in pursuit of the incentive offered by Stanley, since Mikey is, by that point, already dead. Rather, he does so in order to prevent any future rampages, to break the pattern of violence in which Arthur has embroiled his family. In the final scene of the film, Charlie and Arthur are spending their last moments together, seated side by side and watching the setting sun, when Arthur asks, "What are you gonna do now?" Immediately thereafter, Arthur expires and Charlie continues to stare silently ahead, allowing the question to hang in the air indefinitely. With this conclusion, the film reveals as little about Charlie's future as it has about his past, allowing him to remain an inscrutable character defined exclusively in terms of the metaphorical space he occupies: a middle ground between Stanley, who serves as arbiter for a displaced and intrusive British authority, and Arthur, whose socio-pathology dictates a way of life that cannot be sustained. Nonetheless, by raising the specter of a new beginning and an untold future, the film shores up Charlie's circumstantial resemblance to Australia, suggesting that what hangs in the balance in the wake of Arthur's death is not only Charlie's fate but also that of the country whose federation is impending.

In constructing Charlie as representative of a proto-Australian identity that takes shape in contradistinction to a British paradigm that is unresponsive to local environment and exigencies, *The Proposition* bears a resemblance to two other relatively recent contact narratives: Jane Campion's *The Piano* and Michael Mann's *The Last of the Mohicans*, which offer up George Baines (Harvey Keitel) and Hawkeye (Daniel Day-Lewis), respectively, as characters who function in a likewise manner in the New Zealand and U.S. contexts. Despite parallels between their characterization and, by extension, symbolic function, however, Charlie differs from Baines and Hawkeye in a couple of noteworthy ways. First, while Charlie's association with Aboriginal culture is distant, predicated only on his past participation in Arthur's makeshift family and the interracial cooperation and collaboration that it fostered, Baines and Hawkeye have "gone native," fully embracing a hybridized identity and, at least on the surface, divesting themselves of Eurocentricism. Second, as opposed to Charlie, who takes shape relative to two other men, the characters of Baines and Hawkeye are produced through triangulated relations of a different sort; that is, in both cases, their British counterpart is a male competitor with whom they vie for the love of a woman. As a result, they function as romantic leads instead of (*The Piano*) or in addition to (*The Last of the Mohicans*) action heroes. While I have introduced these two distinguishing factors as discrete, they are in fact implicated in each other insofar as it is precisely Baines's and Hawkeye's association with Indigenous culture that signals, if not produces, a capacity for both passion and compassion that eludes their rivals. For this reason, these films are part of a distinct—and distinctly postcolonial—subset of the cinema of new masculinity that, according to Susan Jeffords, emerged in the 1990s.

In "The Big Switch: Hollywood Masculinity in the Nineties," Jeffords argues that a number of sociohistorical factors, including second wave feminism, certain facets of the men's movement, and the end of the Cold War, have produced a new breed of celluloid hero that is "sensitive, generous, caring and, perhaps most importantly, capable of change."[30] While she does not reference either *The Last of the Mohicans* or *The Piano* over the course of her article, she certainly could have, for they share with those films she does cite—for example, *Kindergarten Cop* (Ivan Reitman, 1990), *Switch* (Blake Edwards, 1991), and *City Slickers* (Ron Underwood, 1991)—a commitment to creating male characters that are "kinder" and "gentler" than their cinematic predecessors. Yet the manner in which they do so reveals them to be informed by a postcolonial imperative to produce a kinder and gentler colonialism as well. According to the logic of the films, by renouncing aspects of their British cultural identity, Baines and Hawkeye achieve a degree of critical distance from certain patriarchal practices and thus offer to their partners the possibility of relative "liberation" within the context of a heterosexual union as well as a new national identity. For those white women at the center of *The Piano* and *The Last of the Mohicans*, who "simultaneously constitute 'center' and 'periphery,' identity and alterity" within the colluding and intersecting structures of patriarchy and imperialism, Baines's and Hawkeye's choice to position themselves not quite on the periphery but at least "off-center" of colonial power qualifies them as suitable lovers.[31] In other words, analogous experiences of liminality become the common ground for romantic relations. Yet a relationship of analogy is not a relationship of identity. While Hawkeye's and Baines's hybrid identities serve to define the character of future nations, those of their lovers enjoy no such resolution or consolidation and instead lay bare the extent to which women's relationships to nation are typically and historically mediated by intimate attachments; as E. Ann Kaplan puts it, "Women do not inhabit a space of the state as home: women rather inhabit a space of their family as home, a space of much more local relations."[32]

In 1992, Michael Mann followed the example of countless filmmakers, playwrights, animators, television programmers, and radio performers before him and produced yet another adaptation of James Fenimore Cooper's fictional novel *The Last of the Mohicans: A Narrative of 1757*. Despite the number of past and present literary critics, including most notoriously Mark Twain, who have maligned it for its poor prose and improbable situations, Cooper's quintessentially American story of revenge and rescue, love and rejection, racial difference and cultural extinction in the midst of war between colonial powers has, nonetheless, achieved the status of myth.[33] Yet that myth has proven extremely unstable, since almost every retelling has taken great liberties with regard to plot, character development, and/or theme. According to Jeffrey Walker, Hollywood has been particularly disloyal to the original text, bringing to the screen "those elements of *The Last of the Mohicans* that have little to do with Cooper's original story but have everything to do with twentieth-century American popular culture and taste."[34] Thus, it is no surprise that this most recent cinematic version, which draws more heavily upon Philip Dunne's screenplay for George Seitz's 1936 production than on any other source material, bears scant resemblance to the novel whose title it bears. Like Dunne, Mann and co-writer Christopher Crowe shift the focus of Cooper's tale by treating Hawkeye as the protagonist rather than as a supporting character and by creating romantic pairings that skirt rather than engage the issue of miscegenation; unlike Dunne, they push the envelope of adaptation even further, subordinating all other plot points and narrative concerns to the love affair between Hawkeye and Cora Munro (Madeleine Stowe), one of three British travelers whom Hawkeye and his adoptive Mohican family, father Chingachgook (Russell Means) and brother Uncas (Eric Schweig), save from certain death at the hands of a Huron war party.

In the case of *The Last of the Mohicans*, the third point in the triangle, the man who embodies that which Hawkeye has rejected, is Duncan (Steven Waddington), the British officer who seeks Cora's hand in marriage. With his bright red uniform, ignorance of the terrain, nationalistic arrogance, and unflagging loyalty to the crown, he serves as foil for Hawkeye, whose association with American Indian culture goes hand in hand with his refusal to defer to British rule. In telling Duncan, "I ain't your scout, and I sure ain't no damn militia," he positions himself as a renegade whose cultural hybridity marks his marginalization from any extant social system.

His sympathies lying not only with his almost extinct tribe but also with the settlers living on the frontier whom he and his adoptive family have befriended, he emerges as a proto-American, a nonconformist living by his own moral code, a man of the future whose past has been renounced on the one hand and is vanishing on the other.

When Cora meets up with Duncan upon his arrival in Albany, *The Last of the Mohicans* makes clear that the manner in which Cora is expected to fulfill her role as a respectable British woman is by marrying Duncan. Yet, despite her suitor's persistence and her father's wholehearted support of the union, Cora initially defers and ultimately refuses to accept the marriage proposal because she is not in love. The film frames Cora's resistance as evidence of her independence since Duncan attempts to win her acceptance by employing a rhetorical strategy designed to make her doubt her own feelings and concede to the authority of others: "Why not let those whom you trust—your father—help settle what's best for you [that is, your marriage]? In view of your indecision you should rely on their judgment—and mine." After Hawkeye, Uncas, and Chingachgook rescue Cora, Duncan, and Cora's sister Alice (Jodhi May) from the Huron, however, Cora recognizes Hawkeye's similarly independent will and begins to transfer to him any caring feelings she might have had for Duncan. In a scene establishing her budding attraction to Hawkeye, she tells him that the frontier, with which he is so strongly identified, has defied all of her expectations and "is more deeply stirring to my blood than any imagining could possibly have been." In a metonymic slippage, this visceral reaction to her circumstances bespeaks her nascent passion for Hawkeye, which is finally acted upon at Fort William Henry, where Cora's father is occupying his post as a colonel in the British army.

Cora's independence yields to rebellion when she actually becomes romantically involved with Hawkeye. After arriving at the fort, Hawkeye makes an appeal to Colonel Munro (Maurice Roeves) on behalf of the members of the militia who need to leave the fort in order to return to their homes on the frontier and protect their families from Huron aggression. When his comments are dismissed and the colonials are ordered to stay loyal to British interests by remaining at the fort, he helps a handful of men desert and is subsequently accused of and jailed for sedition. Enraged by her father's decision and Duncan's refusal to support Hawkeye, despite having witnessed the gruesome aftermath of a Huron attack on settlers, Cora takes up Hawkeye's case in his absence and passionately declares, "If [the treatment of Hawkeye] is justice, then the sooner French guns blow the English army out of America, the better it will be for the people here. . . . I know exactly what I am saying and if it is sedition, then I am guilty of sedition too." In this exchange, the personal (Cora and Hawkeye's romance) and the political (the plight of the colonial militia) are conflated as Cora defies the authority of her father and, by extension, Duncan, both of whom presume to know "what's best" for her in their capacity as not only army officers but also men. While she may indeed be guilty of sedition, her traitorous act is not so much that of slandering the British or advocating defiance of the crown as that of refusing to assume the position allocated for her within the British patriarchal nuclear family. Given the nature of women's relationship to nation, the use of the word "sedition" for such rebellion is not just metaphorical; through her involvement with Hawkeye, Cora does indeed compromise her allegiance to Britain, emerging by the end of the film as another representative of a burgeoning American identity founded on an ethos of self-determination. On this count, the last scene of Mann's film, which shows Cora, Hawkeye, and Chingachgook standing together on a mountaintop in the wake of the deaths of Duncan, Uncas, and Alice, is particularly telling. While Chingachgook, as the very last of the Mohicans, represents an ending, Cora and Hawkeye become emblematic of a begin-ning—a new generation, a "new world," a new national identity. As Patrick Brantlinger puts it, "The elegiac loss of history experienced by the Mohicans is the negative or Great Zero from which springs the future-perfect, epic history of the United States."[35]

Like Cora, *The Piano*'s Ada (Holly Hunter) refuses to fulfill the role ex-pected of her when she rejects a man readily identified with the colonizing nation and instead chooses to be with someone who has adapted to his circumstances by partaking of certain aspects of Aboriginal culture. Yet while the staging of that refusal is little more than a means of foregrounding Hawkeye's exceptional nature in *The Last of the Mohicans*, the love triangle at the center of *The Piano* allows for the development of a structural critique of patriarchal authority and the possibility of a heterosexual relationship that does not assume or require female subordination. Set in nineteenth-century colonial New Zealand, *The Piano* tells the story of Ada, a mute Scottish woman who becomes enmeshed in a love triangle after she travels with her daughter, Flora (Anna Paquin), halfway around the world in order to meet Stewart (Sam Neill), the stranger to whom her father has married her. Feeling no affection for Stewart, especially after he fails to understand that she cannot be separated from her beloved piano, Ada becomes involved in an extramarital relationship with Baines, a fellow colonist. While that relationship eventually blooms into a passionate, consensual love affair, it begins as an exploitative bargain whereby Ada agrees to let Baines use her in sexual ways in order to earn back her piano from him after Stewart exchanges it for a parcel of land.

Given the film's ultimate endorsement of a love born of extortion, there is great discord with regard to the issue of whether *The Piano* allows for the emergence of a strong female character, a specifically feminine desire, and/or an empowering point of identification for the (female) spectator.[36] Nonetheless, critics writing in response to *The Piano* generally agree that by challenging the conventionalized male gaze of cinema, Campion is at least able to level a structural critique of the patriarchal power assumed by Stewart, who negotiates relationships with both his wife and his landscape according to the dictates of strictly codified property rights. Indeed, Ada is not only the film's subject but also its source of enunciation, since Campion foregrounds Ada's perspective via a multitude of both point-of-view and reaction shots as well as a soundtrack dominated by her affective piano playing, which one character likens to a "mood that passes into you." Establishing the precedent for this approach are the film's opening moments wherein Campion pairs a highly subjective opening shot of a fragmented world as seen through Ada's spread fingers with a voice-over that attests to Ada's tremendous strength of will: "The voice you hear is not my speaking voice, it is my mind's voice. I have not spoken since I was six years old. No one knows why, not even me. My father says it is a dark talent and the day I take it into my head to stop breathing will be my last." In light of the spectatorial identification that Campion forges with her protagonist consistently from here on in, subsequent attempts on the part of Stewart and, to a lesser extent, Baines to contain her will prove damning evidence of overt abuse and manipulation.

At the start of the film, Ada is already living a life that is severely circumscribed by patriarchal law insofar as her father has just given her away in marriage to a man she does not know. The degree to which she is deprived of agency, however, only escalates once she relocates to New Zealand, where she meets her new husband, who immediately assumes ownership of her piano, and Baines, who takes advantage of the dependency she has on the instrument in order to extort sexual favors. Yet despite the fact that Stewart and Baines are both responsible for using their power to deprive Ada of her instrument of self-expression, the film defines the two characters against each other even before it reveals the "noble" nature of Baines's motives (for him, the bargain is a compromising means to the end of love rather than an end in itself).[37] For example, while Stewart is concerned only with Ada's appearance upon her arrival, wondering aloud if she is stunted, Baines makes a more sympathetic observation when he states, "She looks tired"; while Stewart questions Ada's sanity when he finds her pretending to play the piano on a wood table, Baines is taken in by the imaginative universe created by mother and daughter when they visit the piano on the beach; and while Stewart is clearly unpracticed in emotional or physical intimacy, Baines displays a profound appreciation of the sensual in the way he handles Ada's clothing and cares for the piano.

The most significant difference, however, between the two men is established not in how they initially interact with Ada but in how they react when she withholds that which they desire. When Baines realizes that Ada is not learning to care for him as he had hoped, he calls off their bargain and releases her from any further obligations. In contrast, once Ada enters into a consensual relationship with Baines, Stewart attempts to lay claim to Ada's body and control her behavior in a most brutal manner by, first, attempting to rape her following his discovery of the affair; second, chopping off her finger after intercepting a piano key-cum-love letter being delivered to Baines; and, third, attempting to rape her once again as she lies unconscious while recovering from the aforementioned amputation. It is only in the midst of this last violation that Ada finally succeeds in communicating with Stewart, making him understand through the intensity of her stare her need to leave him. After Stewart agrees to honor her request, she, Flora, and Baines head off to Nelson by boat. While en route to their new home, Ada demands that her piano be thrown overboard and then sticks her foot in the ropes holding the piano so that she too will be pulled into the sea as they unravel. Despite her suicidal impulse, Ada is suddenly overtaken by the will to live while underwater and consequently struggles to free herself from the piano and fight her way to the water's surface. After this incident, the film cuts to Nelson, where, as the penultimate scene of the film reveals, Ada and Baines are living a stable life as newborn New Zealanders. With a metal fingertip crafted by Baines, a more feminized appearance, a job teaching piano lessons, a commitment to learning to speak, and an outlaw status limited to the benign role of "town freak," Ada is well on her way to full assimilation into the prevailing social order.[38]

Signifying Surfaces

For *The Proposition*, *The Piano*, and *The Last of the Mohicans*, part and parcel of consolidating the identity of a settler society is staging a break with Britain, and the most expedient way of accomplishing this is through enmeshing the character who comes to embody the burgeoning nation in a set of triangulated relations. That is, each film is able to establish his most important trait, adaptability, by doing the following: defining him against an unyielding Brit who makes decisions based on an unexamined sense of rectitude and superiority and associating him closely with a character who, for whatever reason, is even more displaced from the center of colonial power and thus occupies a station akin to that of the film's Aboriginal population. Yet what these films also demonstrate is that in the case of cinema, whose melodramatic potential depends upon its ability to communicate information as efficiently and affectively as possible, the antinomy between motherland and rebellious child needs to be both highly charged and immediately legible. Thus, it is not sufficient to rely on narrative action or dialogue to establish the relationship between Britain's embodiment and that of its dominions; rather, the radical alterity of the latter needs to take shape through other means as well. *The Proposition*, for example, characterizes Charlie as not only an outlaw but also Irish, thereby inscribing the situation of Australia within a broader history of conflict, oppression, and racialization.[39] Hawkeye and Baines, in contrast, literally wear their difference, since they are visibly marked by that which distinguishes them from the British norm: their association with Indigenous culture. Or, to put it in terms that more accurately reflect the way meaning is made in film, directors Mann and Campion use appearance to suggest an unrepresented past and to construct an interior self for their characters, both of which serve to distinguish them from their British counterparts. In sum, the hybridity of Hawkeye and Baines is performative, "[constituting] as an effect the very subject it appears to express."[40]

For this reason, these two characters are a fascinating lens through which to examine the construction and circulation of Aboriginality as sign in postcolonial contact narratives—that is, how it is represented; what iconographic, narrative, and ideological functions it serves; and how it inflects other determinants of social position and identity, such as gender. Moreover, they raise interesting questions about the politics of cultural hybridity and its representation. On the one hand, their celluloid presence has the potential to force an acknowledgment of cultural difference, to destabilize the boundaries between self and other, to subvert politically conservative mandates of cultural purity, and, finally, to draw attention to the performativity of all identities. On the other, however, they, like the films Jeffords discusses, redefine the male body without "challeng[ing] the whiteness of that body, nor the special figuration that body demands"[41] and thereby illustrate a point made by Deborah Root when she defines "cultural appropriation" as a term that "signifies not only the taking up of something and making it one's own but also the ability to do so."[42]

The Last of the Mohicans: "Form-Fitting Buckskin"

In conjunction with a visual style that has been described as hypnotic, hyperkinetic, and stylized, Mann's decision to foreground the romance between two dashing figures and to develop that romance through a series of adventurous action sequences results in a film that is more invested in the texture of the image than in the complexities of plot. Because of this privileging of the visceral over the intellectual, Mann constructs character largely through the way his players look and move. For Hawkeye, who is extremely short on words and long on screen time, appearance is particularly meaningful. Although the fact that Hawkeye is a white man raised from infancy as a Mohican may be common knowledge for some due to the number of times that Cooper's tale has played itself out on paper, stage, and screen, for those who are ignorant of this background information, Mann's film offers no explanations until well into its first hour. Instead, it establishes Hawkeye's hybridity by endowing an actor, whose racial identity or "whiteness" is the subject of extratextual knowledge, with those physical markers considered representative of American Indian identity: an occasionally bared chest, buckskin clothing, and long hair. Root summarizes the reason that such markers function so effectively as a visual shorthand when she argues in her book *Cannibal Culture: Art, Appropriation, and the Commodification of Difference* that exoticism is synecdochic. When discussing the means by which the West aestheticizes and consumes cultural difference in order to compensate for its own ambivalence and loss of tradition, she writes, "The particular signs used to represent difference rarely constitute a cultural whole, yet are made to stand for entire concepts and cultural categories. Cultural, ethnic, and sexual difference is connoted by fleeting, fragmentary images."[43]

In *The Last of the Mohicans*, Hawkeye's signs of alterity bear an even greater burden of representation than usual since the cultural whole to which they point, the Mohican people, is rapidly vanishing in the face of colonial invasion and tribal warfare. Had Chingachgook and Uncas, the last living members of the tribe, been more fully developed characters, they might have provided a context for such signs and, by extension, an understanding of the culture with which Hawkeye actively identifies. As it is, however, no such insight is achieved. The tribal identity of the Mohicans is defined not by its specific nature but rather by the way it differs from that of the vengeful Magua (Wes Studi) and the Huron people of whom he is representative. The Huron, like the Pawnee in *Dances with Wolves*, are depicted almost exclusively when engaged in or planning violence and are spurred to action by dubious motives. Yet while *Dances with Wolves* pits "good Indian" against "bad Indian" but still manages to attribute to the former a measure of complexity, *The Last of the Mohicans* not only reproduces historically entrenched stereotypes of American Indians but also fails to endow the Mohicans with any depth of character. Insofar as Chingachgook and Uncas serve as supporting characters both narratively (they dutifully fall in with any plan that Hawkeye hatches and rarely speak to anyone besides one another) and visually (their presence on the screen is almost always conditioned by their proximity to or interaction with Hawkeye), they are depicted as having no autonomous existence. In short, their primary function in the film is similar to that of Hawkeye's long hair: to establish Hawkeye's character by reference to a generic notion of the noble savage.

Yet these synecdochic signs of his alterity evoke for the audience not only the exotic but also the erotic, thereby functioning as fetishes and contributing to Hawkeye's sexualization. Whether doling out a rating of "thumbs up" or "thumbs down," four stars or two, critics of Mann's *The Last of the Mohicans* all agree that Daniel Day-Lewis attained heartthrob status in the film's leading role; for example, while one dubs Day-Lewis's Hawkeye a dreamboat, another refers to him as "a cross between Iron John and romance-novel cover boy Fabio."[44] Moreover, in making a case for Hawkeye's sex appeal, such reviewers inevitably single out those aspects of his appearance that mark his status as cultural hybrid. The reasons for this dual process of exoticization/eroticization are multifarious. First, Hawkeye's role as romantic lead in a narrative of heterosexual attraction conditions the spectator's understanding of him as one who not only feels but also inspires desire. Second, despite the film's expressed goal of featuring authentic and/or historically accurate costumes and props, popular expectations of what an American Indian *should* look like encouraged the display of Day-Lewis's body. Russell Means, a longtime activist within the American Indian Movement who made his acting debut in the role of Chingachgook, explains, "I thought the breechcloths were too small. I told Mann that Indians never wore them that small, but he insisted the costumes were accurate because he'd seen one on a dummy dressed up like an Iroquois in a museum—a white museum, I reminded him. He let me wear the size I wanted, but he left the others small, probably to titillate the women in the audience."[45] While Mann has never spoken to the issue of whether he sacrificed accuracy in the name of titillation, the fact that Hawkeye is bare-chested throughout parts of the film while his Mohican companions always have shirts suggests that the desire to construct Hawkeye as hunk may indeed have informed Mann's decision to ignore Means's protestations. The effect of this decision was not lost on Janet Maslin of the *New York Times*, who writes, "What better way to attract the dating crowd to, say, the French and Indian War than to provide the sight of Daniel Day-Lewis in form-fitting buckskin?"[46]

Certainly, Hawkeye's erotic appeal can, to some extent, be attributed to the small size of his breechcloths; it is more likely, though, the fact that he wears breechcloths in the first place that contributes most to his sexualization. As a result, one must look beyond the text to the third reason for Hawkeye's exoticization/eroticization: dominant cultural assumptions about the sexual/ized other. Historically, popular archetypes of the American Indian male have frequently included a sexual component, but what distinguishes recent depictions of such masculinity from their predecessors is, according to Peter van Lent, the nature of that sexuality: "In past centuries, the vision of violent sexuality was pretty standard treatment of Native men in popular genres such as the Indian captivity narratives. Today, however, Native American men are most often portrayed as sexual in 'good' ways."[47] Part noble savage, part fearless warrior, and part historical victim, the American Indian hunk of contemporary popular culture is a perfect combination of strength and vulnerability, stoicism and sensitivity, carnality and spirituality. Yet, in his analysis of not only cinematic images but also romance novel cover art, greeting cards, and painted portraits, van Lent notes that this hunk is often only part Indian since the men depicted frequently possess Caucasian features and thus appear to be of mixed blood. Arguing that "the exoticism of the Native male is always carefully controlled," he explains this representational trend as a means of creating an image of manhood for white audiences that is not so exotic as to be disconcertingly unfamiliar and not so other as to court social taboos regarding racial intermixture.[48] Bearing out van Lent's point is Day-Lewis as Hawkeye, who offers both Cora and the audience, in the words of M. Elise Marubbio, the "superficial attraction of the exotic within the safety of whiteness."[49]

While Hawkeye's role as romantic lead, frequently exposed body, and association with a culture that is assumed to possess a certain sexual cachet make him the ideal object for a scopophilic gaze, it is the film's cinematography that ensures his specularization. As is demonstrated clearly by the film's opening scene, Hawkeye's function as a point for active spectatorial identification throughout the film cannot be divorced from his repeated objectification as image.[50] *The Last of the Mohicans* starts by dropping the spectator into a forest where three men are quickly and noiselessly pursuing a deer. The first five shots of the hunting sequence feature Hawkeye center frame running toward or away from the camera. In the ensuing shots, he is joined by Chingachgook and Uncas until they eventually stop and Hawkeye takes aim. As he rotates to the left while tracking the fleeing deer, the film crosscuts between hunter and prey, moving closer to Hawkeye with each shot. Once framed in close-up, he aims the gun straight at the camera, shoots, and then lowers his weapon, allowing the spectator the first of many opportunities to gaze upon his intent face. Insofar as the stasis of the body, the lingering of the camera, and the accompanying silence distinguish this moment right after the kill from all the action that has preceded it, this close-up functions as a powerful denouement to the hunt. Captured in this opening sequence of shots is the cinematographic strategy that characterizes the rest of the film. Despite the fact that Hawkeye is the moral and narrative center of the movie, Mann employs very few point-of-view shots from his perspective and instead opts repeatedly to center him in the frame, usually either in a static close-up (the last shot described) or as he moves through the landscape (the first five shots in the scene). While the representation of any person in film always involves some degree of objectification, the fact that the camera studies Hawkeye and the film relies upon his appearance to the extent they do begs the question of how exactly Hawkeye is represented when both at rest and in motion. What the answer makes clear is not only the fact of Hawkeye's objectification but also the stakes involved when displaying a white, male body and the lengths to which a film must go in order to empower that body in other ways.

While each close-up of Hawkeye offers the spectator a brief respite from the flow of narrative events in order to contemplate his visage, the film compensates for this specularization through multiple means, thereby bearing out Peter Lehman's contention that "the apparent role reversal privileging the female gaze and objectifying the male body has to be qualified in several significant ways."[51] The most explicit attempts to qualify Hawkeye's status as object of the spectatorial gaze are contained within those scenes devoted to the development of Hawkeye and Cora's relationship. By abandoning Cora's perspective and privileging Hawkeye's point of view, the film systematically reproduces the male gaze and, in the process, shores up Hawkeye's social power vis-à-vis Cora. Yet, it is not only during his exchanges with the woman on whom he has set his sights that Hawkeye is in control of diegetic looking relations; rather, the potency of his gaze is further (over)determined by the fact that he is an infallible shot. No matter how far his bullet must travel, how fast his enemy runs, how scarce the daylight is, or how many guns he must wield simultaneously, he never once misses his target. Furthermore, in the scene described above, he not only hits his mark but also turns his gun on the spectator such that the power of his gaze reaches beyond the diegetic world and creates a momentary rupture for those consuming his image.

In contradistinction to shots of Hawkeye at rest are those in which he runs swiftly and gracefully toward a given goal (prey, the enemy, Cora's rescue). Shots of Hawkeye in motion and flanked on either side by his father and brother are so integral to the visual texture of the film that Alan Bourassa characterizes the moving body as the film's defining element. He writes, "In *Mohicans* the most powerful detail, in fact the one that dominates the film, is what we might call the complex mobile body, which designates not only the single body, but the system of three bodies working together at top speed. . . . Character is subordinated to this moving body."[52] While Bourassa's argument underscores the film's affective power as well as the perfectly choreographed manner in which Hawkeye, Uncas, and Chingachgook move, his suggestion that the corporeal and the collective are privileged over the internal and the individual fails to take into account the salience of Hawkeye's racial identity and leading man status. Despite an interest in the dynamic triad or what Bourassa calls the "complex mobile body," the film repeatedly singles out Hawkeye's motion by shooting him in shallow focus, centering him in the frame, or featuring him alone in the shot and thereby constructs his as the most important body. Reinforcing the film's form is the fact of Hawkeye's whiteness. While the on-screen presence of Chingachgook and Uncas is primarily iconic in nature, Hawkeye is assumed to have an interior self to which all surface effects refer for the same reason that Hollywood has relocated him multiple times from the margins of Cooper's text to the center of the film screen: whiteness connotes a metaphysics that exceeds the visible bodily surface, a depth of character customarily considered necessary for the protagonist of a (filmic) narrative. Thus, in Hawkeye's case, character is not so much subordinated to as constructed through the moving body, just as it is constructed through his hair and manner of dress.

Like the close-ups of Hawkeye at rest, the shots that position him as the most important mobile body on-screen contribute to his sexualization as well, for he is typically featured running with an open shirt or bare-chested. The fact that he is literally moving the narrative forward in and through such shots, however, serves to align him far more with the archetypal male protagonist posited by Laura Mulvey than with his feminine counterpart. Yet it is not only his gender privilege that is threatened with the display of his body. In his book-length study of the representation of whiteness in Western visual culture, Richard Dyer observes that white men are rarely depicted in any state of undress in cinema and then goes on to note, "This is not so with non-white bodies. In the Western, the plantation drama, and the jungle adventure film, the non-white body is routinely on display."[53] This routine display is both a cause and effect of the commonplace reduction of nonwhite subjectivity to that body that deviates from an assumed white norm. The exhibition of the normative body, which points beyond itself to an individual spirit and mind, however, creates a paradox with regard to whiteness as sign. While visibility of the white body provokes recognition of the corporeal, whiteness in general, like masculinity, signifies a transcendence of that very corporeality and the subjective specificity that it connotes. Thus, the danger of display is that attention to the white male body could result in a loss of legitimacy or a vitiation of those transcendent qualities deemed inherent to whiteness. Within the films analyzed by Dyer, such as those featuring Rambo, Hercules, or Tarzan, this danger is quelled by the qualification of that body as exceedingly muscular or athletically exceptional. Thus, in these cases, both the body and the interior self are superlative.

While Day-Lewis does not possess the brawn of Sylvester Stallone in the Rambo series or the Olympic gold medals of Johnny Weismuller, star of several Tarzan films, his body is exceptional, nonetheless, in the efficiency, agility, and grace with which it moves through any given terrain. Armed with such a body, Hawkeye is capable of leveling all obstacles in his path and performing a succession of valiant deeds in order to save the day. In fact, those characteristics of Hawkeye's that, according to the logic of the film, can be attributed to his socialization outside of European white culture are so fully developed that he repeatedly emerges as the de facto leader of the independent trio. He is not simply *as* knowledgeable about the forest, *as* passionately loyal to those he loves, and *as* capable in the face of danger as Chingachgook and Uncas, but he is *more so*. Running the fastest, shooting the straightest, and desiring the most intensely, Hawkeye is the driving force behind the film visually and narratively. As a result, he is, like Dunbar in *Dances with Wolves*, the singular hero—a role for which his whiteness qualifies him as well as the special figuration that his whiteness demands.

The Piano: "Maori in Spirit"

In the tellingly titled "Forgetting Genocide: Or, the Last of *The Last of the Mohicans*," Patrick Brantlinger argues that Cooper's tale, in its original form and in every one of its subsequent iterations, has contributed to the fantasy of autogenocide. That Mann's version does not escape this ideological fate is not for a lack of trying, since Mann, in Brantlinger's estimation, attempts to erase Cooper's racism by refusing to explain the disappearance of the Mohicans in the terms the novelist employs. Yet insofar as he does not offer any other explanation either, especially that of genocide, he ends up naturalizing the fantasy and thereby reifying the assumption that American Indians were always, already vanishing when first encountered by European settlers. Thus, in the end, Chingachgook remains an object of romanticization, and Hawkeye's ability to adapt shores up his singularity. Unlike Mann's *The Last of the Mohicans*, *The Piano* is informed less by narratives of an (auto)genocidal past (which have dominated the popular imagination of North America for centuries) than by aspirations for a bicultural future (which have heavily influenced New Zealand social policy for over two decades). Thus, in addition to deliberately rewriting conventional gender roles in both history and fiction, it presents the Maori as a vital, if marginalized, constituency in a community characterized by a dynamic interplay of cross-cultural exchange and separatism. Yet, for Anna Neill and Lynda Dyson, such vitality in conjunction with the kinder, gentler colonialism that Baines embodies does not necessarily guarantee exemption from the category to which Brantlinger consigns Mann's work: the "now widely popular genre of nostalgic—or better, amnesiac—imperialist adventure tale."[54]

Both Dyson and Neill take as their starting point the film's function as, in Dyson's words, "a textual palliative for postcolonial anxieties generated by contemporary struggles over the nation's past."[55] Thus, they dedicate themselves to an examination of the means by which the film constructs for Ada, Baines, and, by extension, the contemporary white New Zealander a Pakeha national identity that positions them not as colonial aggressors or European occupants but rather as legitimate members of a bicultural community.[56] For Neill, *The Piano* offers up the Maori as objects of national mourning rather than as agents of historical change in order to construct the subject of the Pakeha in their image. The result is the usurpation of the Maori voice and a depoliticization of the Maori presence as the film refuses to acknowledge any one of the various means of organized resistance that had already been mounted by the 1850s in response to colonial claims on both land and sovereignty. Summing up her argument, Neill writes, "Ada's recovery of language at the end of the film offers a critical narration of the colonial past even as it preserves the colonized as the truly muted subjects of that history."[57] Dyson is most critical of the fact that *The Piano* can realize its postcolonial project only through the deployment of myriad colonial tropes, the most insidious of which is the positioning of the Maori as outside history: "The Maori are located on the margins of the film as the repositories of an authentic, unchanging and simple way of life: they play 'nature' to the white characters' 'culture.'"[58] While Dyson does locate a few rare instances in which the Maori transcend their station of local color and "write themselves back into the script," the fact that she devotes only one short paragraph to their discussion indicates clearly that she does not see them as significantly challenging the film's primitivist discourse.[59]

A close reading of *The Piano* bears out the points made by both Neill and Dyson, for Campion does reify the historically entrenched construction of Aboriginal culture as "ethnographiable." How she does so, however, is a more complicated matter. Campion does not simply locate the Maori in the dreamtime of Maoriland rather than in the national time of New Zealand, which Neill contends, or recycle without interrogation tired tropes, as Dyson argues. Rather, she mounts an (albeit limited) effort to historicize the Maori and thereby acknowledge their ongoing negotiation with the process of European settlement, but she ultimately fails for reasons that are both textual and extratextual in nature. It is precisely this failure that makes this film an interesting case study.

The clearest indication of the strategy Campion employs to this end is on display in the one scene Dyson cites as exemplary of those rare occasions when the Maori insert themselves into a film that otherwise reduces them to stereotypical background color: that wherein Stewart meets Ada and Flora on the beach after their overseas journey. In it, Campion uses the Maori effectively to expose the fissures of not one but two overdetermined systems of subjugation based on difference. During a heated exchange that constitutes the scene's climax, Stewart tells Ada that her piano must stay on the beach for the time being, and Ada, in response, demands (via her interpreter, Flora) that it be taken to the house with her other possessions. As Ada signs to Flora, she shares the frame with the body of a Maori man who, although out of focus, can be seen imitating her gestures. Likewise, as Stewart attempts to counter Ada's protest, he is filmed in a two-shot with another Maori man who stands behind him, parodying his every move in a much more flagrant fashion and spurring on the other Maori men, who begin to make jokes about Stewart's temper. Feeling his authority waning, Stewart ends the conversation abruptly, voicing the final word in the conversation: the piano will stay. This scene, which offers a visual mockery of the colonizing culture at precisely the moment when Ada challenges Stewart's assumption of patriarchal authority, serves two crucial functions. First, it posits the interconnectedness and historical collusion of patriarchal and colonial power and lays the groundwork for a subsequent critique of gender relations that draws heavily on colonialism as metaphor. Second, it displays the tenuous and arbitrary nature of both patriarchal and colonial authority, which Stewart attempts to naturalize but must continually reconstitute as the law. While Ada's challenge to patriarchal power is direct and ultimately recouped, the Maori men's pantomime of the quarreling couple creates a lingering visual mockery of the colonizing culture by employing a strategic relay of gazes that takes Stewart as its ultimate object.

This scene, which exploits the parodic potential of mimicry, exists on a continuum with a range of other moments in the film that cumulatively serve to foreground the ambivalence of colonial discourse and to denaturalize imperial authority. Among such moments are ones featuring actions akin to Tobey's removal of his shoes in *The Proposition*: Stewart's servants singing "God Save the Queen" while they sew, two women trying on Ada's shawl while making coy faces, and a rambunctious group pounding on the piano keys. Enhancing the salience of this occasional behavior on the part of individual characters is the costuming of all the Maori featured since they are, as a group, dressed in a manner that bespeaks multiple cultural influences, combining garments and/or ornamentation from local cultural tradition with items of European clothing such as top hats, suit vests, and long dresses. Through this range of imitative acts and appearances, Campion attempts to draw attention, in an ongoing manner, to the political reality of colonialism, for a gesture, a national anthem, and a top hat all serve as signs of a wider political and cultural hegemony and thus firmly locate the Maori within a history of British authority. Furthermore, in light of the scene on the beach, which so explicitly mobilizes such acts and appearances in service of subversion, Campion ensures that they also defamiliarize certain markers of European identity, thereby turning the gaze of the colonizer back upon itself; as that which was "normal" (the top hat when on Stewart) suddenly calls

A Maori man mimicking Stewart in *The Piano*. (CiBy 2000 and Jan Chapman Productions)

attention to itself (the top hat when on a Maori man or woman), European identity and all its signifiers become occasion for inspection.

Given that the Maori figure and function as just described, Baines's hybridity, which is so central to the plot of *The Piano*, begs further consideration. Specifically, it raises the question of whether a white, Western subject can similarly function as a mimic and enact the same de-essentialization that conditions an understanding of racial and national identity as performative. While Bhabha provides no definitive answer to this query, since he reserves the terms "mimic" and "hybrid" for the colonized who "repeats" the identity of the colonizer, thereby displacing colonial presence and undermining its authority, a consideration of *The Piano* may. Indeed, examining the function of Baines's hybridity in comparison to that of the Maori sheds light not only on representational issues specific to *The Piano* but also on those visual and epistemological conventions that inform the construction of any number of (white) hybridized heroes from recent years, including Dunbar and Hawkeye. Like the latter of these two, Baines is visibly marked as hybrid: he wears on his white skin *moko*, or traditional facial tattoos, which serve as a synecdochic sign of Maori culture. Yet his body does not bear the burden of signification to the same extent that Hawkeye's body does, since his physicality (constructed at the level of the image) and certain components of his character (established at the level of the narrative) serve to support one another. That is, as an extension of his dual cultural inscription, his literal in-corporation of the other, Baines is renowned among the colonists for having gotten in "too deep with the natives," since he shares many of the values and customs the film ascribes to the Maori: he speaks their language, he empathizes with their outraged refusal to sell a sacred burial ground to Stewart, and he participates in their open, relaxed conversations about sex. All of these factors lead critic Carol Jacobs to characterize Baines as "European by birth, but Maori in spirit."[60]

At the same time, however, because of his skin color and British birthright, Baines is systematically empowered and thus has the political and economic leverage to own property, keep a Maori woman as a house servant, and purchase from Stewart the piano he knows Ada will do almost anything to recover. Given Baines's failure to divest himself of such colonial privileges, Mark A. Reid designates him as the good cop to Stewart's bad cop and as a character whose participation in certain Maori ways serves only to obscure for viewers like Jacobs "his important 'civilizing' role in a patriarchy and colonialism."[61] Yet to regard Baines as fully assimilated into Maori culture, as Jacobs does, or to reduce him to the role of Stewart's co-conspirator, as Reid does, is to ignore the ways in which he is, in fact, a liminal character and representative of a self-fashioned Pakeha identity. Insofar as his association with the Maori isolates him even further from the many settlers whose class privilege and educational background he already does not share, he is both inside and outside of colonial culture, invested in and excluded from the center of colonial power. As such, Baines is in a position to call into question certain colonial tenets, the most significant of which is related to property rights. Even though he does in fact own property, he is not, like Stewart, driven by the thrill of acquisition or convinced of his unmitigated entitlement to Maori land; instead, he forces Stewart on occasion to reconsider his terms of ownership. Interestingly enough, the scene in which he does so most patently, however, is one having to do with appropriation in the name of patriarchy rather than of colonialism. In it, Baines responds to Stewart's bafflement over the recently returned piano by granting Ada a degree of autonomy that both Stewart and the law would deny her: "It was more to your wife that I gave [the piano]." That Baines fails to challenge Stewart's proprietary assumptions as directly when it comes to Maori land, restricting his reprobation to a look or a meaningful silence, is symptomatic of the fact that his liminality serves less to foster a critique of colonial practice than to qualify him as the film's romantic lead.

Within the logic of the narrative, Baines's association with the Maori endows him with a sensitivity to Ada's social marginalization as well as with two other character traits that prove germane to their romance. First, the film capitalizes upon historically entrenched stereotypes of nonwhite peoples as closer to nature and less sexually repressed than those with fairer skin in order to construct Baines as having a vital sexuality. The film establishes that sexuality, which in turn prompts a type of sexual awakening in Ada, through a number of means. Not only is Baines willing to engage in casual conversation about sex with the Maori and request sexual favors from a woman he barely knows, but he is also shown to be quite at ease with his body, appearing naked—either alone or in Ada's company—in a total of three scenes, one of which contains full frontal nudity.[62] Second, Baines also demonstrates a profound capacity for emotional understanding and display. For example, after calling off the deal when he realizes it "is making [Ada] a whore," he treats Ada with only kindness and concern. In so doing, he distinguishes himself from Stewart, who goes so far as to chop off Ada's finger after she disobeys him, and from the settler community as a whole, which is shown to be complicit in such acts of violence when it eagerly takes in a shadow play about Bluebeard that foreshadows Ada's punishment.

In sum, while signs of European identity on the Maori body are occasion for mimicry/mockery and uncanny displacement, signs of Maori identity on Baines's body serve to construct his character, define his "spirit," and posit him as a sexually and emotionally liberating force for Ada within a narrative in need of a sensitive hero. In other words, *The Piano* suggests that there are indeed limits to the notion of mimicry and to the acts of estrangement it conditions, thereby raising the following question: what cultural assumptions and/or representational conventions with respect to an Aboriginal character ensure the production of the slippage necessary to construct him or her as a menacing mimic rather than as an integrated hybrid like Baines? In other words, why is hybridity not incorporated into his or her identity as it is for the First World subject? To a certain extent, the answer lies in Campion's tendency to use the Maori as foils for her protagonists. While *The Piano* does attempt to position its Maori characters within colonial history and thus render them "historifiable," it nonetheless relegates them to supporting roles such that they have no direct involvement in the central plot of the film. As a result, they function exclusively as silent pundits who provide an effective backdrop against which the constructedness of European identity is thrown into fresh relief. Yet, even in their capacity as spectacle, they only confound First World expectations of Aboriginal authenticity at an exterior or superficial level. In other words, it is not the case that Campion "tosses to the wind any pathos of native purity," as Jacobs contends.[63] First, the little that the film does reveal about the Maori through dialogue and plot, as opposed to appearance, suggests that they maintain a high level of cultural autonomy despite a colonial presence. For example, they never speak English throughout the film and are profoundly naive about aspects of settler culture, as evidenced by their disruption of the community's production of the story of Bluebeard. Yet even more salient than this disjuncture between a hybridity established through the image and a purity suggested by the narrative is an issue that exceeds the terms of this particular film. That Campion ultimately maintains a distinction between the colonizers as civilized and the colonized as primitive, despite her attempts to engage history and distinguish her work from colonialist paradigms, demonstrates the extent to which the specter of colonialism haunts the "postcolonial" present, continuing to condition the way racial identity is codified and bodies are read. Indeed, it is because of the persistence of the stereotype of "the native"—that is, the native *as image*—that the notion of the authentic Maori reappears in *The Piano* right at the site of its very denial, right in the heart of the act of mimicry.

When examining the identity of the native, Rey Chow warns that we must be particularly aware of the centrality of the visual image in its conception. Working from Gayatri Spivak's argument that the subaltern cannot speak in part because the act of speaking itself belongs to a long history of domination, she designates the native as voiceless image within the realm of Western discourse.[64] According to Chow, the native becomes image when the pre-imperialist gaze of the colonized prompts the objectifying gaze of the colonizer, which, in turn, renders and fixes the native as an object in the process of consolidating the ontology of the European self. That this process is a hostile one is made clear when Chow brings Fredric Jameson's identification of the visual as essentially pornographic to bear upon a consideration of colonial and postcolonial representation and asserts, "The image is what has been devastated, left bare, and left behind by aggression."[65] The native subsequently remains image, impervious to change, even in the face of geographical displacement, cross-cultural exchange, and the influence of technological and industrial development. Thus, by invoking a metaphysics of surfaces, Chow suggests that the identity of the native is two-dimensional such that appearance does not create the effect of an essence but rather constitutes essence. In other words, while whiteness automatically connotes a metaphysics of depth, the native is essentially surface, essentially appearance.

According to Bhabha, it is precisely by engaging in a play of surfaces that mimicry unanchors identity from a unified self and confounds the metaphysical opposition between appearance and essence. While Bhabha theorizes the colonized mimic as capable of drawing attention to the manner in which appearance constructs essence with regard to the Western subject, Chow's argument reveals why the white Westerner cannot do the same with regard to Aboriginal identity: for the native, robbed of any discursive or subjective depth, there does not exist the gap between essence and appearance necessary for a theorization of a productive relationship between the two (that is, a relationship in which one produces the other). As such, Chow's theory supplants a relationship of productivity with one of identity, flattening to two dimensions the three-dimensional terrain necessary for Bhabha's deconstructionist play and, in so doing, elucidating the reasons that hybridity inscribes itself on the white European body and the Maori body in such divergent manners. On the one hand, because the native's essence is so fully identified with his or her appearance, the Maori are fixed in the image of the other, reduced to two-dimensional signifiers of a cultural purity that defies history. As a result, attempts to historicize them through the incorporation of aspects of Western identity result in a parodic displacement that serves to deconstruct Western identity but leaves the equation between native, image, and essence intact. On the other, Baines is another hybridized hero, whose association with an oppressed culture (as opposed to a culture of oppression) imbues him with emotional depth and desirable sensitivity. In short, due to dominant assumptions regarding their respective racial identities, both Baines and the Maori emerge in *The Piano* as "Maori in spirit." Deployed within a text in which the Western subject commands discursive primacy *and* within a context in which the Western spectator has already been taught to read the native as sign of the primitive, Campion's critique of imperialism is limited in ways that her critique of patriarchy is not. As a result, the voice that emerges out of the ambivalence of colonial authority is not that of the Aboriginal subject but that of his or her Western informant.

2. SWAN SONGS
Speaking the Aboriginal Subject

The year 2002 marked the release of two Australian features engaged in a common project: the narration of certain events in the life of a particular Aboriginal Australian and, more generally, an examination of the heretofore marginalized history of oppression and resistance to which those events attest. First, in *Black and White*, director Craig Lahiff relays the story of Max Stuart, an Aboriginal man accused and ultimately convicted of raping and killing a nine-year-old girl, despite the prodigious efforts made on his behalf by his underdog lawyers and a populist press in search of scandal. Second, Phillip Noyce's *Rabbit-Proof Fence* is an adaptation of Doris Pilkington Garimara's literary account of her mother Molly and aunt Daisy's escape at the ages of fourteen and seven, respectively, from the Moore River Settlement, where "Stolen Generations" of biracial children from Western Australia were interned in an initiative to breed the black out of them. What is even more noteworthy than their shared interest in individual experiences of systemic racism, however, is the rhetorical strategy that both films employ in order to make their narratives as resonant as possible. Namely, both *Black and White* and *Rabbit-Proof Fence* conclude with a coda featuring the actual people upon whom these stories are based—Max in the former film and Molly and Daisy in the latter—so as to authenticate their fictional versions (played by David Ngoombujarra, Everlyn Sampi, and Tianna Sansbury, respectively), ground their stories both spatially and historically, and position the spectator as a witness to, as well as a consumer of, their travails.

Having ended *Black and White* by indicting the Australian legal system but leaving the question of Max's guilt or innocence unresolved, Lahiff includes footage of the real Max Stuart that underscores the ambiguity of the film's resolution. In it, a shot of the landscape as seen from a moving car is accompanied by Max's voice-over: "Yeah, some people think that I'm guilty, and some people think I'm not." As the scene continues with a medium close-up of Max behind the wheel of that vehicle, he concludes his noncommittal testimonial by saying, "Some people think Elvis Presley is still alive, and most of us think he's dead and gone." In a similar vein, *Rabbit-Proof Fence* ends with Garimara's mother, Molly Craig, resuming the voice-over she initiated at the start of the film in order to explain the aftermath of her 1,500-mile walk home with sister Daisy and, until her recapture, cousin Gracie in tow: "We walked for nine weeks, a long way, all the way home. Then we went straightaway and hid in the desert. Got married. I had two baby girls. Then they took me and my kids back to that place, Moore River. And I walked all the way back to Jigalong again, carrying Annabelle, the little one. When she was three, that Mr. Neville took her away. I've never seen her again. Gracie is dead now. She never made it back to Jigalong. Daisy and me, we're here living in our country, Jigalong. We're never going back to that place." Just before mention of Gracie, shots of the landscape give way to one of Molly and Daisy. Like the performed version of their younger selves, they are walking, but their stride is slow and measured as befits two women in their eighties who are no longer in imminent danger of forced displacement.

In closing the gap between documentary and fiction, these endings foreground the voices of their Aboriginal subjects, literally letting them have the last word in the relay of their experiences. Yet if these films can be said to facilitate the speech of the subaltern, it is due not only to these denouements but also to the manner in which Lahiff and Noyce prepare for them by creating, over the entirety of their films, a context in which Max and Molly can speak and, moreover, be heard. Indeed, as Gayatri Spivak herself has noted numerous times when clarifying her oft appropriated and oft misunderstood axiom, "The subaltern cannot speak" is a function less of voice (or lack thereof) than of interlocution. In an interview with Donna Landry and Gerald MacLean, for example, she says plainly, "By 'speaking' I was obviously talking about a transaction between the speaker and the listener."[1] Clarifying the conditions of such a transaction further, she tells Sneja Gunew, "For me the question 'Who should speak?' is less crucial than 'Who will listen?' 'I will speak for myself as a Third World person' is an important position for political mobilization today. But the real demand is that, when I speak from that position, I should be listened to seriously."[2] In other words, some of the most important work that *Black and White* and *Rabbit-Proof Fence* do is that of producing a spectator that is ready to question received versions of reality and history and is capable of hearing a counterhegemonic perspective without necessarily reducing it to the logic of the status quo.

Felicity Collins and Therese Davis speak to the means by which these films accomplish such a feat when they describe *Black and White* and *Rabbit-Proof Fence* as part of a contemporary Australian cinema that is both informed by and productive of a sense of disorientation. In their book *Australian Cinema after Mabo*, Collins and Davis examine the body of work that has emerged since the Mabo decision of 1992, which officially dismantled Australia's founding doctrine of *terra nullius* and thus acknowledged, for the first time in the nation's history, the legitimacy of land claims on the part of Aboriginal Australians. By no means do Collins and Davis limit the category of post-Mabo cinema to films that explicitly acknowledge the landmark legal decision or, for that matter, foreground the status of Aboriginal Australians; rather, they define it more broadly to encompass a wide range of films that recognize the need in a contemporary context to engage actively with issues related to history, memory, and national identity. In describing the nature of that engagement, they appeal to the notion of rupture as a means of addressing and imbricating the ideological and aesthetic features of the films at hand. Specifically, in discussing works made by Australian directors over the last fifteen years, they make a link between, first, the phenomenon that the films respond to and, in turn, lay bare—that is, in terms derived from Walter Benjamin, "the shock of recognition of historical discontinuity"[3]—and, second, the form such negotiations take, namely that of trauma cinema, to which they ascribe a combination of generic hybridity and formal fragmentation, which results in abrupt shifts in tone and affect, time and space. Insofar as they serve to disorient the spectator, it is precisely these ruptures, both aesthetic and ideological, that condition the speech of the subaltern in *Black and White* and *Rabbit-Proof Fence*.

Like the work of Lahiff and Noyce, the contact narratives I examine in this chapter also confront the marginalization of Aboriginal experience in popular memory and public record through the inclusion of perspectives that have too often fallen on deaf ears, yet they do so without "rupturing" the diegetic frame or, in other words, introducing a documentary component into otherwise dramatized material. They are *Utu* (Geoff Murphy, 1983), *Map of the Human Heart* (Vincent Ward, 1993), *Dead Man* (Jim Jarmusch, 1995), and *The New World* (Terrence Malick, 2005), all of which structure their narrative arcs around the life (and death) of a single Indigenous character.[4] In approaching these texts, I examine their capacity to articulate an Aboriginal subjectivity, bearing in mind that such an exercise requires producing both a speaking, as opposed to a spoken, subject and a spectator capable of seriously listening. In light of another Spivakian axiom, such an articulation seems unlikely, especially in the case of a narrative form that depends both thematically and structurally on a racialized divide across which encounters take place and along which identities take shape: "No perspective critical of imperialism can turn the Other into a self, because the project of imperialism has always already historically refracted what might have been the absolute Other into a domesticated Other that consolidates the imperialist self."[5] Yet rather than obviating the need for an exploration of texts containing said perspective, Spivak's comment highlights what is to be gained from their close examination: an understanding of the specifically cinematic means by which domestication is achieved, history is refracted, and subaltern selfhood is not—but also potentially is—produced.

At the same time that I am interested in assessing the feasibility of articulating Aboriginal subjectivity from within the narrative structure demanded by a contact scenario, I am also interested in the possibility of an intervention in dominant culture and, moreover, dominant cinema that is not circumscribed by dualistic logic and the counterpoint stratagem of critique. Thus, I conclude this chapter with a consideration of two intertexts that not only dovetail in interesting ways with the texts already mentioned but also pave the way for a consideration of the Indigenous media that features prominently in part 2. Specifically, I examine the relationships between two recent documentary shorts, *Rosalie's Journey* (Warwick Thornton, 2003) and *Yellow Fella* (Ivan Sen, 2005), and the landmark features that they respond to and thereby transform: *Jedda* (Charles Chauvel, 1955) and *The Chant of Jimmie Blacksmith* (Fred Schepisi, 1978), respectively. Featuring Aboriginal subjects who speak in and on their own terms, these documentaries manage, in the words of Margaret L. Andersen and Patricia Hill Collins, to "shift the center" of discourse and thus to facilitate the performance of a self-determined Aboriginal identity.[6] In the process, they imbue two contact narratives of paramount importance in the history of a cinema of Aboriginality with considerable complexity and, moreover, showcase a variety of subaltern speech that is not conditioned by ruptures, be they linked to the disorientation effected by trauma cinema, the discontinuity associated with historiographic shock, or some other phenomenon altogether.

Tragic Fates

Before concluding, in her landmark essay, that the subaltern cannot speak insofar as he or she cannot be heard, Spivak thinks through the possibilities of a subaltern speaking subject by examining the way the practice of *sati* has—and has not—been narrativized. Between the rhetorical position proffered by (post)colonial culture ("White men are saving brown women from brown men") and that associated with the Indian nativist camp ("The women wanted to die"), Spivak argues, there is no space for the participating widows to speak their desires for themselves: "One never encounters the testimony of the women's voice-consciousness." Continuing, she clarifies the nature of her hypothetical subaltern speech: "Such a testimony would not be ideology-transcendent or 'fully' subjective, of course, but it would have constituted the ingredients for producing a countersentence."[7] In other words, when envisioning a woman capable of intervening in the discourse that surrounds her, Spivak refuses to ascribe to her those things that post-structuralism has systematically dismantled—the status of a sovereign subject and an unmediated knowledge of her situation—but she nonetheless imagines that woman as producing utterances that are both grounded in her own experience and capable of cohering into a position of resistance, a "countersentence." Ultimately, though, the only means of discursive intervention Spivak is able to conjure is a woman's body, and that only in death: she concludes her essay with a discussion of Bhuvaneswari, a sixteen-year-old woman who purposely waited until she was menstruating to kill herself so as to make clear to her survivors that her self-immolation was not a response to illicit pregnancy. This "unemphatic, ad hoc, subaltern rewriting of the social text of *sati*-suicide" serves to underscore the desperation of the situation Spivak is describing, for it is effective only insofar as it annuls the possibility of any future rewritings.[8]

In light of the tragic ending of both Bhuvaneswari's life and Spivak's text, it is imperative to note at the outset of this chapter a trend that is so pervasive as to almost qualify as a defining characteristic of the subcategory of contact narratives under examination here: the decision to conclude such films with the death of their Aboriginal protagonists. In his discussion of *Map of the Human Heart*, Christopher Gittings identifies the effect of this type of ending when he describes the death of Avik, the film's half-Inuit lead, as "the ultimate whiting-out of the Aboriginal."[9] In so doing, he links Avik's fate with a series of other problematic practices, including not only those on display in the film (that is, the various means by which Avik's conformity with white norms is ensured) but also those enacted by it, such as the casting of Jason Scott Lee, a non-Inuit actor, in the film's leading role. As a critical shorthand for the very phenomenon with which Spivak is concerned—a process of projection that conceives of the other in terms of the self and thus reduces difference to the logic of the same—the term "whiting out" is quite useful. Yet I am concerned with the fact that Gittings assumes rather than proves its applicability to *Map of the Human Heart*. To regard as a foregone conclusion the role, both narrative and ideological, that death plays in the film (or for that matter, all films in which Aboriginal characters die) is akin to treating Spivak's definitive "The subaltern cannot speak" as the last word on a subject of tremendous complexity, for both moves forestall rather than facilitate analysis. To be sure, it is quite possible—in fact, probable—that a film featuring the death of an Indigenous character has a purchase on the same logic as those narratives of cultural extinction examined in chapter 1 (*Dances with Wolves, Black Robe*, and *The Last of the Mohicans*) and thus functions to perpetuate the myth of a vanishing race. Yet this need not be the case, as indicated by Catherine Russell.

In *Narrative Mortality: Death, Closure, and New Wave Cinemas*, Russell uses the textual treatment of death as a site of differentiation between a variety of new wave cinemas on the one hand and their classical predecessors on the other. While the latter frequently employ death as a means of closing down a film's story and significance, including it in a final act where it "has an ostensible authorization of 'meaning,' uniting the film's imagery into a single figuration of identity," the former exemplify "narrative mortality," which Russell identifies as "an 'undoing' or 'reading' of the ideological tendency of death as closure" and moreover "a violent means of condemning 'closure' as a narrative and historical event."[10] Following Russell's lead, it is possible then to conceive of death as a means of not only reification but also rupture and, by extension, to concede the following: while a scripted death like that to which Avik is fated proscribes his future speech, never mind subject status, the manner in which it affects his past utterances as well as the film's function as discourse is a more complicated matter. Indeed, when it is one among a network of textual ingredients produced in the spirit of a countercinematic sentence, death *on-screen* (as utterly distinct from death on a funeral pyre) can effect a rewriting of the representational, if not social, status quo.

Deferring a more thorough discussion of *Map of the Human Heart* at the moment, I turn instead to another text that has much to reveal about the relationship between mortality, voice, and narration within the context of a contact narrative, Geoff Murphy's *Utu*. Made during a period marked by widespread support, both institutional and popular, for a redefinition of New Zealand along bicultural lines, *Utu* plumbs the historical past for a precedent to this initiative. The result is a text that confronts squarely the reasons, both political and personal, that battle lines get drawn and alliances get made in the midst of colonial contests for land rights, institutional power, and cultural hegemony. Set in 1870 during the land wars that engulfed New Zealand from 1840, when the Treaty of Waitangi was signed and the nation was founded, through the end of the nineteenth century, *Utu* features prominently a wide array of representative types, each positioned uniquely within the cultural landscape. Among the Maori characters are Te Wheke (Anzac Wallace) and Wiremu (Wi Kuki Kaa), both of whom start the film as loyal soldiers in the British army. While Wiremu continues on in this capacity, ultimately coming to exemplify a perfect meld of European refinement and Indigenous soulfulness, Te Wheke sets the film's events in motion by going renegade after his family is massacred and his village destroyed by another army squadron. The three most significant white characters include the stridently British and relentlessly condescending Colonel Elliot (Tim Elliot); the far more likable Lieutenant Scott (Kelly Johnson), whose status as a Pakeha causes his loyalties to vacillate over the course of the film; and the eccentric Williamson (Bruno Lawrence), a fellow New Zealander who sets out on an unauthorized mission of vengeance after Te Wheke murders his wife.

Although Te Wheke does not have more screen time than any of the other key players in the film, it is his short yet action-packed stint as rebel leader that provides the story its structure. That is, the film starts with his apostate turn during which he declares his intention to seek "utu" (variously translated as "revenge," "retribution," and "balance") for atrocities his people have suffered and then receives a traditional *moko* on his face; it follows his lead as he and his recruits move around the countryside, killing those who cross their path and fleeing those who seek their capture; and finally it concludes with his tragic end. Given this trajectory, the event toward which the entire film builds is Te Wheke's court-martial, where he is found guilty on numerous counts of murder and sentenced to death. At this point, multiple people affected by his violent acts vie for the opportunity to serve as executioner, but it is Wiremu who ultimately assumes that role when he dramatically declares himself to be not only the most impartial of the trial participants but also Te Wheke's brother.

Utu has been released in two versions: a 124-minute one, which premiered at the 1983 Cannes Film Festival and was distributed in domestic markets, and a 104-minute one released in the second half of 1984. Given that the latter was prepared specifically for international circulation, there can be no doubt that a primary impetus behind its production was a desire to clarify the historical situation under examination in order to avoid alienating viewers unfamiliar with New Zealand's colonial past. Yet, ironically, the two most extensive revisions that distinguish the shorter version from the longer one diminish rather than enhance the legibility of the events on display. First, the re-edited version excises approximately eight minutes from the original's expository material, eliminating, among other things, the footage that introduces Te Wheke while engaged in routine activities with his fellow officers in the British army and thus establishes the equilibrium soon to be disturbed. Second, the re-edited version handles the climactic episode described above, Te Wheke's trial and death, in a different manner. While the original presents this material in its entirety at the end of the film such that plot corresponds with story chronologically, the re-edited version fragments it in order to use it as a framing device. As a result, portions of the trial are included earlier in the film (as early, in fact, as the second scene), while the rest of the material comes to constitute a protracted flashback, the past with which the trial is reckoning. The outcome of these two changes is a film whose start in medias res is even more demanding on viewers than the original since they are thrust into not only the narrative action but also a disjointed mode of narration that implicates the enigma of Te Wheke's character in that of the film's structure.

In both cases, Te Wheke's character hinges on a particular disjuncture, a contrast between what he is and what he becomes. In the longer version of the film, it is his transition from confederate to enemy of the British army that defines Te Wheke, a shift that is crystallized by the pronouncement he makes after committing his first retaliatory killing. In Maori he says, "I must kill the white man to avenge what he has done. The spirits of my people command me. I cannot live this life"; concluding in English, he adds, "I would rather die." Insofar as this moment is immediately followed by a title credit with the word "utu" ablaze, it moreover privileges Te Wheke's mission as primary exemplar of the concept invoked with the film's title. The second cut of the film, by comparison, underscores the contrast between Te Wheke at the start and the end of his run as rebel leader, such that the shift in allegiance that propels the film's action is read in terms of the outlaw he will come to be rather than the loyalist he once was. In this version of the film, Te Wheke first appears on-screen while on trial. Explaining the realization that made further support of the British untenable, he prepares the way for a flashback to the events with which the other version begins: "I joined your army and wore your uniform to gain peace for my people. But that same army I fought for destroyed my family. For you, they were just victims of a conflict. For me, they were the source of life itself." With the edit that follows this speech, the film initiates a brief crosscutting sequence through which it links past and present. Specifically, it moves on to the scene that culminates in the declaration of vengeance cited above; that is, Te Wheke is shown encountering the carnage in his village, killing a fellow soldier, and describing his actions in terms of an ancestral imperative ("I must kill the white man to avenge what he has done. The spirits of my people command me. I cannot live this life"). Yet before Te Wheke can complete his thought, the film cuts back to the trial where Lieutenant Scott is reading Te Wheke's list of offenses and sentencing him to death. Only then does the past materialize again, so that Te Wheke can conclude his incendiary statement with "I would rather die."

While this last statement functions in the longer version of the film as a strongly worded refusal to continue living a life in collaboration with an entity that does not have his people's interests in mind, it has a different resonance in the second cut. Divorced from the mission of vengeance that he is assuming and instead offered up as a rejoinder to his future death sentence, it takes on a note of resignation, as if Te Wheke is knowingly subscribing to the fate he has just been assigned. The result is a shift in emphasis from the course of action Te Wheke is compelled to take to the tragic end in which it inevitably culminates. The manner in which the trial is handled throughout the remainder of the film serves to underscore this shift. Once Te Wheke's fate has been sealed, footage from the trial is included intermittently as a means of introducing a particular series of events. Specifically, the film features footage of each aggrieved party saying his or her piece at Te Wheke's trial immediately before footage of the events to which that party is responding, thereby systematically pairing action with reaction and incorporating the concept of *utu* into its very structure. While this approach indeed "allows the arguments to surface more sharply," as one reviewer notes, it does so at Te Wheke's expense by highlighting the catalyzing rather than retributive function of his deeds and thus precluding a protracted consideration of the well-founded ire and sense of betrayal motivating his behavior.[11]

In short, the producers of *Utu* do not make a bid for international currency in the ways one might expect. They do not, for example, simplify the film's structure or develop and, in turn, elucidate the complex situation at the film's start. Instead, they construct Te Wheke at the film's outset as an internationally recognizable type: the doomed separatist who demands nothing short of liberty or death, the last of the unassimilable natives. Even in the first cut of the film, "the character of Te Wheke as a human presence gradually diminishes," as demonstrated by Kenneth Marc Harris; yet in foretelling his death and thereby anticipating the state of equilibrium achieved with the story's end, the re-edited version contains his disruptive potential to an even greater degree, leaving it to Te Wheke's charisma alone (which is, incidentally, substantial) to lend his protest any weight.[12] As much as this move suggests about the cross-cultural currency of a character like Te Wheke, who makes flesh assumptions about vanishing races and in the process serves a reassuring function for audiences confronted with unfamiliar circumstances, to argue that Te Wheke's death constitutes the ultimate whiting-out of the Aboriginal would be to ignore other aspects of the film that have proven compelling to a variety of critics.

Significantly, it is Wiremu who functions throughout the film as, in the words of Harris, "a projection of a New Zealand ideal."[13] Granted, what qualifies him as that ideal is his moderation, his occupation of a middle ground between the equally strident Te Wheke and Colonel Elliot, both of whom he kills. Yet in occupying that terrain, he is not forced to abdicate the advantage he has over the Pakeha with whom he aligns himself, and consequently he comes to assume a role reserved for white heroes in the films from chapter 1. In short, as much as Lieutenant Scott and Williamson are akin to Baines from *The Piano*, *Utu* ultimately locates the origins of the nation in Wiremu, whose actions eliminate the specter of both British imperialism and Maori separatism and therefore make possible a bicultural future. While such a move might seem perverse given the marginalization of the Maori historically, it nonetheless also provides occasion for a reappraisal of the nation, especially when coupled with the film's representation of the egregious abuses exacted in the name of colonial expansion and settlement. Martin Blythe for one argues as much when he reads the film as committed to biculturalism rather than bicultural nationalism due to the fact that "a blood bond is sealed between the characters, not necessarily in terms of national unity, but in terms of a Maori sense of utu which may be interpreted as a 'higher' ethical code, if one chooses to think of it that way."[14] For Blythe, such a move has potentially profound effects, for it not only privileges Maori culture epistemologically but also, in the process, enables an interrogation of national sovereignty: "Just as culture can be seen to be a national historical construction when viewed from a New Zealand perspective, so the whole apparatus of nation and history can be seen to be a cultural construction when viewed from the perspective of Maori culture."[15]

Whether one concurs with Blythe's assessment of the film's ideological work or finds within the text a much more conservative impulse, as does Harris, for example, the film's purchase on biculturalism is beyond dispute: confronted with the question of whether a future of mutuality, cooperation, and collaboration is feasible, *Utu* responds optimistically in the affirmative by providing a precedent from the past.[16] *Map of the Human Heart*, in contrast, is far more despondent in its reply to the same question. One thing that makes this difference so poignant is the common ground Vincent Ward, the director of *Map of the Human Heart*, shares with Murphy: not only were they both born and raised in New Zealand, but they were also among a small group of directors who gained prominence both nationally and internationally in the 1980s, the decade during which the New Zealand film industry experienced an unprecedented boom and the bicultural initiative gained considerable momentum among policy makers and the general public alike.[17] Of course, one factor contributing to this difference is the fact that *Map of the Human Heart* is set in Canada and thus is reflective of a nation with a more complicated history and a more fractured populace than New Zealand. Another factor, however, has to do with the act of representation itself. While both Murphy and Ward explore in earnest the binary oppositions and social hierarchies that characterize colonial discourse and order life in settler societies, only Murphy success-fully confounds them in the process. Ward, in contrast, reifies them to the detriment of his protagonist. As a result, Gittings is ultimately right about the ideological function of Avik's death despite the fact that he reaches his conclusion without adequate analysis: *Map of the Human Heart* does indeed white-out the Aboriginal insofar as Avik's death is symptomatic of a more general inability to envision an alternative for Aboriginal peoples other than hopelessly self-abnegating compromise or extinction.

At the center of *Map of the Human Heart* is Avik, a biracial man raised as Inuit after his father, a white hunter, goes missing from his life. Epic in scope and structure, the film covers in episodic fashion the bulk of Avik's life, show-ing in flashback those events that an aged Avik conveys to a visiting cartog-rapher (John Cusack). While Avik is at home amidst a landscape of snow and oil fields when this narration starts and ends (the first and last few minutes of the film, which are identified as taking place in the year 1963), the remainder of the film features him taking flight, both literally and metaphorically, as he travels beyond the Arctic. The event that sets the story in motion is a fateful meeting in 1931 between eleven-year-old Avik and Walter Russell (Patrick Bergin), a British cartographer whose work has brought him to Nunataaq. After developing a bond with Avik, Walter ushers him into a new life, flying him to Montreal once he shows symptoms of tuberculosis and in the process instilling in him a passion for flight. It is only a decade later, however, after another fateful encounter with Walter, that Avik figures out a way to pursue his passion: by journeying southeast once again in order to participate in World War II as an aerial photographer and bombardier in the British air force. Aside from the desire that Walter ignites in Avik—to fly like a bird, as he tells an Inuit woman he meets while en route to Europe—there is another that compels Avik throughout all these episodes: the desire that he feels for Albertine (Anne Parillaud), a Métis woman whom he first befriends at the sanatorium and later reunites with in London where she works at Bomber Command and lives with Walter. In Albertine, Avik finds a kindred spirit whose biracial heritage likewise fosters feelings of confusion and a fervent desire to fit into existing social categories at all costs.

Map of the Human Heart typifies the white culture to which both Avik and Albertine gain conditional access by way of a series of associations straight out of Jean-Louis Baudry's work. That is, white identity comes over the course of the film to be identified with two things that confer on the subject a position of mastery. The first of these is the experience of transcendence, which is most readily enabled by a series of vehicles associated with Walter's and, in turn, Avik's work (airplane, bomber jet) but can be achieved even by simply climbing. To wit, Avik and Albertine's most momentous encounters take place in an upper tier of some sort, be it on the roof of the sanatorium, in the rafters of Prince Albert Hall, or on the topside of a moored dirigible. The second is the penetrating vision associated with various imaging technologies, including X-rays and photography. Consistently over its duration, the film sites the convergence of these two attributes in the cartographic enterprise, particularly as it is practiced by the imperialistic Walter and by Cusack's mapmaker, who is in the employ of an oil company. Nonetheless, they are taken in tandem to their most violent extreme in the episode with which Avik's life in flashback ends, the bombing of Dresden. While he starts this episode at a safe remove from the destruction he is wreaking, he is eventually forced to parachute to the ground, where he is engulfed by flames and confronted with the lives and landmarks that are nothing but abstractions from the air. In the wake of this life-threatening confrontation, Avik abandons Albertine and returns to the Arctic, convinced, as he puts it, that "all white people were cannibals and I couldn't live among them."

While perhaps not as extreme as Avik in his condemnation of white people, *Map of the Human Heart* is certainly, at its most explicit level at least, critical of the means by which white culture attempts to map the Aboriginal other, securing power through the production of knowledge. Not only is Ward's attachment to Avik as sympathetic protagonist unwavering, but he also constructs Walter, the film's avatar of white culture, as an arrogant adventurer, capable of increasingly greater acts of insensitivity as he ages. At the start of the film, the brusque manner in which he overrides the protests of Avik's grandmother in order to take him to Montreal serves to define him as presumptuous: "He has the white man's disease. He needs white man's medicine. . . . I'm taking him." By its end, however, the film annuls any purchase Walter may have had on cultural authority or spectatorial sympathy by showing his support of the Allies' attack on Dresden to be an act of personal vengeance (targeting a woman who spurned him long ago) as much as political stratagem. Yet despite its attempts to distance itself from Walter's perspective, the film cannot help but relish the view that perspective affords. As J. A. Wainright aptly observes, "Ward is fascinated by the telescopic gaze from above" and consequently inattentive to that which it occludes: "[N]ot once in Ward's glittering display of the eastern Arctic seascape does the viewer glimpse an iceberg. There are extraordinary shots of pan and floe ice breaking up and redolent of map configurations, but none where the camera gaze slips beneath the surface to examine the nine-tenths of an ice formation that defies surface interpretation."[18]

For Wainright, Ward's propensity for bird's-eye views is not a downfall of the film, but his association of that perspective with absolute authority is. Noting "how ice and light combine to create mirages and extraordinary difficulties with scale and depth perception," he argues that the Arctic has historically proven resistant to being mapped and thus concludes that "Ward's metaphor of the map essentially fails."[19] Yet given the way Ward (mis)uses the metaphor of the map—that is, the way he does link the bird's-eye view with power—it is noteworthy that he relies so heavily on this point of view, never finding for his own camera a place outside of the scopic economy from which Avik divests himself in disgust. In other words, while Wainright takes issue with Ward's ascription of unmitigated power to the bird's-eye view, I highlight the converse: Ward's inability to image another site/sight of power. Throughout much of the film, particularly the portion that details Avik and Albertine's childhood experience in the sanatorium, the appeal of higher ground is understandable. Conveyed via shot–reverse shot editing that makes palpable the experience of being confronted, scrutinized, and disciplined, their experiences as part of the throng on the ground are fraught for not only Avik and Albertine but also the spectator. Of particular note are Avik's encounter with the X-ray technician who wants to "take a look inside" him and Albertine's exchange with the nun who is determined to erase any traces of Albertine's half-breed status; in both cases, the adults making their entreaties are tightly framed as they address the camera directly. Given the sense of entrapment these confrontations—and their presentation—incite, the distanced vantage achieved during Avik's first plane ride and the twosome's excursions to the roof are a welcome relief. By its end, however, the film has produced no other sustained formal strategy for allaying said entrapment, just as it has not produced any images of Aboriginal fortitude or resilience. Like his grandmother, who is so lacking in survival skills that she commits suicide when separated from her grandson the second time, Avik draws very little strength from his Inuit heritage, relying on the resources that white culture provides to make his way in the world.

Avik's double-bind—assimilation or subordination—is made painfully evident in the film's final sequence, which employs one of the two means Russell cites as typical of films in which death produces closure, both formal and ideological. While *Utu* in its re-edited state exemplifies the first of these, opening "with the death"—or, for that matter, death sentence—"to which the narrative will return," *Map of the Human Heart* illustrates the second: the use of a "montage of images that precedes, follows, or is intercut with a character's death."[20] Just prior to this concluding montage of images, Avik meets the daughter he never knew he had when she visits the Arctic to invite him to attend her impending wedding and to reunite with her mother, Albertine. After some initial reluctance, he decides to take her up on her offer and begins his journey back to his lost love by speeding toward his destination on a snowmobile. While en route he crashes and is thrown onto the surface of an ice floe, where he remains inert as the final minutes of his life play themselves out amidst a steady stream of images. In addition to shots that feature Avik's current reality, the montage sequence that ensues contains a number of other fanciful images, some of which showcase Avik and Albertine as children and derive from the film just watched, and others of which envision a hypothetical reunion with Albertine at their daughter's wedding. At one point during this sequence, two of these three lines of action converge in order to conceive of Avik in terms of two oppositional selves. In his fantasized rendezvous with Albertine, the couple climb into a hot air balloon awaiting them at the wedding reception and ascend into the sky, taking great joy in each other's company as well as in the view below. At one point in the course of their trip, they float over an injured Avik lying prostrate on the ice and unable to move, never mind make the journey required to change the course of his life and integrate into the family unit that awaits him. Cutting between Avik and Albertine in the air and their view of Avik on the ice below,[21] the film lays bare Avik's limited options: to transcend his reality by assuming a (subject) position that is the object of both critique and fascination for the film, or to be subjected, vulnerable to the gaze and episteme of others.

Mortifying Measures

In Russell's hands, narrative mortality is a concept of considerably density that has cinematic, philosophical, and ideological dimensions. As both a writing and reading strategy, it is an occasion for the "mortification," as she puts it, of not only the subject but also the classical realism of so much prewar cinema as well as of the hermeneutics encouraged by that cinema, one that privileges the search for meaning to the exclusion of other textual pleasures. As such, it provides an opportunity for an exploration of the transient, the contingent, the spectacular, and the meaningless, and it functions as a site of potential social change. Identifying the most important influence on her work, Russell asserts that narrative mortality "is, in keeping with Walter Benjamin, unapologetically idealist in its emphasis on redemption, renewal, and social transformation"; explaining the reasons for such idealism, she cites its function as "vehicle of an antiauthoritarian challenge to the discourses of control."[22]

Charting no outside to the vantage it proposes and exhibiting no self-consciousness about the death with which it predictably concludes, *Map of the Human Heart* functions as a well-intentioned lament far more than a challenge, antiauthoritarian or otherwise. As a result, it bears little resemblance to the types of films Russell takes up in her study and, by extension, provides little fodder for the kind of reading strategy that she both promotes and models. Like *Map of the Human Heart*, *Utu* also frames its protagonist's death as inevitable and in the process naturalizes a particular historical trajectory in order to shore up a contemporary political and social agenda, especially in its re-edited version wherein it forecloses the possibility of Te Wheke's triumph. Nonetheless, in articulating a variety of subject positions, lending agency to an array of characters, and entertaining, at least temporarily, a plurality of political possibilities, *Utu* clears a space for a pointed protest. It is precisely in this space that Blythe sites his reading of the film.

Despite this significant difference, however, both of these films do handle death as a closure device that functions as "an ostensible authorization of 'meaning,'" to quote Russell again, a fact that is indicative of their compliance with the paradigm of the three-act structure as defined by Deidre Pribram. Within the context of a study of contemporary independent film, Pribram thinks through the possibility of an independent narrative by adopting an "integrationist approach" to the study of narrativity in which she, in contrast to a formalist scholar like David Bordwell, refuses to create absolute divisions between narrative and narration—or, by extension, content and form, politics and aesthetics. In so doing, she expands the notion of three-act structure so that it "does not refer solely to a narrative's structural aspects (although that too) but to all aspects of textuality, including subject matter, point of view or perspective, principles of continuity (unity of time and space), psychological realism, cause-and-effect ordering—indeed many of the traits of normative realist film."[23] She then goes on to argue that while a rejection of this dominant paradigm might legitimately qualify a film as independent, many films that get marketed and received as such are, in fact, quite conservative, buttressing the ideological status quo despite the use of certain stylistic flourishes and working in tandem with story arcs that foreground familiar themes, such as redemption or, in the case of both *Map of the Human Heart* and *Utu*, personal sacrifice.

Two American contact narratives that come by the independent label easily due to the fact that their directors have made long careers of being Hollywood outsiders are Jim Jarmusch's *Dead Man* and Terrence Malick's *The New World*. Insofar as they deviate from the three-act structure described by Pribram, in part through their embrace of narrative mortality, they differ considerably from the films just discussed and, for that matter, from Mike Leigh's *Naked* (1993), which Pribram reads as surprisingly conventional in many ways when proving her point. With respect to both these films, narrative mortality is a symptom of something more thoroughgoing: a refusal of both traditional character psychology and a strong narrative drive that links cause with effect in a definitive manner. In the case of *Dead Man*, that refusal allows for a self-reflexive meditation on and intervention in the conventions that prevail in popular (hi)storytelling; in that of *The New World*, it facilitates an exploration of the metaphysics of contact within a world(view) that decenters the human subject in multiple ways.

The exact nature of *Dead Man*'s relationship to the Western has been a subject of much discussion, as evinced by the sheer variety of adjectives—from psychedelic to comedic, anti- to postmodern—that critics regularly employ when qualifying its status as such. What is beyond dispute, however, is its active and critical engagement with the formal conventions and ideological assumptions typical of the genre. Such an engagement is on most blatant display in the film's final scene wherein its American Indian protagonist, Nobody (Gary Farmer), dies. Having already resolved those narrative strands of greatest concern—the state of the relationship between Nobody and his white traveling companion as well as the fate of the latter—Jarmusch stages an unexpected final showdown in which Nobody and a depraved bounty hunter shoot each other dead. Attempting to account for Jarmusch's decision to end *Dead Man* thus, especially in light of the fact that Nobody qualifies as his most well-developed and fully realized character to date, critic Jonathan Rosenbaum makes two critical moves. The first is to cite Jarmusch's active and moreover critical engagement with the formal conventions and ideological assumptions typical of the Western genre; as he puts it, "To my mind, Jarmusch's somewhat disrespectful treatment of the Western as a genre is a function of several intertwining impulses, including . . . an impatience with certain Western conventions such as The Final Shootout that encourages him to use them derisively."[24] The second is to characterize Jarmusch in terms of his stylistic inheritance: "As a sort of stepson of the French New Wave,

Jarmusch may have even been guided by the frequent practice of ending New Wave features with the gratuitous death of leading characters."[25] With these two explanations, he forges, inadvertently perhaps, the very link that Russell makes when examining the work of the French New Wave's most quintessential *enfant terrible*: "In Godard's genre revisionism, the representation of death contributes to a mortification of genre and its mythic dimensions."[26] Jarmusch's inheritance is precisely an embrace of narrative mortality and its mortifying effects, for he stages a final shootout not in obedience to a historically entrenched imperative to end the lives of Aboriginal characters tragically but rather in order to amplify the arbitrariness of Nobody's death and thus draw attention to its status as dramatic convention.

The New World, like *Dead Man*, revisits a mythologized terrain that has been traversed by scores of filmmakers over the past century, yet in this case that terrain is a figure (Pocahontas) rather a ground (the West) with particular resonance in the history of American settlement. Unlike *Dead Man*, however, Malick registers little to no concern with previous iterations of his tale, preferring to eschew sidelong glances at other incarnations of Pocahontas in favor of a penetrating gaze that seeks to uncover some truth that, paradoxically enough, both exceeds and reveals itself in its representation. To be sure, that truth is not a historical one; like so many before him, Malick reproduces a specious version of the colonial past by romanticizing the association between Pocahontas and John Smith despite copious evidence that their relationship was platonic at best and exploitative at worst due to a profound age difference. Yet he does so as a necessary precondition in pursuit of the truth he is after, one of the metaphysical variety. Indeed, it is in part by evoking viscerally the experience of falling in love that he is able to capture the sense of wonderment that colors an encounter with the unknown, a world that is utterly new. Given his interest in experience over event, contingency over continuity, "discontinuity and ellipsis are at the heart of Malick's aesthetic," as Kent Jones explains. Yet, he continues, "it hardly matters, because Malick is interested in time only to the extent that it allows his films to perpetually crash-land in a primordial vision of Life on Earth."[27] In other words, Malick defies a linear sense of time, attending more to the texture of events than to their chronology and refusing to moor himself in the present at the exclusion of past and future. Indicative of this is Pocahontas's death, which is not treated with any finality. Evoked but never made visual, it pales in comparison to her presence, which lingers on-screen in vibrant form even after mention of her fate, giving way only to images of the natural landscape with which she is so closely associated, to which she relates in filial terms.

Dead Man: "Why is it that the landscape is moving, but the boat is still?"

Dead Man features an unworldly accountant named William Blake (Johnny Depp) who travels by train from Cleveland to Machine, Oregon, in order to take up a position he believes to be waiting for him at Dickinson Metal-works. After learning that his job has been given to another man, he meets up with Thel (Mili Avital), who takes him back to her room for a drink and some company. When Thel's former boyfriend Charlie (Gabriel Byrne) walks in to find the two of them together, he kills Thel and injures William with a single bullet. William, in turn, shoots Charlie with Thel's pistol and flees town on Charlie's horse. In his escape, he meets up with Nobody, an American Indian who nurses his wound and helps him elude the bounty hunters on his trail. While Nobody initially comes to William's aid for no explicit reason, he is compelled to continue in his capacity as caretaker and guide when he learns William's name and assumes his new companion to be an incarnation of his favorite poet, who has come back to this world to write verse with the blood of white men.

What distinguishes *Dead Man* from the archetypal Western is the manner in which it characterizes its pair of protagonists. A hapless hero, William bears more resemblance to a Hitchcock protagonist than to the typical gunslinger. Even more important, however, he undergoes a trans-formation over the course of the film, gradually identifying more and more with Nobody—an act that, as suggested by this play on words, involves both community (the movement toward one cultural milieu) and isolation (the movement away from another). This transformation reaches a visual and narrative culmination when William encounters a pair of U.S. mar-shals and boldly claims the renegade identity that Nobody has constructed for him: his face decorated in war paint, he responds to their query, "Are you William Blake?" by answering, "Yes. Do you know my poetry?" and then shooting them dead. In short, after transgressing the law by killing Charlie, William begins to transgress the boundary between (white) self and (Aboriginal) other that is of structural importance to the conventional Hollywood Western.

Unto itself, William's alterity does not qualify *Dead Man* as singular. From Jack Crabb (Dustin Hoffman), whose movement across cultural boundaries in *Little Big Man* is an occasion for absurdity, to John Dunbar, the hybridized hero of chapter 1, numerous characters like William have populated the Western, particularly in its revisionist variety. Rather, what distinguishes *Dead Man* is the irony of William's situation. In identifying with Nobody, he does not, as have his predecessors, tap into a resource constructed as culturally pure, for Nobody is a syncretic subject himself. Born of parents from different tribes and educated in English schools after being kidnapped by soldiers at a young age, he occupies a space between communities, a fact made most apparent by his speech, which is peppered with lines from Blake's poetry. Indeed, even when William mimics Nobody and thus pledges his identification with American Indian culture, as he does after gunning down the marshals mentioned above, he recites a line penned by Blake: "Some are Born to Endless Night."

For Mary Katherine Hall, Jarmusch's decision to make Nobody a mouthpiece for Blake's poetry is a betrayal of sorts, for it evacuates the film of an Indigenous voice and moreover does so in a manner that is distractingly clever. She argues, "While *Dead Man* criticizes what white society has done to Nobody—kidnapped him, paraded him, erased his identity—it exempts Nobody's absorption of Blake from censure and celebrates it instead. Blake's voice in effect replaces Nobody's voice."[28] As she fleshes out the effects of this exemption, she describes a phenomenon much akin to that which Gittings designates as "whiting-out": "The absenting of the Indian's voice is part of the larger project of absenting the Indian, whose consent to authoritative representation by a white man amounts to consent to his fate as Vanishing American."[29] To a certain extent, Hall has a point, since many of Nobody's most colorful lines are derivative; cases in point include not only the excerpt from Blake's "Auguries of Innocence" cited above but also Nobody's sage advice to William ("The eagle never lost so much time as when he submitted to learn of the crow") as well as his acerbic response to a prejudiced priest ("The Vision of Christ that thou dost see / Is my Vision's Greatest Enemy"). Yet rather than facilitating a whiting-out, an absenting where there should be a (re)presentation, Jarmusch's construction of Nobody lays bare the limits of the generic Indian while simultaneously confounding assumptions animating him. In other words, he is that which he cannot be other than: the "domesticated Other" that Spivak posits, the "always already historically refracted" subject of fiction whose diegetic status as subject informed by a white European cultural tradition underscores his extradiegetic status as product of a white American representational tradition. Trapped within that role, he nonetheless confounds and confronts it, lampooning the convention of representing American Indian characters as repositories of Aboriginal authenticity and calling the genre, by way of its hero, on lapses in logic with his oft-repeated refrain: "stupid, fucking white man."

While Jarmusch undermines the mythology of the Western from within through his characterization of Nobody, he points beyond the genre to a reality that has escaped it with his representation of the Makah village, where Nobody takes William after he suffers his second gunshot wound. Unlike the Plains tribes from which Nobody hails (Blood and Blackfoot), the Makah are relatively new to the Western genre. Yet even more remarkable than their lack of a screen presence historically is the fact that in *Dead Man*, they assume the position of the "absolute Other," to invoke Spivak: they are outside the comprehension of both William, who stumbles through their settlement in a semiconscious haze, and the spectator, who is offered no sub-titles for lines spoken in Makah and whose vision is limited through a series of vertiginous camera movements that ensure an unstable and fragmented impression of William's surroundings. In other words, Jarmusch resists all temptation to make them immediately and utterly legible to the average film-goer by sacrificing their cultural specificity to some generic Indianness or by attempting a facile translation that inevitably, even if inadvertently, involves transformation as well. For this reason, the representation of the Makah culture, albeit brief, is pivotal; it is precisely the moment when the field in which *Dead Man* stages an intervention extends beyond the Western genre to an episteme wherein domestication is a precondition of representation. In his bravura analysis of *Dead Man*, Justus Nieland captures the delicate balance involved in representation without reduction when he describes Jarmusch as a "visionary archivist" and his project as a dual one of making whole and making holes.[30] Crystallizing this is the scene in the Makah vil-lage. The result of painstaking attention to historical accuracy, it serves a restorative function, yet at the same time "Jarmusch troubles the complete-ness of his records at precisely the moment of its greatest 'accuracy.'"[31]

William's, and our, encounter with the Makah in *Dead Man*. (12 Gauge Productions)

Insofar as the Makah are a fleeting presence and are not endowed with the capacity to speak in a manner that is comprehensible to most audiences for the film, they hardly constitute speaking subjects—that is, subjects capable of both speaking and being heard. Nonetheless, they open up a film that is otherwise hermetic due to its extreme self-reflexivity and a genre that is thoroughly codified on account of its historical entrenchment. In sum, while Nobody, in his life and death, is an instrument of critique or "antiauthoritarian challenge," the Makah are a site/sight of revision. For this reason, I would argue that their representation constitutes the moment toward which the film builds from its pre-credit sequence on. In that opening sequence, William is aboard a train traveling west when its fireman (Crispin Glover) takes a break from his work chores and initiates conversation by posing a confounding question: "Look out the window. And doesn't it remind you of when you're in the boat, and then later that night you're lying, looking up at the ceiling, and the water in your head was not dissimilar from the landscape, and you think to yourself, 'Why is it that the landscape is moving, but the boat is still?'" Nieland accurately describes this monologue as "oddly prophetic of the film's closing scene," during which a dying William floats out to sea in a boat that Nobody has prepared for him with boughs of cedar. Yet, as much as this monologue is about a boat, it is also about a fundamental shift in perspective, which is precisely what William's encounter with the Makah incites, especially when compared to the earlier scene that is its visual, thematic, and structural counterpart: one wherein William, new to Machine, takes a walk down the town's main thoroughfare in order to reach Dickinson Metalworks.

Without actually linking the juxtaposition between these two scenes to the fireman's speech, Rosenbaum nonetheless identifies the shift in perspective I am proposing when he writes the following: "Blake's delirious impressions of the Makah village, fading in and out of legibility and consciousness, perfectly illustrate the film's overall strategy of 'making strange': on the one hand a simple itinerary of prosaic and everyday sights and events, rendered almost anthropologically; on the other hand, a series of slow lap dissolves that merge and confuse these simple perceptions. This sequence forms a precise inversion of the equally subjective and no less disorienting glimpses of various grim events on Machine's main street, where the style is relatively straightforward and the content is considerably more grotesque."[32] During his walk through Machine, William takes in a number of unsavory sights that mark the limits of civilization, encapsulate capitalist exchange at its most primitive and primal, and raise the specter of death; included among them are a coffin under construction, a horse urinating, a collection of animal and human skulls, and a prostitute servicing a male customer at gunpoint. In contrast to the grim underside of Western expansion on display in Machine, village life among the Makah is less menacing, more mysterious, and markedly other, creating the impression of a culture that is not necessarily pure or untouched but that operates by way of a logic that is distinct from that on display in the Western genre. Aside from the occasional (re)establishing shot, the scene in Machine consists of shots of William in alternation with eye-line matches that capture the mundane yet menacing activities he observes, all of which are mobile in order to keep apace with William's stride. In the Makah village, the same editing pattern prevails, but in this case the camera drifts and sways in such a manner that William and the spectator experience a profound disorientation as they catch sight of, rather than survey, components of tribal life in fragmented form. The result is as the fireman predicts: it is the landscape (and its inhabitants) that seems to be moving, in the process eluding capture, resisting fixation, and defying facile interpretation. While hardly a forum for American Indian voices, *Dead Man* does clear a space for those voices by enacting a shift in perspective and pointing beyond a Western representational regime wherein "great care was taken to obliterate the textual ingredients with which [a non-European] subject could cathect."[33]

The New World: "He floats through me"

In *Dead Man*, Jarmusch signals his self-reflexive engagement with the Western genre through the names he chooses for his lead characters, one signifying presence and absence simultaneously, the other staking out a subject position associated with the unconventional, mystical, marginal, and visionary. In *The New World*, names—or the lack thereof—are equally telling, encapsulating in shorthand Malick's atypical approach to character construction. In this case, however, they are less overdetermined than under erasure since Pocahontas (Q'Orinanka Kilcher) is never actually called such, and John Smith (Colin Farrell) concludes a rumination on the steps involved in creating a satisfying future thus: "Start over. Exchange this light for a true one. Give up the name of Smith." In short, Malick reveals names (particularly those that have accrued tremendous connotative baggage in their intertextual travels) to be wholly inadequate to the task of figuring identity, which he constructs as elusive through the manipulation of both image and sound.

Like Malick's other films, particularly *Days of Heaven* (1978) and *The Thin Red Line* (1998), *The New World* is characterized visually by an accretion of details drawn from a natural world wherein humans are no more or less important than any other entity. Malick privileges images that offer up fragments of larger wholes—a single leaf, a human hand, a river current, a bird in flight—and editing patterns that grant those fragments an independent existence rather than subordinate them to the logic of a sequence wherein a close-up functions as insert. The result of this representational strategy is a privileging of the fragmentary and fleeting over the integrity of bodies and events. People, as a result, come to figure in the film as the sum of parts, subjects that take shape in their gestures, impulses, hesitations, and glances. Yet even more salient in the creation of a dispersed subjectivity is Malick's manipulation of sound. One of the most distinguishing characteristics of Malick's body of work in general is his idiosyncratic use of voice-overs. Rather than providing explicit narration or granting access to a character's thoughts on a particular topic at a decisive moment, they are typically meditative, wide ranging, and sporadic, serving to infuse his films with a sense of disembodied consciousness. In *The New World*, it is Pocahontas, Smith, and eventually John Rolfe (Christian Bale) who speak themselves via voice-over repeatedly, lending their voices to moments of action and inaction, silence and synchronous dialogue. As a result of this strategy, especially in concert with an image track that caters to the sensuous, the contingent, and the ephemeral, the reified category of "identity" gives way to a dispersed subjectivity. When Pocahontas says of Smith, "He floats through me," she captures the effect of Malick's voice-overs in general. Unmoored from yet hovering in close proximity to the world of the image track, the voices of Pocahontas, Smith, and Rolfe function as sonic wisps that circulate independently, giving rise to sentiments both partial and variable, and that intermingle with resonant results.

In light of Malick's general approach to film form, which regards not only people but all aspects of the natural world as they are unto themselves, David Sterritt identifies the director's project as a quintessentially Bazinian one: that of striving to "unify the natural and the cinematic" such that "cinema itself can function as an organic part of the natural world" rather than as a means of dominating it.[34] Yet I would argue that Malick's work aligns him even more so with another champion of realism, Siegfried Kracauer, since what he achieves above and beyond all else is "a redemption of physical reality."[35] Strategically defamiliarizing the mundane, he cultivates a capacity to see in all its specificity the natural world to which people have become inured and from which they have become alienated. The opening of *The New World* is a case in point. With the first shot, Malick presents an image that recurs repeatedly, one wherein the world is seen as reflected in a body of water; then in the series of images directly following the credit sequence, he builds upon this representational trope, with its capacity to invert, double, and render strange, through a succession of underwater images wherein the familiar, be it the world below or above the water line, is distorted. In light of this redemptive project, the film's title refers less to the oft contested myth of European "discovery" of the Americas than to that which Malick offers viewers with not only this film but all his films: a new world, as in the capacity to view the world anew. Hence, *The New World* is a contact narrative, but one quite different in ilk from many discussed thus far insofar as it engages in a protracted meditation on the very notion of contact—what it feels like, what it entails, what it does and undoes, confirms and confuses.

Contributing to this meditation is the relationship between Pocahontas and John Smith, which Malick refuses to press in the service of any larger historical narrative, be it one of progress or genocide, the birth of one nation or the displacement of another. Forcing the spectator to see their relationship anew as well, Malick de-emphasizes those plot points that are so familiar—Pocahontas throwing herself on the body of Smith in order to save him after his capture, Pocahontas offering food to the starving settlers—so as to devote equal attention to that which surrounds them: moments of profound intimacy in which the discovery of another person, along with the world of experience he or she represents, inspires wonder and awe. The scenes depicting the burgeoning love between Pocahontas and Smith are among the most affecting of the film due to their exploration of the unknown in its capacity to confound and comfort, to evoke both fear and desire, and to test the limits of one's own subjectivity. To that end, the film frames their interactions from a position of close proximity, with the camera highlighting those incidents of literal contact that condition Pocahontas and Smith's developing bond. Only with their final farewell, the moment when Pocahontas actively chooses to remain with Rolfe, whom she married after being told Smith had died at sea, does the film offer up a conventional shot–reverse shot sequence: situated between the two former lovers, the camera isolates each in its field of vision and thereby makes palpable the gulf between them.

To be sure, Malick not only elects to narrate a relationship in which white Americans have a much greater stake than American Indians but also romanticizes that relationship by perpetuating the mythology of a grand interracial love affair and representing the union, at least initially, as edenic. While such a move leaves Malick open to charges of mystifying the reality of colonial expansion, to focus on narrative to the exclusion of narration would be to invert the formalism that Pribram associates with Bordwell and thus, again, to deny the imbrication of form and content, aesthetic

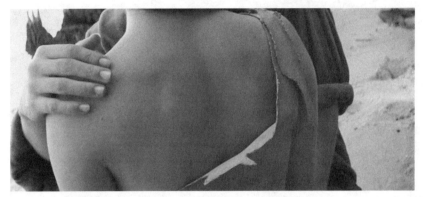

The type of contact at hand in *The New World*. (New Line Cinema)

and politics. Fraught as it may be, the project of *The New World* is that of bringing complexity to characters and contexts that have come to assume two-dimensional form, both literally (Disney's *Pocahontas* [1995]) and figuratively, in American culture at large. The result is a film that contemplates an encounter between two people without recourse to reductive antinomies such as those between villainy and victimhood or savagery and civilization. Immediately following the underwater shots described above, the film depicts the first moments of that encounter, presenting images of three British ships approaching the coast of Virginia from vantages afforded by both land and sea. Captured summarily therein are the divergent experiences of the film's future lovers: Pocahontas stands among other members of the Powhatan community as they respond with confusion and excitement to the view from shore, while Smith catches his first glimpse of land through a small window below deck where he has been imprisoned on charges of sedition. This even-handed alternation of perspectives, with its capacity to highlight the mutuality of the encounter, is repeated again when Pocahontas and Smith see each other for the first time in a field of tall grass.

It is primarily through voice-over that Malick indicates clearly that the encounter at hand is not merely one of two people or, for that matter, two peoples but also that of two epistemes. Lending her voice to the first frames of the film, Pocahontas establishes a precedent for all her ensuing speech by directly invoking her relationship to a spirit greater than herself as well as to a land that serves both material and metaphorical purposes: "Come, spirit. Help us sing the story of our land. You are our mother. We, your field of corn. We rise from out of the soul of you." Later she continues in this vein but incorporates Smith into her reverence as well: "Mother, where do you live? In the sky? The clouds? The sea? Show me your face. Give me a sign. We rise. We rise. Afraid of myself. A god, he seems to me. What else is life but being near you? Do they suspect? Oh, to be given to you, you to me. I will be faithful to you, true. Two no more. One. One. I am, I am." With its shifting "you," which imbues Smith with a degree of divinity, and its refusal of division between interior and exterior, self and other, Pocahontas's language conceives the world as a site for protean forces, profound connections, and ongoing interpenetration. In contrast, Smith's idealistic, albeit presumptuous, worldview bespeaks a relationship with the land that is more instrumentalist than intimate and a sense of self predicated on autonomy rather than communion: "What voice is this that speaks within me, guides me toward the best? We shall make a new start. A fresh beginning. Here the blessings of the earth are bestowed upon all. None need grow poor. Here there is good ground for all, and no cost but one's labor. We shall build a true commonwealth, hard work and self-reliance our virtues. We shall have no landlords to rack us with high rents or extort the fruit of our labor. None shall eat up carelessly what his friends got worthily or steal away that which virtue has stored up. Men shall not make each other their spoil."

In growing to love Pocahontas, Smith comes to question the very self capable of such pronouncements, a process crystallized in the pair's playful exchange of breath and culminating in his desire to "give up the name of Smith." Yet he does so only temporarily, for upon returning to the James-town encampment he dutifully resigns himself to the leadership position foisted upon him, coming to regard his time with the Powhatan as a dream from which he has woken. Malick, in contrast, is unwavering in his identification with Pocahontas: his film is, from start to finish, animated by the same worldview that he ascribes to her, one that stresses vital connections, levels differences between the human and nonhuman, and promotes an expansive understanding of self. To be sure, to retell the most mythologized of contact stories with an overriding concern with presence and the present is a risky venture, for it demands holding in abeyance a history that is far too often forgotten, romanticized, and/or constructed as inevitable. Nonetheless, the gains are profound as well, for *The New World* affords a sustained survey of that which is only glimpsed in *Dead Man*: an alternative to the epistemic and representational regime associated with colonial power. While it is the voice of Malick, the singular auteur, rather than that of Pocahontas that is amplified in the process, the rupture that voice conditions enables a renunciation—if not of the name Smith, then of the subject position with which it is associated.

Shifting the Center, Re-viewing the Past

Writing in her capacity as "Indigenous curator" for the online archive *Australian Screen*, Romaine Moreton ends a generally favorable synopsis of Fred Schepisi's *The Chant of Jimmie Blacksmith* thus: "Films such as *The Chant of Jimmie Blacksmith* are strictly organized in terms of 'us' and 'them,' or 'non-Aborigine' and 'Aborigine,' and while true to the era before Federation, there is the possibility that such a story would have been told differently by an Indigenous filmmaker."[36] No doubt, the caveat with which she concludes this sentence could easily be applied to any of the films discussed thus far in this chapter, for even though they feature Aboriginal characters with a degree of both narrative agency and discursive authority, those characters remain nonetheless a construction refracted, to paraphrase Spivak, through the lens of colonial history. In other words, while these films can be credited with producing ruptures of various sorts—be it through content or form, for a fleeting instant or their entire duration—and thereby creating space for a subaltern counterhistory, the conditions of their production guarantee an Aboriginal subject that is more spoken than speaking. This proves as true for films that subvert the codes and conventions of dominant cinema (*Dead Man* and *The New World*) as for those that adhere to them (*Map of the Human Heart* and *Utu*); to be spoken with an ironic inflection, as is Jarmusch's Nobody, or in sentence fragments that only sporadically cohere, as is Malick's Pocahontas, is to be spoken nonetheless. In this final section, however, I take on two films that manage not only to prepare the ground for a legitimate counterhistory but also to vocalize one. The way they both do so is by taking as their subject the actor behind an Australian Aboriginal cinematic icon.

Warwick Thornton's *Rosalie's Journey* focuses on Rosalie Kunoth-Monks, the actress who played the eponymous lead in Charles Chauvel's feature *Jedda*, released in 1955, while Ivan Sen's *Yellow Fella* features Tom E. Lewis, an actor whose most notorious role was that of the titular character in *The Chant of Jimmie Blacksmith* from 1978. Strictly speaking, *Rosalie's Journey* and *Yellow Fella* fall outside the parameters of this project since they are documentary shorts, yet in responding to they also transform *Jedda* and *The Chant of Jimmie Blacksmith*, two features that are strikingly similar to *Utu*, *Map of the Human Heart*, *Dead Man*, and *The New World* on multiple meaningful counts: the presentation of an Aboriginal protagonist who is portrayed sympathetically but fated to die and the use of such a protagonist to grapple actively with a tangle of difficult questions related to race, identity, and power in a colonial context. The extent to which the subjects of these two documentaries talk about—and, at times, back to—the feature films with which they are indelibly associated varies. On the one hand, much of Kunoth-Monks's narration, which is delivered in her native language of Arrernte, concerns *Jedda*, such that her involvement therein comes to function, for the purposes of the film at least, as the central event around which her life prior and subsequent are organized. The English-speaking Lewis, on the other, makes only passing reference to *The Chant of Jimmie Blacksmith*, noting at the outset of the film that it is precisely what he shares with Jimmie—the status of "yellow fella"—that compels him to search for traces of his father with filmmaker Sen in tow. Despite this difference, however, both documentaries demand to be read in relation to the feature films they reference, creating an intertext that has the potential to expand the possibilities of the latter by complicating the manner in which their Aboriginal protagonists both figure and function. In so doing, they bear out Moreton's speculative comment. While Chauvel's and Schepisi's films designate any position between "us" and "them," "non-Aborigine" and "Aborigine" as an impossible one capable of achieving resolution only in death, be it realized (*Jedda*) or impending (*The Chant of Jimmie Blacksmith*), *Rosalie's Journey* and *Yellow Fella* do not demand the sacrifice of their central players in the name of tragedy.

Made during a decade when the Australian film industry's average rate of production was slightly more than one film per year, *Jedda* was a rarity at the time of its release due to its status as a local product. That it also featured in leading roles Aboriginal characters played by Aboriginal actors and, moreover, dared to call into question the logic governing certain policies and practices that were in effect at the time qualified it as an utterly singular phenomenon. In the film, director Charles Chauvel uses a white couple's adoption of an abandoned Aboriginal child as opportunity to rehearse the debates about racial difference and assimilation that had great currency in Australia throughout the middle of the century. That is, the film pits the wife's investment in racial uplift against her husband's cultural relativism, ultimately making a more compelling case for the latter. One of multiple factors contributing to that case is the behavior of Jedda, the adopted girl, who both exhibits and articulates a strong desire to live like "her people," which, according to the logic of the film, entails sleeping outdoors, preferring to read animal tracks over the alphabet, participating in walkabout, making rhythm rather than melody, and, finally, casting her lot with a man whose traditional ways are far more seductive than those of her assimilated "half-caste" suitor. While *Jedda* is easy to dismiss, since the wife and husband, Sarah and Doug McMann (Betty Suttor and George Simpson-Lyttle), are, for all their differences, united in a paternalistic and racist conviction that the Aboriginal culture to which Jedda is so drawn is inferior to white culture, certain critics—Stuart Cunningham and Karen Jennings being chief among them—have insisted that the film is nonetheless more complex than the points of view it has the couple articulate. For example, Cunningham finds in the text evidence of Chauvel's "desire to document and *narrativise* the full range of the black 'condition'" in an effort "to prevent the suturing of the 'wound' of race relations, to maintain the disparity and inadequacy of both central positions—the crude versions of assimilationism and of cultural integrity espoused by Sarah and Doug McMann respectively,"[37] while Jennings builds on his argument by emphasizing "both the ambiguities within [the film's] characterization and the contestation between them."[38]

According to Cunningham, who has written extensively on Chauvel's body of work, it was not until *The Chant of Jimmie Blacksmith*, made twenty-three years later, that another Australian feature would "treat the wound," as he puts it, and "[dramatize] black experience with a force and centrality" equal to that on display in *Jedda*.[39] By the time Schepisi began production on his film, the Australian industry had begun to recover from the period of extreme atrophy that marked the heyday of Chauvel's career; this was due to the establishment of the Australian Film Commission and a commitment on the part of the government to help fund the development of a local infrastructure for film production in the mid-1970s. Like so many of those films that were part of the revival that ensued over the next decade and thus took as their charge not only the creation of a specifically Australian cinema but also the consolidation of a specifically Australian identity, *The Chant of Jimmie Blacksmith* is set at the turn of the twentieth century, around the time of Australian federation. Yet rather than perpetuate a version of nascent nationhood available to only a portion of the population—namely, white men capable of proving their mettle in the outback or at war (Bruce Beresford's *Breaker Morant* [1980] is archetypal in this regard)—it complicates that hegemonic paradigm, in the process raising important questions about racial difference, cultural assimilation, and political protest. In the estimation of Neil Rattigan, it is for this reason that the film was received so poorly in Australia at the time of its release: "The time was not yet ripe to suggest that something was rotten at the core of Australian society when the core itself still needed to be rediscovered."[40] Only with the passing of time and a favorable reception internationally (from Pauline Kael, most famously) has its ambitious singularity become apparent and its reputation grown within Australia.

Rosalie's Journey: "They slowly broke my law and made me act"

The most oft noted text to revisit *Jedda*, at least among contemporary film critics, is *Night Cries: A Rural Tragedy* (1989), wherein filmmaker Tracey

Moffatt replicates two elements that dominate *Jedda*'s first half hour—the home of the McManns, which positions signifiers of "civilization" against a painted backdrop of the outback, and the interaction between Jedda and her adoptive mother—in order to revise them. The result is a short film that wittily demystifies *Jedda*'s textual and ideological operations by simultaneously exaggerating the artificiality of the mise-en-scène and infusing the filial relationship on stage with a sober ambivalence. *Rosalie's Journey*, in contrast, functions more as a rejoinder to than a rewriting of Chauvel's original, focusing on extratextual factors by way of Rosalie Kunoth-Monks's recollections of her involvement in the landmark project. Specifically, she and by extension the film position the production of *Jedda* within a larger narrative of her life as a biracial girl growing up in Central Australia, in the process suggesting her performance to be one in a long series of capitulations to an assimilationist imperative. Almost the first half of the twenty-four-minute film is taken up with descriptions of Rosalie's life prior to the day when she met Charles and Elsa Chauvel for the first time. Via voice-over, Rosalie recounts her experiences at St. Mary's Children's Hostel, a boarding school in Alice Springs where, at her father's insistence, she spent six years learning how to do those things that would allow her to integrate successfully into dominant Australian culture: reading, writing, and speaking English; completing household chores; playing popular team sports; and worshipping a Christian god. Paired with this voice-over are authentic home movie footage and dramatic reenactments of the events being described, both of which underscore the regulatory nature of Rosalie's training by frequently featuring uniformed girls working and playing in highly organized fashion.

When recounting her memory of those experiences, Rosalie paints a portrait of herself as a reluctant participant, unsure as to the purpose of her education and disconcerted about the prospect of becoming further alienated from her land, culture, and people—in short, herself. Rather than marking a turning point in this developmental trajectory, her involvement in the production of *Jedda* only intensified her feelings of unease. Her description of the first stages of the audition process, her unwitting initiation into the project, is telling: "All the girls were lined up. [The Chauvels] came and looked at their faces and teeth. They looked at their eyes and hair. They looked at them very closely, and then they went away. . . . I didn't know why they were looking at us." Just like this voice-over, the footage accompanying it is more evocative of ethnographic research than of a casting call, suggesting that, in this case at least, the line between an exercise in dramaturgy on the one hand and typology on the other is quite thin. In it, a succession of representative girls pose for the camera in accordance with instruction: frontally first and then in profile, in adherence with what Fatimah Tobing Rony identifies as the "codes of anthropometric photography."[41]

Subsequent stages in the production process inspire similarly ambivalent commentary. For example, when explaining the final step in casting, Rosalie expresses dolor about losing the comforting camaraderie of the other potential Jeddas; when recounting the shoot, she lays emphasis on the strict division of labor that prevailed on-set and thus the extremely limited nature of her contributions; and, finally, when describing the injunction placed on her to look into the eyes of her male costar and feign desire, she speaks in terms of transgression and betrayal: "They slowly broke my law and made me act." This last statement is particularly salient since it speaks to a point that Rosalie returns to multiple times over the course of her commentary: that she was pressed into the service of acting without her explicit consent or fulsome understanding of the project at hand. In fact, she expresses a profound suspicion of the kind of (dis)simulation on which filmmaking, particularly that of the fictional dramatic variety, depends. Certainly, one could attribute such sentiments to her naïveté; after all, she freely admits that prior to making *Jedda*, she had seen only one film in her life, and it had been a source of much bewilderment. At the same time, however, the kind of (dis)simulation of which she speaks suggests that more is at stake than mere discomfort with the unfamiliar. Despite Chauvel's claim, made via *Jedda*'s opening intertitle, that the story to come is "founded on fact," the process Rosalie describes via voice-over is that of becoming a "domesticated Other" and experiencing the kind of self-alienation that such entails: speaking a language with which she has little facility; being pressed to engage, over her protestations, in activities that are taboo in her culture; and performing a version of self that is defined in terms of what she rejects (for example, clothing, domesticity, and written language) rather than of what she embraces. As a result, what lends Rosalie's narration authority is not a claim to some purported authenticity but rather a pursuit of self-determination.

Yet in addition to providing Rosalie with a forum in which to describe and thus interrupt that process, *Rosalie's Journey* allows for the restitution of that which was evacuated in the production of *Jedda*: a voice that both speaks on its own terms—that is, in Arrernte—and bespeaks a self-determined identity. That this is the case is most apparent in the film's closing minutes during which Rosalie offers her final thoughts on *Jedda*. Over a series of still images from Chauvel's film, she starts, "Other people may look at me and say 'There's Jedda.' I am a Pengart and my name is Rosalie. I am from Utopia and my father is from Alice Springs. I don't think about films.

I left all that. I now think of the fact that I am a mother and a grandmother. As for the film *Jedda*, I think my daughter has a copy of it. I don't bother looking at myself." As she continues, the stills give way to traveling shots of the landscape with which Rosalie repeatedly associates herself over the duration of the film: "I am an old woman now and feel good. My purpose now is to retain our language and our land. To hold onto our corroboree and our rituals. I do not worry about films or making films. I am not an actress." At this point, an older Rosalie, the one who has been narrating all along, appears on-screen for the first time in order to complete her concluding thoughts while directly addressing the camera. She says, "I went and made that picture show *Jedda*. I went for a long time. I lived in Melbourne. I got married there. From there I came home to here. I am back to where I was born, at Utopia. I come home for good, I hope to stay here until I die. I am glad I still have my language."

With this series of statements, Rosalie distances herself from a number of things—the character of Jedda, the acting profession, and film culture in general—in order to speak (for) herself and direct the viewer's attention *away* from the surface appearances by which she is most widely (mis)known and *toward* those things with which she actively identifies: the land surveyed, the kin invoked, and the language she so gladly uses throughout the film. In providing her a platform for such, however, Thornton does not engage in the same kind of retreat. Rather, he uses Rosalie's journey as an opportunity to interrogate and explore his medium of choice in multiple ways. He interrupts film history by revealing the culture whose call Jedda cannot resist to be one derived from the white imagination, one that regards the other in terms of the same. He opens up Chauvel's film text by pairing the very images that Rosalie doesn't bother to look at with a soundtrack that lends them historical dimension. Finally, he points the way toward an Indigenous film aesthetic by allowing Rosalie's voice to drive the film, thereby reversing the typical relationship between sound and image. The result is a link with traditional Aboriginal culture wherein, according to Jane Lydon, the ear, not the eye, was considered "the organ of intellection" and "meaning was found in a wider range of less overt signifying practices" than mechanical reproduction of a visual field.[42]

Yellow Fella: Tom's Journey

Like *Rosalie's Journey, Yellow Fella* also features its subject's voice prominently, but that voice is not divorced from the image to the extent that it is in Thornton's text, since Tom Lewis appears on camera frequently throughout the film. Nonetheless, because it is Tom's voice that articulates his presence most forcefully and continually, be it via voice-over, direct address, or a conversation with one of his traveling companions, this film privileges its soundtrack as well, using it strategically to deliver information, establish tone, create transitions, and, in general, make meaning. At the very start of Sen's documentary, Lewis explains via voice-over the circumstances that led to his acting debut and, in the process, establishes the representational precedent against which his story takes shape. Over a series of clips from *The Chant of Jimmie Blacksmith*, the first of which presents Jimmie engaged in the historically salient and symbolically charged activity of building a fence for a white landowner, he declares, "In 1977 I was approached at an airport by a stranger, a director named Fred Schepisi. He went on to cast me in the lead role of his film *The Chant of Jimmie Blacksmith*. The life of the character I played was hauntingly close to my own: a young man of mixed heritage struggling to find his place on the edge of two cultures." In *The Chant of Jimmie Blacksmith*, the young man of mixed heritage proves a tragic figure insofar as his inability to fit into existing categories and, by extension, communities produces a wellspring of anger that ultimately gains expression through acts of brutal and fatal violence. That Jimmie's "half-caste" status deprives him of the security of belonging to any given community is expressed quite powerfully by the film's form. Specifically, Schepisi creates a film text as lacking in coherence as Jimmie's identity by moving from one scene to the next rapidly, favoring tight framing over establishing shots and withholding expository information that might contextualize Jimmie's activities at any given moment. Yet even as the viewer experiences a fragmentation and displacement that aligns him or her with Jimmie, he remains opaque as a character insofar as he expresses himself only with the bluntest of tools: an ax initially and then a shotgun. In other words, the film points clearly to Jimmie's interiority, humanizing him in the process, but it fails to construct that interiority and thereby extricate him from the status of other. As Marion Wynne-Davies says of both the film and Thomas Keneally's novel upon which it was based, *The Chant of Jimmie Blacksmith* makes clear that "the final irony of the subaltern's voice is that it may only be heard at the moment of its negation."[43]

Yellow Fella, in contrast, follows a different developmental journey as Sen accompanies Tom and his Aboriginal mother, Angelina, on a road trip, the goal of which is to find traces of Hurtle, the Welsh father Tom barely knew. In the process, they visit the cattle station where Tom's parents met, the rodeo where father and son enjoyed a reunion many years earlier, and, finally, a graveyard where Hurtle's remains may or may not be buried. Moreover, unlike Jimmie, who has no verbal language with which to protest his treatment or even name himself, Tom is both expressive and articulate, functioning in the capacity of narrator and detailing not only every step of his physical journey but also every nuance of his emotional one. Even during scenes when his immediate response to events lacks in eloquence, his voice-over provides an aural counterpoint wherein he approaches those events from the distanced vantage of one who has had time to make sense of his experience by naming it. As a result, over the course of the film he identifies with utter frankness and clarity his reactions to a wide variety of stimuli: the excitement and fear he feels approaching an impending stop on their itinerary, the pain and comfort he takes in knowing his father tried to marry his mother, the beauty of the moment when his father first called him "son," the heaviness that comes with discovery that some of his family members were massacred by white stockmen, and the uncertainty he faces when trying to guess how Hurtle would have responded to such violence at the hands of his compeers.

Given the story of Jimmie Blacksmith (as well as of Jimmie Governor, the infamous bushranger on whom he was based), one of the most interesting scenes in *Yellow Fella* is one that showcases Tom's facility with language as a means of not only personal reflection but also social protest. In it he identifies a rock that he is driving past as a sacred site in the eyes of his people and then launches into an indignant line of questioning: "How come we can respect your church, how come, but you got no respect for our church? You don't see our church. You don't see the colors of our churches. You reap and you rape and you tear up—in my church. And you imagine if I gone and done the same thing in your church? Sometimes I['d] like to blow them up. I['d] like to go and sit and put a big firecracker. Boom. See what happens then. You wouldn't like it, would you?" In the wake of this confrontational challenge to the spectator, he stops speaking, heaves a sigh of relief, laughs, and says the following: first, "I feel better now," and then, playfully assuming the role of a morning talk show host, "Good morning, Australia. This is the black fella Australia." Engaging in a strategic reversal in order to lay bare the ongoing desecration of his people's land, Tom puts into words a key cause of the indignation that inspires Jimmie's killing spree as well as the popular support thereof in the second half of *The Chant of Jimmie Blacksmith*. Moreover, in speaking those words in the name of "black fella Australia," he draws attention to the power they accrue when broadcast widely, be it by a variety of quotidian programming, such as that which he fancifully imagines, or the very film in which he is candidly starring.

Perhaps the most pointed way in which the film emphasizes the power of Tom's speech, however, is through the term "yellow fella," which Tom and, in turn, Sen use to forge an alternative to the established dichotomy of black and white. With such an alternative, Tom's identity does not necessarily enjoy resolution. On the contrary, the category of "yellow fella" speaks of an experience of liminality that is, at turns, frustrating and fulfilling. Exemplifying the former are multiple moments in the film when Tom's characterization of his life evokes terminology employed by Spivak to describe the figure of the Third World woman: "a violent shuttling."[44] Such moments culminate in his final on-camera interview, which he gives after failing to find his father's gravesite. Demonstrably frustrated and disheartened, he describes the experience of being pushed from one side of a frontier to the other and then back again, likening his life to a series of movements over which he has little control and against which he must steel himself. At times, however, the language of both/and supplants that of either/or, as in Tom's concluding voice-over, which ends the film on an optimistic final note: "When Gatjimarra, my stepfather, passed away, I feel I took on a part of his spirit. I feel the same way I do feel for Hurtle. I share my heart to them both. I love them both. I respect them in my heart, true. And all this made me understand now I got a good balance in my heart and I want to hang onto that." In claiming a rhetorical space outside of the social landscape from which Jimmie could find no escape, *Yellow Fella* and its subject chart the space between direct address and voice-over, between the language of reaction and that of reflection, and in the process allow for a violent shuttling to give way, at least provisionally, to an integration with transformative potential.

PART TWO

Mapping the Fourth World

At the conclusion of his essay "Lawrence of South Dakota," Ward Churchill calls into question the purportedly noble intentions fueling the production of a film like *Dances with Wolves* while simultaneously articulating requirements for a cinema capable of affecting popular opinion and effecting political change: "If Kevin Costner or anyone else in Hollywood held an honest inclination to make a movie which would alter public perceptions of Native America in some meaningful way, it would, first and foremost, be set in the present day, not in the mid-19th century. It would feature, front and center, the real struggles of living native people to liberate themselves from the oppression which has beset them in the contemporary era, not the adventures of some fictional non-Indian out to save the savage. It would engage directly with concrete issues like expropriation of water rights and minerals, involuntary sterilization, and FBI repression of Indian activists."[1] While Churchill's comments are specific to the United States, they have relevance in all the national contexts under consideration in this project since what he takes issue with is not the nineteenth century per se or even the presence of "some fictional non-Indian" but rather the types of stories in which these things are typically implicated: narratives of cultural extinction that propagate the myth of a vanishing race. (*Dances with Wolves*, after all, could just as easily be called "The Last of the Lakota Sioux" as "Lawrence of South Dakota.") Indeed, for Churchill, the most compelling fodder for a relevant cinema of Aboriginality is a present of colonial sovereignty—precisely that which is obscured by the euphemistic term "settler society"—rather than a past of colonial expansion. To focus on such a present, however, is not to ignore the past; on the contrary, the contemporary problems that Churchill names, as well as others that disproportionately affect Aboriginal communities in both North America and the Antipodes, such as poverty, unemployment, violence, and alcohol abuse, cannot be understood without reference to a history of colonial exploitation, dispossession, and displacement. As such, their narration demands the production of a temporality that conceives of history as exceeding the past and inhering in the present.

Three years before *Yellow Fella*, Australian filmmaker Ivan Sen released *Beneath Clouds* (2002), a narrative feature that is, in its broadest strokes, remarkably similar to *Walkabout*, the ur-text of contact narratives, which I used to introduce part 1. It too features a teenaged girl and boy who meet while traveling on foot, routes their journey toward an urban destination through largely rural spaces, and relies heavily on images of landscape and local fauna to lend their experience texture. On all these counts, however, there are also salient differences that signal Sen's commitment to the kind of storytelling that Churchill demands and Nicolas Roeg, like Costner, refuses. First, the male protagonist in *Beneath Clouds*, Vaughn (Damian Pitt), is not a noble savage of yesteryear but a contemporary Aboriginal boy on the lam after escaping from a juvenile correctional facility, and his female counterpart, Lena (Dannielle Hall), is not a displaced girl of British pedigree so much as a biracial girl performing as such: not only can she pass for white (which she does with Vaughn), but she also identifies her father's homeland of Ireland as hers as well, even though her knowledge of it is limited to some photographs she keeps in an album. Second, the spaces through which they travel are hardly the stuff of classical poetry: the "land of lost content" that A. E. Housman and, in turn, Roeg evoke gives way to long stretches of empty road along which Vaughn and Lena encounter a wide variety of people, from kindly gentlemen to abusive husbands, from indigent field hands to opportunistic thieves. Finally, unlike the wide array of animals featured in *Walkabout*, which contribute greatly to the exoticism of its landscape, the animal imagery in *Beneath Clouds* is dominated by shots of roadkill.

A far cry from Roeg's romanticized vision, *Beneath Clouds* functions more as an exploration of grim realities. At various points in the film, Lena and Vaughn each search a family photograph for evidence of lost filial connections. Uncannily similar in both content and staging—both feature a mother flanked by her daughter on the right and her son on the left—these photos serve to crystallize the portrait of a typical Aboriginal family that emerges over the course of the film's duration: one made up of an absent father, uncaring mother, pregnant daughter, and criminal son. Yet both Lena and Vaughn are attempting desperately to escape the fate prescribed them by this image and, more generally, to break the cycles of deprivation, compromise, and neglect by which the past continues to determine the present. Lena sets out for Sydney in search of the Irish father she barely knows after two events convince her that she must: her friend reveals that she is pregnant and thus will follow in the footsteps of so many girls in the film, including Vaughn's sister, by becoming a teenaged mother, and her younger brother gets arrested for a petty crime to the seeming indifference of her hard-drinking mother ("[It will] give me a fuckin' break from him, anyway") and stepfather ("Do the little prick good to get sent away. It'll toughen him up a bit"). Vaughn, in contrast, is already ensnared in a pernicious cycle, one wherein rage begets violence, which results in internment and even more rage; thus, he literalizes the theme of escape when he manages to stow away on a milk truck and leave the confines of the facility where he has been housed for years. His escape attempt, however, involves more than a short-sighted bid for freedom, since the impetus propelling his actions is a desire to visit his dying mother and thereby give her the support she has withheld from him.

By its end, *Beneath Clouds* has not entirely thwarted Lena and Vaughn in their pursuits. Indeed, there is occasion for some hope insofar as the final scene has Lena boarding a train for Sydney, Vaughn eluding police custody, and both of them enjoying the fulfillment of a newfound relationship. Nonetheless, the odds are clearly stacked against them. While Lena's access to mobility, both geographical and social, is predicated on a fragmentation of her identity and a disavowal of the Aboriginal portion thereof, for Vaughn, who is both darker-skinned and fugitive, the horizon of possibility is even more limited: in a social context wherein racial profiling is commonplace among police officers and regular citizens alike, any move he makes attracts surveillance and suspicion. In short, by foregrounding those social and systemic forces that prove a match for any individual will, no matter how determined, the film constructs history as something lived in an ongoing manner due to the legacy of past events rather than as something revisited via memory from a safe temporal remove. At the same time, however, history—or, more properly, historiography–emerges as a site for productive intervention as well, as evinced by an exchange that Lena and Vaughn have after Lena reveals that she is an avid reader.

VAUGHN: Yeah, well, I wouldn't believe everything you read. All written by white fellas anyway.
LENA: Not all white fellas are the same.
VAUGHN: Don't make no difference where they come from. They all fuckin' white, and they all took our fuckin' land.
LENA: You were the ones who gave it up.
VAUGHN: We didn't give it up. It was all them disease and shit they brought here. That's what fucked it up.

LENA: How do you know?
VAUGHN: I just know.
LENA: Yeah, you know because someone wrote it in a book, that's why.
VAUGHN: Anyway, the war ain't fuckin' over.

On the one hand, this exchange points to a phenomenon that Peter Burke summarizes well when he writes, "It is often said that history is written by the victors. It might also be said that history is forgotten by the victors. They can afford to forget, while the losers are unable to accept what happened and condemned to brood over it, relive it, and reflect how different it might have been."[2] On the other, it also points to an existing counterhistory that scholars of all sorts have already begun to write and that may be the most important ground on which to stage contemporary battles in the ongoing war to which Vaughn refers. Hence, the importance of *Beneath Clouds* and Indigenous media in general, for the relative lack of interest that Aboriginal filmmakers have in the contact scenario that so fascinates their white counterparts goes hand in hand with a dedication to the subject matter suggested by Churchill.[3]

Because films made by Aboriginal filmmakers about the present day are the most determined and, in turn, successful at producing representations of Aboriginality that do not cohere only insofar as they differ from a white norm, they dominate part 2 of *Unsettling Sights*, but not to the exclusion of texts created by non-Native artists. Indeed, just as this part marks a move away from the contact narrative, it refuses to replicate the dichotomous logic that the contact narrative depends upon. As such, it is not dedicated to defining a (singular) countercinema so much as to continuing the project initiated in part 1 by examining the multiplicity of strategies, be they visual, narrative, or rhetorical, that accounts for the trends within as well as the diversity across contemporary films that represent Indigenous peoples. In the case of the films discussed in chapters 3 and 4, however, Aboriginal identity is not constructed strictly in reactive response to a colonizing presence nor fixed to reflect some purported authenticity. Rather, these films acknowledge the precarious space that is (not) the Fourth World as well as the conflicts that are specific to the social location that Fourth World status engenders. In the process, they provide Native audiences with recognizable images of themselves and non-Native audiences with a reminder of that which they have the option of forgetting: the colonial past—and present—of the place they call home.

Of particular interest are the multiplicity of strategies employed in achieving the temporality described above, one that allows for a representation of Aboriginal identity on its own terms as well as an awareness of the history that has produced that identity at the individual and communal levels. Specifically, in chapter 3 I examine how films implicate questions of time in those of space, thereby highlighting the particular resonance that Homi Bhabha's notion of the unhomely has in the context of the Fourth World, which is not identified with a particular geographical terrain, as are its First and Third counterparts, but defined instead by its lack thereof. Chapter 4, in turn, foregrounds the role that aesthetic forms and modes of cultural transmission play in ensuring historical continuity, thereby building on a point made by Steven Leuthold within the context of an examination of Indigenous documentary filmmaking: that there is an "internal consistency" between the older narrative forms of a particular culture and newer ones, such as film and video, which serves to "establish a close connection between the past and present day realities."[4]

3. LAND CLAIMS
Dramas of Deterritorialization

Within Canada, the filmmaker who has broached land issues most persistently, publicly, and passionately is Alanis Obomsawin, whom Randolph Lewis describes as "the grande dame of Canadian documentary filmmaking, if not the Canadian film industry in general" in his recent book on her work.[1] In her capacity as a filmmaker with the National Film Board, she has produced multiple films since the early 1970s dedicated to the ongoing struggle on the part of First Nations peoples for title to and/or usage rights for Native land. Among them are four that foreground the Oka crisis of 1990, which involved a two-and-a-half-month-long standoff between representatives of the state—first, the provincial police of Québec and then the Canadian army—and a group of activists dubbed the Mohawk warriors over a tract of land slated for development into a golf course, despite its longtime function as a Mohawk graveyard. According to Lewis, the most significant of these four films—and indeed of Obomsawin's entire body of work—is *Kanehsatake: 270 Years of Resistance* (1993), a first-hand account of the conflict, which is widely considered to be the most fraught and volatile between Native and non-Native interests in recent Canadian history. Composed primarily of footage that Obomsawin shot from behind the barricade erected by the protesters, a position that she assumed early on in the crisis and maintained, despite substantial danger, until the day before the Mohawk surrender to Québec officials, it "represents one of the great acts of courage in the history of documentary filmmaking."[2] Moreover, it has enjoyed the widest distribution of any of Obomsawin's films nationally and internationally and thus has served in myriad quarters as both a pedagogical tool and a corrective to mainstream media coverage of the event, which typically showed little sympathy for the Mohawk cause.

In comparison to *Kanehsatake: 270 Years of Resistance*, few films from any settler society showcase as dramatically the tension and hostility that has so often attended recent interactions between First Nations and the nation-state or render as explicitly the links between a past of colonial invasion and a present of ongoing deterritorialization, be it realized through sudden land seizures or the gradual erosion of Native territorial rights. Despite this, however, I do not turn my attention here to Obomsawin's work or even, for that matter, Gil Cardinal's *Indian Summer: The Oka Crisis* (2006), a recent dramatization of the event. Rather, I am interested in the more mundane reality of deterritorialization experienced by Indigenous populations; thus, the films addressed in this chapter contextualize the relationship between people and place within a wider field of experience conditioned not by heated conflicts with mutually exclusive "sides" but by the daily negotiation—and often provisional integration—of dual national allegiances and competing cultural influences. For this reason, a more appropriate documentary counterpart to the fiction films I take up in this chapter is Clint Alberta's *Deep Inside Clint Star* (1999). Exploring the issues of identity, sexuality, and love with utter candor, the film features interviews with a cross-section of the young director's contemporaries, all of whom identify as Native, often in the face of potentially mitigating factors, such as biracial parentage, adoption into a white family at an early age, and little, if any, knowledge of reserve culture. The result is a portrait, at turns capricious and poignant, of a resilient group of Canadians who have successfully weathered a host of traumatic experiences, ranging from suicide to incest, rape to alcoholism, confusion over their identity to mistreatment because of it.

While one participant, Michael, speaks frankly about feeling removed both historically and emotionally from struggles over land waged by prior generations and therefore committing himself to "dealing with the now," the film as a whole bears traces of those struggles nonetheless in its subtle yet profound evocation of the experience of deterritorialization. More specifically, Alberta shows how "the now" with which Michael, for one, is concerned is shaped by "the then" of his ancestors by staging the majority of the film's action—that is, its numerous interviews with his peers—in liminal and anonymous spaces, such as a moving car, a generic hotel room, or various outdoor and public locales. Indeed, it is not until he interviews his (non-Native) mother late in the film that he crosses the threshold of the domestic sphere and broaches in any way the comforts it may (or may not) offer. By thus implicating temporal relations in spatial ones, using place to represent history as that which exceeds the past and inheres in the present, *Deep Inside Clint Star* bears a resemblance to the films discussed in this chapter. Yet rather than minimizing mention of home in order to create a portrait of a generation in limbo, the filmmakers I engage below instead employ home as a persistent point of reference, even for those characters whose narrative development is bound up with a physical journey away from it. In so doing, they are capable of illustrating vividly the condition of "unhomeliness," which Homi Bhabha designates as a particularly estranging effect of postcoloniality and postmodernity in his essay "The World and the Home."

In that essay, Bhabha conceives of history as a kind of spectral presence with the capacity to penetrate seemingly insular contexts and, consequently, to blur the boundaries between assumedly discrete spaces: "In a feverish stillness, the intimate recesses of the domestic space become sites for history's most intricate invasions. In that displacement, the border between home and world becomes confused; and, uncannily, the private and the public become part of each other, forcing upon us a vision that is as divided as it is disorienting."[3] While Bhabha associates unhomeliness with the types of intricate invasions described above, it is not only the experience of disorientation that such invasions incite but also a consciousness of that experience—"the shock of recognition of the world-in-the-home, the home-in-the-world"—that properly defines the unhomely.[4] Taking as his object of analysis contemporary world literature, Bhabha posits two fundamental steps in the raising of that consciousness. The first is enacted by the writer, who employs an aesthetic process that does not take as its aim the transcendence of historical time but rather engages with temporality in a dynamic manner. In Bhabha's words, that "process introduces into our reading of social reality not another reified form of mediation—the art object—but another temporality in which to signify the 'event' of history."[5] The second is enacted by the critic, who must identify the history that informs the fiction and thereby "attempt to fully realize, and take responsibility for, the unspoken, unrepresented pasts that haunt the historical present."[6] Throughout the article, the works to which he turns his attention as critic are Toni Morrison's Beloved (1987) and Nadine Gordimer's My Son's Story (1990), both of which are affective narratives of displacement and fictions infused with historical dimension. In narrating moments of personal history in such a way that the specter of a wider communal history is raised and the past is evoked without being mimetically represented, Gordimer and Morrison both express and produce the blurring of boundaries between the world and the home, the public and the private, as well as, by extension, the social and the psyche, the political and the personal. In short, they forge an aesthetic of the unhomely by producing a fiction haunted by history.

While Bhabha has singled out literature as the nexus for displaced characters, the site for historical hauntings, and the grounds for critical engagement, the cinema also creates a sense of the unhomely, as demonstrated by Powwow Highway (Jonathan Wacks, 1989) and Smoke Signals (Chris Eyre, 1998), Once Were Warriors (Lee Tamahori, 1994) and Stryker (Noam Gonick, 2004). All of these films mandate a political reading that takes into consideration, at least to some extent, the effects of imperialist history and structural racism, yet they do so without dwelling in the contact zones that serve as mise-en-scène for the films discussed in part 1 or on the boundary between settler and Aboriginal culture that such zones condition. Instead, they locate themselves in spaces that are in some way local or insular—"on the road" in the case of the first pair and "in the hood" in that of the latter—and that thus allow for a degree of separation from the dominant culture associated with the nation-state as well as for a focus on the ways identity is negotiated within a given ethnic community rather than across cultural divides. Nonetheless, by employing a variety of visual and rhetorical strategies, these films make clear that these spaces are not impervious to what lies outside their boundaries, that they—and, by extension, the people occupying them—are affected by and constituted within a much larger political and social context. In short, these films not only depict the lives and experiences of those who have been subject to a variety of intricate invasions but also facilitate the "shock of recognition" that Bhabha associates with the unhomely. In the process, they implicate the cinematic medium itself in the very history they evoke by self-reflexively calling attention to the way that visual media have contributed to the colonialist project by propagating reductive and oftentimes malevolent stereotypes of Indigenous communities.

Intricate Invasions on the Rez

Although Sherman Alexie denies that Jonathan Wacks's 1989 sleeper *Powwow Highway* had a significant influence on his screenplay for *Smoke Signals*, the much celebrated film directed by Chris Eyre and released in 1998, the two movies share too many common elements to escape comparison. Equal parts buddy film and road movie, each features an unlikely pair of American Indian men who are forced by circumstances to venture off the reservation and make a journey that not only results in the attainment of their immediate goal but also proves a personally enriching bonding experience for both men involved. The specifics of the pair, the journey, and the goal vary from one film to the other. At the center of *Powwow Highway* are Buddy (A Martinez) and Philbert (Gary Farmer), two Cheyenne Indians who drive Philbert's 1964 Buick from Montana to New Mexico, where Buddy's sister has been arrested on a bogus charge. *Smoke Signals*, in contrast, follows the duo of Victor (Adam Beach) and Thomas (Evan Adams) as they travel together by bus from the Coeur d'Alene reservation in Idaho to Phoenix, Arizona, in order to retrieve the ashes of Victor's recently deceased father. Despite these differences, the films, as dictated by the particular genres in and with which they are working, share a common plot structure, emotional arc, and narrative resolution and thus qualify as complementary texts that make for interesting analysis when taken as a twosome or read against each other.

Assuming Alexie's comments to be sincere and the similarities between *Powwow Highway* and *Smoke Signals* to be coincidental, one might ask why, when there are so few films with contemporary American Indian protagonists, these two both gravitate toward the dual generic tradition of the buddy film/road movie, following in the footsteps—or, better yet, tire tracks—of films such as *Midnight Cowboy* (John Schlesinger), *Butch Cassidy and the Sundance Kid* (George Roy Hill), and *Easy Rider* (Dennis Hopper), all of which were released in 1969. While there are several possible answers to that question, the most compelling is the simple fact that the buddy film/road movie is ideally suited to the project at the center of both these films: an exploration of the contours of masculine identity and the vicissitudes of male friendship. As a site that has been defined, populated, and given significance historically by personages ranging from Lewis and Clark to John Steinbeck, the road is a profoundly masculine location. By extension, the road on-screen, especially since the publication of Jack Kerouac's *On the Road* in 1957, has served as stomping ground for many individual men and even more male duos, whose physical movement serves as both catalyst and metaphor for a more internalized type of journey.[7] Although the buddy film/road movie is capable of being regendered, as in the case of Ridley Scott's *Thelma and Louise* (1991), such revisionist representations are exceptional and owe their potency to the fact that the road has been so thoroughly defined as masculine territory.[8] While Thelma and Louise are the exception, it is Velma and Lucy (Michelle St. John and Elaine Miles), characters in *Smoke Signals*, who more accurately capture the way that women are typically represented in relation to travel; riding backward around the reservation while drinking refreshments and listening to music, these two women are getting nowhere fast. Unlike Velma and Lucy, Buddy and Philbert on the one hand and Victor and Thomas on the other successfully take trips off the reservation, and in both cases, the journeys that ensue serve as impetus and opportunity for the various characters to reflect upon themselves in relation to their personal pasts as well as the histories they share with their individual families, reservation communities, and tribes at large. The conclusions they reach about those things, however, are quite different.

Powwow Highway: Envisioning Resistance

What emerges most clearly in a review of the critical literature on *Powwow Highway* is the extent to which the film is, in the estimation of many viewers, riddled with contradictions. While its vacillation between comedic slapstick antics and serious political commentary makes for a text that is uneven tonally, its simultaneous capitulation to and revision of existing stereotypes render its politics equally inconsistent. In "Driving the Red Road," Eric Gary Anderson describes these contradictions as the result of the film's attempt to infuse Hollywood genres with an American Indian point of view. Examining how the film alternately preserves the politically complex vision of David Seals's novel, upon which the film is based, and succumbs to the narrative simplification demanded by generic formulas, he shows this effort to be an "imperfect process."[9] Yet imperfection is not, in his opinion, grounds for dismissal. On the contrary, Anderson suggests that it is these textual tensions that make *Powwow Highway* so enriching for both American Indian and white audiences alike and that lead him ultimately to endorse it as a film that "Americanizes Native Americans and Native Americanizes the movies, while at the same time respecting the sacred traditions of both the Hollywood Western and the Cheyenne Indians."[10] While this conclusion may prove a bit too enthusiastic, particularly for viewers like Toby Langen and Kathryn Shanley, who responded to the cross-purposes of the material with far more ambivalence than Anderson, the desire to explore those tensions resulting from the film's integration of Native and non-Native elements is instructive.[11] For while the demands of genre do at times contribute to the production of a representation that is reductive, the mere fact that Buddy and Philbert, the twosome at the center of this buddy film/road movie, are Cheyenne demonstrates that the film is also committed to an ongoing engagement with issues of Indigenous identity and reservation politics.

The credit sequence begins with a slow-motion shot of an American Indian man bathed in golden light, dressed in traditional garb, and riding a horse through an unpopulated landscape. With a dissolve, the film gradually supplants this romantic image with one of a very different environment, which is characterized by ramshackle homes, abandoned cars, and barren patches of ground and identified via subtitle as the Northern Cheyenne reservation in Lame Deer, Montana. While the juxtaposition of the first two shots in *Powwow Highway* creates a disjuncture between past and present and thereby raises the specter of a history of exploitation, the sense of the unhomely engendered is further developed as the film explores scenarios of corporate expansion and intratribal factionalism, both of which incite conflict over the issue of how large a role the "world" of white America should play within the "home"land of the reservation. The first such scenario is introduced early on in the film when the Cheyenne tribal council is shown listening to Mr. Youngblood (Geoffrey Rivas), an American Indian who, as a representative of the Overdine Corporation, makes a pitch for the renewal of his company's lease and the continued mining of reservation land. While Youngblood's argument rests on the fundamental contention that Overdine's presence on the reservation has proven economically advantageous in the past, it is Buddy's retort that explains the film's opening images and thus proves more convincing: "You get what you want and we get the shaft. . . . This ain't the American Dream we're livin'. This here's the Third World." With this argument, Buddy poses to Overdine a threat so formidable that the FBI decides to intervene on the corporation's behalf by framing and jailing Buddy's sister, Bonnie, so as to lure Buddy off the reservation while the council is engaged in deliberation over the lease renewal issue.

Later in the film, Wacks introduces the second scenario of reservation politics when Buddy and Philbert stop off at the Pine Ridge reservation while en route to Santa Fe in order to visit Buddy's friends Wolf and Imogene (Wayne Waterman and Margot Kane). While in Pine Ridge, they learn of the intimidation tactics being employed by Bull Miller (Adam Taylor), a man who in vying for power on the reservation defines himself against those, like Buddy and Wolf, who have been involved in the American Indian Movement (AIM). Explaining their intention to leave Pine Ridge, Wolf relays a story of Miller's "gestapo" vandalizing his machine shop, and Imogene laments, "There's a shooting a week, Buddy. It's like living in Belfast." That the violence caused by differences within this particular community does not respect private/public boundaries is evident in the fact that when Buddy and Philbert arrive at the home of their friends, they are greeted with a view down the barrel of the shotgun that Wolf must wield for protection.

In advocating for the interests of big business and squelching any political activity on the part of AIM activists, Mr. Youngblood and Mr. Miller, respectively, are defined in terms of a desire for assimilation rather than for autonomy; they thereby serve as foils for Buddy and Philbert, both of whom actively embrace their identity as Cheyenne. Yet what distinguishes Buddy and Philbert from each other and therefore provides fodder for dramatic tension throughout the pair's journey is whether that identity is conceived of primarily in political or cultural terms and how it is claimed in the context of a necessarily hybridized existence. With his old Buick, which he has dubbed "Protector, the War Pony," Philbert is on a modern quest for an "authentic" experience that will allow him to forge a spiritual connection with his ancestors. Regarding the trip to Santa Fe as an opportunity to gain wisdom and collect the tokens needed for his warrior medicine bundle, he makes a series of unscheduled stops at various sacred locations, including Sweet Butte State Park in South Dakota, and sites of historical importance to his tribe such as Fort Robinson, where 149 Cheyenne were imprisoned in 1878. While Buddy responds to Philbert's interest in traditional Cheyenne culture with frustration and annoyance (at least initially), others are compelled by it. For example, Wolf and Imogene are genuinely entertained by the story of Wihio, the trickster, that Philbert relays to them over lunch one day, and a truck driver whom Philbert contacts with his CB radio is greatly heartened when Philbert identifies himself as "Whirlwind Dreamer" and proves both interested in and knowledgeable about Indigenous theology. Furthermore, the spectator too is encouraged to share in Philbert's regard for the "old ways" insofar as the film includes a series of fantastic images that are reminiscent of the film's opening shot yet explicitly constructed as Philbert's point of view. Typical of these images are the shots of a pack of horses, bathed in golden light and running free, which constitute Philbert's first glimpse of the junkyard where he buys his jalopy, and the shot of a man in traditional costume who visits a meditative Philbert upon his pilgrimage to the Black Hills. With such moments of subjective narration, the film makes Philbert's view of the world its own and thereby presents the past as intimately bound up with the present while emphasizing cultural continuity over intergenerational difference.

In contrast to Philbert, Buddy is an AIM activist who has participated in the conflicts at both Oglala and Wounded Knee; as such, he is outspoken about his distrust of the U.S. government and corporate America and willing to take any measure necessary to preserve what little sovereignty and few resources his community may still have. Serving as evidence of his determination is the fact that Buddy is a favored member of the tribal council whom the chief credits with many accomplishments when he declares that Buddy "has done more for this tribe than anyone." Going hand in hand with his commitment to political resistance is his impatience with what he sees as apolitical celebrations of American Indian culture. While Philbert participates eagerly in a powwow that the pair attend while in Pine Ridge, Buddy is more cynical, remarking, "I hate these goddamn things. Look at these people traipsing around a basketball court. They think a few lousy beads and some feathers are a culture or something." For Buddy, the affirmation of Aboriginal traditions obfuscates the ways in which those traditions have been impoverished by white America and, even more important, diverts attention away from the pressing need for active, organized, and, when necessary, armed resistance to political and economic cooptation. Arguing that the problems facing Americans Indians in the contemporary United States are distinctly modern and therefore demand distinctly modern solutions, he regards the ways of his ancestors as having little political efficacy or relevance. Buddy articulates his position most forcefully right after Philbert tells Imogene and Wolf the story of Wihio:

BUDDY: You tell everybody fairy stories.
PHILBERT: Stories of our ancestors, how the old ones dealt with problems. Often the problems never change. Nor the people.
BUDDY: Well, it's just too bad that those stories don't tell us how to keep our reservations from turning into sewers.
PHILBERT: But they do.
BUDDY: Look, Phil, I don't mean to step on your show, but white America ain't going to hold off much longer, man. They're hungry. They want our coal and our oil and our uranium, and they're going to take it, wherever it is.
PHILBERT: No, they won't. Wihio the trickster won't let them, for Wihio is also the creator of the universe.

That Philbert has the last word in the above exchange is highly significant, since the resolution of the film's plot serves to lend credence to his convictions. Philbert does, arguably, become more radicalized over the course of the trip, for he demonstrates an utter disregard for the law when he helps himself to a bundle of cash from the vault at the Santa Fe town hall and then breaks Bonnie out of jail. Nonetheless, it is Buddy who realizes the more profound transformation. Despite his reservations, Buddy does, over the course of the film, come to embrace, at least in part, the old ways, thereby bridging the personal and ideological differences between the pair of protagonists and propelling the film toward the type of closure expected of a buddy film/road movie. While Buddy is furious when he awakens to discover that Philbert has taken a significant detour while driving through their first night on the road in order to visit the Black Hills, he resigns himself to Philbert's subsequent stops and even comes to share in Philbert's spiritual quest. For example, by following Philbert's lead, Buddy finds himself at one point in the film standing in the middle of a river, up to his thighs in water and chanting, and at another, dancing at the powwow that he had been so reluctant to attend in the first place. His participation in Philbert's journey culminates in the chase sequence that ensues after Philbert breaks Bonnie out of jail. As a police car closes in on Philbert's "pony," Buddy pulls the window out of Philbert's door, assumes a position in the middle of the street while letting out a holler, and then throws the window toward the oncoming cruiser, causing it to crash. At the crucial moment of action, however, the film presents an image not of Buddy and the plate of glass but rather of the traditionally clothed Indian from earlier shots as he hurls a tomahawk into

the air. While it is the case that all of the other shots featuring an embodiment of Philbert and Buddy's ancestral past (except for that with which the
film opens) are from Philbert's perspective, Buddy's shape-shifting takes
place in Philbert's absence and thus independently of Philbert's gaze. In
short, Philbert's individual perspective is generalized as the film comes to
regard Buddy as infused with the spirit of the past.

In general, *Powwow Highway* is fairly savvy in its identity politics, es-
chewing depictions of Aboriginal authenticity in favor of moments of postmodern incongruity, such as those produced when Philbert uses a Her-
shey bar as a sacred offering and when his Aunt Harriet (Maria Antoinette
Rogers) lampoons his spiritual quest by taunting, "What'd you do? Find a
token in a Cracker Jack box?" Yet the rhetorical power of such moments,
which testify to the thoroughly syncretic nature of contemporary culture,
is vitiated when Wacks ultimately reinscribes the very same iconography
that he initially attempts to demystify. While the majority of romanticized
images from a hypothetical past are presented as Philbert's point of view, the
last one, which, as described above, transforms Buddy into a traditionally
outfitted Indian during the climax of a fraught confrontation, is like the
film's opening shot insofar as it is divorced from such a subjective context
and thus represents the vision of the film(maker). At this crucial moment,
Powwow Highway suggests that it is unable to envision Buddy's strength in
contemporary terms; as a result, his resistance to white law, which is bound
up with his participation in AIM, not his investment in traditional culture,
is translated into a traditionalist trope nonetheless.

The film's inability to envision Buddy's strength on Buddy's own terms
corresponds to its inability to envision a feasible alternative to a reservation
that is the site of continual struggle rather than communal support and of
mere survival as opposed to actual living. While Buddy and Philbert are each
engaged in a personal struggle for sovereignty, be it in the realm of politics
or culture, the forces that they are up against—corporations in cahoots with
the federal government on the one hand and a lack of will, even on the part
of older community members, to observe the traditional ways of the tribe
on the other—are formidable; furthermore, the acts of rebellion that they
do successfully mount (for example, vandalism, theft, a jailbreak) do not, in
the end, contribute at all to their work on behalf of the reservation and its
resident community. As a result, the only point of reference that the film has
for its vision of the ideal home is the hypothetical past invoked by the trope
above, a time when the reservation was not in the clutches of corporations
and people had access to the "good old Indian wisdom" at which Philbert's
Aunt Harriet scoffs.

Smoke Signals: On the Road, Take Two

While the popularity of *Powwow Highway* has been enduring enough to secure it cult status, *Smoke Signals* has emerged as a definitively mainstream hit since its release in 1998 when it won accolades from critics and average filmgoers alike, who were as enthusiastic about the film's conditions of production as they were about the film itself.[12] That not only the text but also its authorship inspired such a response is not surprising. The first feature written, directed, and co-produced by Americans Indians, *Smoke Signals* is a landmark movie and, as suggested by director Eyre, inherently political due to its novelty.[13] Furthermore, for many spectators, the film's appeal lies precisely in the fact that the perspective that director/co-producer Eyre and screenwriter/co-producer Alexie bring to bear upon the narrative[14]—a perspective that is remarkably unique since American Indians have almost always assumed a position in front of rather than behind the movie camera—is so palpable; Roger Ebert, for one, writes, "The film is so relaxed about its characters, so much at home in their world, that we sense it's an inside job."[15] Given this insider perspective, *Smoke Signals* succeeds where *Powwow Highway* falters: in the integration of a conventional story and unconventional protagonists. Whereas the uneven *Powwow Highway* occasionally compromises its re-vision of Indigenous subjectivity (as is the case, for example, when generic demands for action and romance lead to, respectively, Buddy's senseless vandalism of a stereo supplies store and a forced flirtation between Buddy and his sister's best friend), *Smoke Signals* is characterized by a much greater degree of consistency—in tone, story, and characterization. In short, it can be argued that Wacks privileges the road movie/buddy film formula over the integrity of his subject matter, while Eyre and Alexie do exactly the opposite, thereby employing generic conventions on their own terms.

At the same time that *Smoke Signals* is a largely self-determined vision of American Indian life, it is not a film "about" Indian issues. In this regard, the perspective that it brings to mainstream cinema is one not only marked by ethnicity but also heavily influenced by generation. Wryly humorous and profoundly self-aware, the film distances itself from the type of stridency commonly associated with social movement politics of the 1960s and 1970s. Furthermore, in structuring the film's emotional arc around the anger of a son whose father has abandoned him rather than that of an AIM activist, Eyre and Alexie refuse to limit their subject matter to those concerns specific to the American Indian community. Explaining the potentially universal appeal of *Smoke Signals*, Alexie argues, "I think you'd find the same thing in every ethnic or racial community, that it's fathers who are missing. I was doing an interview yesterday, and it came to me that brown artists—African-American, Chicano, Indian, and so on—write about fathers who physically leave and don't come back. White artists deal with fathers who leave emotionally, who sit in the chair in the living room but are gone. It's a theme that resonates."[16] Given Alexie's expressed interest in those familial experiences that are common to a variety of cultural communities, the film's concluding voice-over—Thomas's recitation of the poem "How Do We Forgive Our Fathers?" by Dick Lourie, a non-Native author—is especially fitting.

Refusing a pedantic approach, *Smoke Signals* does not dwell upon the fact of colonial oppression in the United States (although it does certainly acknowledge it); as a result, it does not represent the reservation as the besieged site that it is in *Powwow Highway*, defined solely in relation to that which threatens its autonomy or renders it uninhabitable. Instead, the reservation is constructed in a much more inviting manner, as indicated by the way it is introduced. While Wacks begins his film by offering up the Cheyenne reservation as an impoverished version of some idealized past, Eyre and Alexie establish the Coeur d'Alene reservation as a self-sufficient and supportive community with the film's first scene. In an opening that is evocative of Spike Lee's *Do the Right Thing* (1989), the voice of an agreeable deejay broadcasting over KREZ radio links a series of establishing shots. Providing an element of continuity between the different locations pictured, this voice serves to delineate the reservation as a specifically local space and to create a sense of shared experience among his listeners. The ties that bind individual members of this community are further established as the film goes on to introduce Thomas and Victor as infant survivors of a tragic fire that takes place on the night of the American bicentennial. Via voice-over, an adult Thomas narrates the events being depicted on-screen, detailing how his parents died in the blaze while he was rescued by Arnold Joseph (Gary Farmer), Victor's father who would subsequently walk out on his own family twelve years later. Once the film jumps ahead twenty-two years in time to the year 1998 and the day when Victor and his mother, Arlene (Tantoo Cardinal), learn of Arnold's recent death from his neighbor in Arizona, it becomes clear that even though they are not close by any means, these "children of fire and ash," as Thomas identifies himself and Victor, still share a connection. It is due to this connection that Thomas offers to finance Victor's trip to retrieve Arnold's ashes in exchange for the opportunity to tag along.

To provide evidence of the film's identification of the reservation with a strong social network is not to suggest that that this space is free of conflicts.

In fact, those moments of Victor's childhood that are captured in subsequent flashbacks are ones in which his alcoholic father turns from affable to abusive with no warning or in which he and Thomas trade barbs or blows with each other. Yet even though these events, particularly those involving his father, hurt and in turn embitter Victor, they do not threaten the fabric of the community as a whole. In fact, Arnold removes himself from his family's life and the reservation in general so as to avoid doing further damage, while Victor (as well as others of his generation, such as Velma and Lucy) swear off alcohol, presumably in order to avoid the fate of their elders. Thus, even in the face of individual problems, the reservation proves itself to be an adaptable community, no more a victim of self-destruction than of corporate conspiracies. The reservation is further consolidated when Velma and Lucy define it against that which lies outside its boundaries. After giving Thomas and Victor a lift to the bus station, the two women bid them good-bye with the following banter:

> VELMA: Do you guys got your passports?
> THOMAS: Passports?
> VELMA: Yeah, you're leaving the rez and going into a whole different country, cousin.
> THOMAS: But it's the United States.
> LUCY: Damn right it is. That's as foreign as it gets. Hope you two got your vaccinations.

In likening movement off the reservation to foreign travel, Velma and Lucy clearly distinguish between the "us" of the Coeur d'Alene nation and the "them" of the nation-state and thereby imbue the borderline between the two with profound significance.

Even though the reservation border is assumed to be important symbolically as that which demarcates a culture that is reassuringly familiar from one that is relatively other, it is nonetheless a very permeable threshold: while it may discourage the movement of populations across it (particularly for those moving in the direction that Thomas and Victor are), it in no way prohibits such crossings. Yet even more important to the film's vision is the fact that the border poses no obstacle whatsoever in the trafficking of images, either. While *Smoke Signals* is relatively uninterested in the threat that corporate America, the FBI, or factionalism pose to reservation life, it is fascinated with intricate invasions of a more intangible and therefore insidious variety—that is, those realized by satellite and cyber technologies, mass media, and consumer culture—which contribute so greatly to a contemporary youth culture that is syncretic in nature. Continually mentioning television and cinema, Victor, Thomas, and their contemporaries are extremely conversant in the language of pop culture, just like their creator Alexie, who identifies such populist fare as Stephen King and *The Brady Bunch* as among his primary influences.[17] In making explicit reference to the extensive reach of written and visual media produced by the dominant culture, the film illustrates Thomas and Victor's experience of hybridity with savvy self-reflexivity. It is by additionally drawing attention to the frequent (mis)representation of Indigenous culture by that media that the film moreover engages in its most incisive cultural critique, proving that what supplants the political vision of decades past is a decidedly contemporary brand of identity politics informed by a postmodern concern with signifiers and their appropriation.

Among the film's many intertextual references to other depictions of American Indians are those that occur when Thomas and Victor repeatedly parody the fatalistic line "Some days it's a good day to die" from *Little Big Man*; when the two discuss John Wayne's closed-mouthed performance style and then break into spontaneous song about his enigmatic teeth; when Victor ridicules Thomas for having watched *Dances with Wolves* over a hundred times; and when a woman makes a comment comparing Thomas and Victor to the Lone Ranger and Tonto, to which Thomas responds, "It's more like we're Tonto and Tonto." Even when such representations are not explicitly mentioned, their potency is hinted at by characters who demonstrate a hyper-awareness of how their culture has been and continues to be constructed within dominant discourse. For example, Velma and Lucy jokingly demand that Victor and Thomas give them something in exchange for a lift to the bus station ("We're Indians, remember? We barter") and then compliment the story that Thomas offers up in trade by designating it as "a fine example of the oral tradition," while Victor later instructs Thomas to "get stoic," lest he not be seen by others as a "real" Indian. An examination of these various instances reveals that the spirit in which the film's self-reflexive comments are made varies greatly, ranging from celebratory to challenging, ironic to revisionist. Thus, in the case of Thomas and Victor, the relationship between text and reader is revealed to be an extremely complex one involving a dual process of consumption and critique, especially when the text in question is an image of one's own culture. Crystallizing this tension is a moment in the film that occurs once Thomas and Victor have reached their destination and are in the home of Suzy Song (Irene Bedard), the neighbor who discovered Arnold's dead body and oversaw its cremation. As the three sit down to eat dinner while an old Western plays on the television, Thomas remarks, "The only thing more pathetic than Indians on TV is Indians watching Indians on TV." Yet, despite this comment, no one changes the channel.

In sum, rather than suggesting that a vital present for American Indians depends on a firming up of boundaries—between cultures, between spaces—*Smoke Signals* accepts unhomeliness and the hybridity that it engenders as an indisputable component of contemporary life. Indeed, just as Thomas and Victor, Velma and Lucy, and, for that matter, Eyre and Alexie enjoy the type of banter that their extensive knowledge of dominant media allows them to engage in, their reservation homeland is constructed as a very habitable place with a host of quirky personalities, a beautiful natural landscape, a tight-knit community, and a number of comfortable living spaces. In fact, the character who most profoundly feels a discrepancy between the home he inhabits and the home he seeks is not a member of the extant reservation community at all; it is, rather, Arnold, who continues to define his place in the world in terms of that which he left behind when he moved to Arizona. A photo that Victor finds among his father's belongings is telling in this regard. On the front is an image of Arlene, Arnold, and Victor embracing and laughing for the camera, and on the backside is written the single word "home." While this image of home at its most idyllic is rooted in the past, that past is one specific to Arnold's actual family history rather than the hypothetical yesteryear evoked by *Powwow Highway*. Thus, *Smoke Signals* is able at least to envision, if not to realize (since Arnold dies before returning to the reservation), a homecoming worth feeling hopeful about.

Urban Initiatives

Despite the fact that Buddy and Philbert on the one hand and Victor and Thomas on the other are, like so many male duos before them, on the road for the majority of *Powwow Highway* and *Smoke Signals*, they still define their respective journeys in relation to the site from which they have departed and to which they will return, just as they define themselves in relation to the family members from whom they have been separated and with whom they seek some sort of reconciliation. In other words, both Wacks and Eyre route a meditation on home—specifically, the reservation—through the vast network of highways that traverse the American West. Yet each film also contains at least one character who opens the door onto another experience of Indigeneity, one that is not bound up with reservation life and the specific variety of community that it fosters. In *Powwow Highway*, that character is Buddy's sister, Bonnie, who left the reservation for Santa Fe and severed ties with her family ten years earlier after concluding that "nobody gave a damn about her when she was a kid." Bonnie's counterpart in *Smoke*

Signals is Suzy Song, who served as a companion to Arnold Joseph in the last years of his life. Born and raised in New York City and traveling frequently for her job as a hospital administrator, she lacks the kind of geographical moorings that ground Arnold, even if only through memories of his past and intentions for his future. At the same time that they represent an alternative to reservation life, Bonnie and Suzy also serve to suggest that to live off the reservation is to be outside the fold of an Indian community. Specifically, Bonnie's most significant relationships of the last decade have been with non-Native people, namely her former partner with whom she had two children and her close friend Rabbit, who comes to her rescue with bail money, takes care of the children in her absence, and identifies herself to Buddy as "the one who stuck by [Bonnie] while you were out saving the world." Suzy, in contrast, lacks ties not only to a traditional homeland but also to a past or future family of any sort and thus is responsible for the caretaking of no one but herself.[18]

The characters of Bonnie and Suzy notwithstanding, recent census data suggest that urban living need not entail such a lack. With three-quarters of self-defined American Indians living in cities as of the year 2000,[19] urban populations are large enough not only to problematize Native people's status as those "conceptually sited far beyond the horizon" of the cityscapes associated with white settler and/or immigrant culture but also to ensure the possibility of an Aboriginal urban community.[20] Bearing this out is recent research and scholarship on emergent urban social configurations such as that being produced by Susan Lobo, Angela A. Gonzalez, Terry Straus, and Debra Valentino.[21] No doubt, similar arguments can also be made in relation to the other countries at issue in this project since urban residency rates for Aboriginal populations therein are also high, even if, in the case of Canada and Australia, they do not quite approach 75 percent. Indeed, the most recent statistics on this issue are as follows: 84.4 percent of Maori live in cities, according to data collected for New Zealand's 2006 census; 49 percent of those who identified as members of First Nations in 2001 do so in Canada; and, as of 2001, 30 percent of Australian Aborigines lived in major urban centers, with another 43 percent residing in inner and outer regional areas as opposed to remote ones.[22] Even in the face of such realities, however, traditional associations between Aboriginality and rural environs sustain popular assumptions that urban living tempers claims to Aboriginal authenticity. As a result, participation in city life and the nontribal forms of social organization to which it may give rise frequently result in a combination of social invisibility and (further) political disfranchisement that, as Jeffrey Sissons demonstrates, gains its most pointed expression when crystallized into public policy. In a discussion of recent New Zealand legislation regarding fishing quotas, Sissons explains how the interests of urban Maori get sidelined in a postsettler context where the power to engage in negotiation and self-representation is predicated either on one's status as an individual who has fully assimilated into New Zealand (read white) political life or on membership in one of the tribal collectivities that has represented Maori interests since the earliest days of European settlement. As Sissons notes at the conclusion of his article, policies that more readily recognize Aboriginal persons who have maintained residence on traditional lands are common in other settler societies as well, including Australia, where the Native Title Act awards land rights based on the ability to demonstrate a "continuous traditional connection" to the parcel under consideration; Canada, where reserve Indians have far greater access to social services than do those who live elsewhere; and the United States, where the Indian Arts and Crafts Act of 1990 prohibits Indians who are not certified by federally recognized tribes from claiming Indian origins for their work.

As literary critic Carol Miller notes, for a number of reasons, including those that Sissons speaks to, American Indian authors frequently represent cities and towns as particularly fraught contact zones where the differences between Native and non-Native culture are thrown into fresh relief and Aboriginal people are most vulnerable to a host of ills, from disfranchisement to discrimination, poverty to abuse. At the same time, however, as settings for both fiction and reality, they also offer a horizon of possibility, as suggested by the query fueling Miller's analytical work: "To what degree, if at all, may this movement [to urban environments] be understood as a '(re)taking place'—a double breaking out—both from federally designated boundaries historically intended to isolate and contain Native people and from an equally pervasive confinement within the anachronistic fantasy-wilderness of the white imagination?"[23] In the following sections, I take up two films, Lee Tamahori's *Once Were Warriors* and Noam Gonick's *Stryker*, that break out of extant paradigms, be they social or cinematic, by dramatizing urban Aboriginal life and focusing on varieties of community that are not visible in *Powwow Highway* and *Smoke Signals*. In so doing, they clarify both the terms and the stakes of the issue Miller broaches by raising an additional question: how does a text acknowledge the myriad hardships associated with urban living without supplanting "the anachronistic fantasy-wilderness of the white imagination" with another, equally confining paradigm, namely, that of a fantasy-underworld in which lack of initiative and agency ensures for urban Aboriginal peoples a precarious existence of social deprivation and downward mobility? As I grapple with this question throughout the remainder of this chapter, considerations of space, once again, give way to those of time as I foreground the extent to which the films at hand contextualize the present by speaking to the historical past that has produced it and/or by envisioning a future made possible by social change.

Once Were Warriors: "Taking Care of Her Green Stone Wall"

In 1994, Lee Tamahori's debut film, Once Were Warriors, made history in its native New Zealand, where it earned $6 million at the box office and became the highest grossing movie in the country's history. The film's overwhelming popularity in its domestic market came as quite a surprise to its director, who was anticipating a backlash against the film, particularly from Maori viewers. Even though the cast and crew were made up largely of people of Maori ancestry, the fact that the film was adapted from a novel by the highly controversial author Alan Duff, whom Jonathan Dennis, founding director of the New Zealand Film Archive, has described as "a mouthpiece for Maoribashing," made it, prior to its release, a cause for disquietude on the part of many.[24] Yet, once viewed, the film proved more compelling than repelling, as reported by Tamahori: "Maori are going to this film in unprecedented numbers, like no other movie ever. We sent it out to provincial centers and they broke all box office records. Every Maori in the country is going to see it. . . . It happens to be a bleak vision but it is our vision. It's not the only one, but it is one, and they're proud of that."[25] Whether or not it is indeed the case, as Tamahori suggests, that the film's success can be ascribed to a pride born of self-recognition is difficult to ascertain. What is indisputable, however, is that Once Were Warriors struck a chord in its homeland, making a significant social impact in a couple of ways. First, it raised awareness around the issue of domestic violence, sparking a national dialogue on what has come to be known as "the warrior problem" and encouraging both men and women to enlist the services of hotlines and counseling centers in order to address their roles in abusive situations.[26] Second, by surpassing even Jurassic Park (Steven Spielberg) in popularity the year of its release, it earned for cinema a certain pride of place in a country where "nationalist identifications have historically been located in sport, rather than in film."[27] Yet the success of this film was in no way limited to its domestic context. Once Were Warriors also became an international hit, particularly on the festival circuit, where it garnered copious praise and over sixty prizes and thereby confirmed what many had come to suspect after the release of Jane Campion's The Piano and Peter Jackson's Heavenly Creatures (1994): that the New Zealand film industry, albeit small, was hitting its stride.[28]

At the center of *Once Were Warriors* is Beth Heke (Rena Owen), who lives with her husband, Jake (Temuera Morrison), and their five children in a run-down section of South Auckland. Having cut herself off from her noble heritage when her decision to marry the descendant of a slave tribe was greeted with family-wide disapproval and skepticism, Beth has spent her marriage determined to prove the prudence of her life choices. Yet as the years have passed, this task has become increasingly more difficult. Drawing a comparison with the similarly paired Stanley and Stella of Tennessee Williams's *A Streetcar Named Desire* (1947), Richard Alleva writes, "The Hekes are the Kowalskis after twenty years of marriage and there have been too many drinks, too many brawls, too much brutality."[29] Early on in *Once Were Warriors*, Jake loses his job, proclaims his intention to put the family on the dole despite Beth's protestations, and dedicates himself full-time to drinking with his friends at the local pub during the day and back at the Heke home after hours. Emotionally volatile, easily enraged, and frequently intoxicated, Jake proves a callous father and abusive husband who does not think twice about beating his wife to a pulp when she gets "lippy" with him or breaking promises made to his children so that he can drink the day away. Over the course of the movie, Beth attempts to hold the family together even in the face of her husband's uncaring behavior, but it is only after the rape and subsequent suicide of their thirteen-year-old daughter, Grace (Mamaengaroa Kerr-Bell), that Beth realizes she must leave Jake in order to ensure her family's survival.

As is evident from this synopsis, *Once Were Warriors* presents a narrative of relentless violence, which contains scenes of barroom brawls, domestic abuse, hazing, rape, suicide, and retribution of the eye-for-an-eye variety. For critic Leonie Pihama, author of "Repositioning Maori Representation: Contextualizing *Once Were Warriors*," this focus on brutality within the Maori community is worrisome since it threatens to eclipse a more quotidian reality, especially in the minds of those viewers, both inside and outside of New Zealand, whose exposure to Maori culture is limited to mediated encounters. Pihama designates the film's images as negative not simply because they serve to embroil the Heke family in violence but because they are not paired with representation of the historical conditions that have produced such violence. She writes, "*Once Were Warriors* as a representation of Maori is particularly problematic because it is not located within historical realities of this land. The issues raised within the movie are not read in light of the wider context and experiences of colonization and the impact of that upon Maori people."[30] As the crux of her argument, this quotation should elucidate her case, yet instead it in fact complicates it. While the subject of the first sentence is clear, Pihama's use of the passive voice in the second creates a certain ambiguity, raising the question of whether the one doing the reading is the film(maker) or, alternately, the film's hypothetical viewer. A stronger case could probably be made for the former understanding of the sentence given the syntax of the passage as a whole; at the same time, the latter option actually speaks to what seems to trouble Pihama even more than *Once Were Warriors* per se: the absence of any representational tradition that might have contextualized—and thereby prepared contemporary audiences for—the negative images that Tamahori presents. In the absence of such a tradition, Pihama cautions, *Once Were Warriors* may do more harm than good.

What is most interesting about this critique is not Pihama's concern with negative images, for on this count she falls in line with myriad critics before her in acknowledging that texts featuring underrepresented populations bear a greater representational burden than those that position themselves in closer proximity to what Audre Lorde calls the "mythical norm."[31] Rather, it is her suggestion that the only way *Once Were Warriors* could have skirted the danger of negative stereotyping is with "discussion of the impact of colonization and the acts of violence perpetrated upon our tupuna."[32] For what exactly would constitute said discussion—mimetic representation of the colonial past, an opening intertitle providing expository information on lives lost and spoils gained, frequent dialogic allusion to a personal and/or communal history of violation? Although Pihama does not specify, Jane Smith offers up the possibility of an answer to this question when she produces a closer reading of the film in order to reach a similar conclusion about the film's ultimate message.

In "Knocked Around in New Zealand: Postcolonialism Goes to the Movies," she argues that *Once Were Warriors* starts out locating the lives of the Hekes within a larger context by drawing attention to the legacies of colonialism (seen in the depressed urban neighborhood in which they live) and intertribal discrimination (heard about when Jake and Beth argue). Approximately a third of the way through, however, the film, according to Smith, loses its historically informed and socially inflected perspective. The specific turning point for Smith is a brief but brutal scene wherein Jake beats Beth after she refuses to cook some eggs for their partying friends. Setting the bar with regard to the severity of the film's violence and the graphic nature of its depiction, this scene constructs Jake as monstrous villain and, conversely, Beth as victim/survivor. These roles are further consolidated when the film surveys the morning aftermath in the next scene, the first shot of which presents a bird's-eye view of the couple lying in bed. While the positioning of Jake's body ensures that the spectator has limited access to him visually and, in turn, emotionally, Beth's bruised and swollen face is on full display. From this point on, according to Smith, the film's "narrative aperture begins to close": "Prior to [the beating Jake gives Beth], the film seemed to be arguing that the difficulties facing the Heke family—unemployment, depression, imprisonment, alcoholism, and interfamily violence—arose from past and present discrimination, but now *Once Were Warriors* tempts viewers to read the Hekes' troubles as springing from the incontestable differences between bad men and good women. Surreptitiously, a symptom of colonialist oppression becomes the origin of modern-day Maori misery."[33] In reading *Once Were Warriors* thus, Smith identifies it as one of a triad of recent films—the other two being *The Piano* and *Broken English* (Gregor Nicholas, 1996)—that engages in a very particular ideological project: the reduction of social relations to "the age-old, nothing-to-be-done-about-it battle between the sexes," which serves both to naturalize gender and to deny the divisive role that race, class, and ethnicity have played and continue to play in New Zealand.[34] For Smith, such a cinematic slight of hand is part and parcel of a broader cultural initiative to position New Zealand favorably within a new world order dictated by global capitalism. In such a context, "attention to the domestic frontier helps prevent questions about the relationship of the national to the global."[35]

Thus, for Smith, the "discussion" that Pihama calls for, which takes the shape of various visual and aural traces of a social reality that extends beyond the Heke household both spatially and temporally, is initiated but not sustained. Once the film foregrounds the issue of domestic violence, it devolves into melodrama, retreating into the private sphere, foregrounding gender at the exclusion of other determinants of social power and position, and engaging in a discourse of moral rather than political dimensions. In short, Smith posits as mutually exclusive the "domestic frontier" invoked above and that which lies beyond it: the urban landscape, the public sphere, and culture at large with all its racial, ethnic, and class diversity. Yet, it is not the film but Smith herself who instates this boundary between spaces and, by extension, discourses. *Once Were Warriors*, in contrast, relentlessly narrates the breakdown of such a boundary and thus the manner in which gender, race, and class are defined and inflected, experienced and understood in and through one another. In the process, it routes questions of the national, the global, and perhaps even their relationship through the domestic frontier, thereby showing the family home to be a space that is not impervious to that which lies beyond it.

The first third of the film serves to provide not simply a narrative context for the events to follow but also a discursive framework in which to understand those events. More specifically, after establishing at its outset the extent to which the past haunts the present and the public infuses the private, *Once Were Warriors* goes on to explore in a highly dramatic manner the potentially devastating effects of such blurred boundaries as they are experienced by one couple and their children. Thus, it can be argued that the film undergoes a racking of its focus as opposed to a closing of its aperture. While it is indeed true that Beth and Jake's troubled and troubling relationship takes center stage once the punches have started to fly, to argue that the film then becomes myopic, incapable of engaging with issues such as race, class, and colonialism, is to ignore key elements of the film's narration, such as the emphasis placed on Beth and Jake's personal history and the interest shown in other characters' negotiation of tribal tradition. Moreover, it is to ignore the role of space in the film, for the manner in which it is made up, lived in, moved through, talked about, and fought over serves to link the phenomenon of domestic violence with the experience of deterritorialization that is commonplace for Aboriginal populations like the Maori.

From its outset, *Once Were Warriors* raises the specter of a history that provides context for the story to unfold. The film opens with what appears to be an extreme long shot of a landscape made up of snow-capped mountains, sun-drenched fields, and a serene lake. After a moment of quiet and stillness, the blare of a car horn sounds, and the camera pans left and cranes down to reveal that this view is actually a photograph on a billboard positioned on the side of a busy highway along which Beth walks with a shopping cart. Presenting an initial image that obscures the reality of urban modernity and instead resonates with colonialist tropes of a pristine and peaceful "virgin" land, the film quickly reveals that image, which has been appropriated for exclusively commercial purposes, to be rooted in the hypothetical past of this particular contemporary context. This disjuncture is exacerbated by Beth's appearance. Isolated on-screen in a medium close-up that reveals her to be wearing a black leather vest, smoking a cigarette, and sporting dark sunglasses while an electric guitar supplies nondiegetic musical accompaniment, Beth, like her stomping ground, defies popular expectations: she is not the primitive native assumed to populate the unspoiled terrain of the billboard. With this opening shot/"shock," as well as subsequent shots/"shocks" that introduce the spectator to other members of the urban Maori community, Tamahori plays with and, in the process, draws attention to contemporary cinema's preference for romanticized representations of the precolonial or colonial past over depictions of a devastated "postcolonial" present characterized by extreme economic disparities. Furthermore, he also draws attention to the colonialist history that haunts the events to be depicted by leading the spectator to consider what series of historical events connects the disparate images of past and present.

In keeping with an unhomely aesthetic, it is not simply the intrusion of history on the present but also that of the public on the private that the film narrates. After Beth is introduced in the film's opening shot, she looks across the highway to her backyard, where Grace sits with the two youngest children and reads aloud from the journal that serves as her constant companion. Presenting the trio as just beyond a foreground dominated by passing cars, barbed wire, and a chain-link fence, Tamahori highlights the public nature of this domestic and typically private space. Once Beth returns home, it is revealed that the story Grace relays is, fittingly, one of a border and the omnipresent threat to its stability. Introducing a fantastic creature named Rahey, Grace explains: "She lived at the bottom of a huge lake. She spent most of her time taking care of her green stone wall. The wall stopped the water from flooding over the people who lived by Rahey's lake. Once a month the people would bring a huge piece of green stone to help Rahey keep the wall strong." While the fate of Rahey's wall is left undetermined, the boundaries that distinguish home from world for the Hekes and thus could potentially safeguard their privacy are like the border between highway and backyard: full of holes and lacking in substance.

Since they are bound to the family home at both the conceptual and phenomenological levels in their capacity as caretakers, the female members

The home as site of intricate invasions in *Once Were Warriors*. (Communicado Productions)

of the Heke family are the ones who bear the brunt of this dissolution of boundaries. It is certainly not the case that Beth and Grace are confined to the domestic space in any absolute sense. Beth, after all, is first introduced while walking on the shoulder of a highway, and Grace makes frequent visits to her best friend, Toot (Shannon Williams), who lives in a broken-down car located under an overpass. Nonetheless, the home is clearly their domain insofar as they are the only ones who look after the two youngest children and attend to household chores such as cooking, cleaning, and laundry. As a result, they contrast sharply with Jake, who treats the Heke house as a pit stop between beers with his buddies; the eldest son, Nig (Julian Arahanga), who is seen at home only when on his way in or out; and the teenaged Boogie (Taungaroa Emile), who spends the majority of the film living in a reformatory as a ward of the state. Crystallizing perfectly the extent to which the home is constructed and perceived as a female space and, moreover, a "woman's lot" is an exchange between Nig and Grace that takes place the day after the raucous party that culminated in Jake's abuse of Beth. As Grace starts to clean up the living room, Nig teases his sister:

NIG: You should leave it. There'll be plenty of time for you to clean up after drunken fuckin' parties.
GRACE: What do you mean?
NIG: When you get married, girl.
GRACE: Who said I want to?
NIG: It's just the way things are.
GRACE: Nah, fellas around here are too ugly.
NIG: *(Laughs)* It's just a matter of time.

Due to the extent to which Beth and Grace are identified with domestic space, they are the ones most profoundly affected by the intricate invasions Bhabha associates with postcoloniality. In fact, for them the blurring of boundaries between home and world is experienced not simply as a disorientation but also as a violation—a fact made literal by the film's two rapes.

The culture of violence that gains its most dramatic expression in these rapes is established shortly after Beth makes her initial appearance on-screen, for on display in the streets through which she walks her shopping cart is a masculinity predicated on physical strength and the power to intimidate. Punctuating this opening sequence, which serves to introduce the film's key players one by one, is the appearance of Jake, who stares down a passerby who has carelessly bumped into him, and then Nig, who lifts weights with his friends. The violence that is only posed as threat initially becomes a reality in a subsequent scene when a bemused Jake watches a brutal fistfight and then picks his own while out at the neighborhood pub. As per the condition of unhomeliness, however, physical abuse is not limited to the public arenas of the streets and the pub. Instead, it travels over the course of the film into increasingly more intimate recesses until it is apparent that there is no space, domestic or corporeal, safe from invasion. The geographical progression of violence moves from the local, public space of the pub into the home when Jake abuses Beth in the scene mentioned above. In the process of the thrashing, they move from the kitchen to the living room and finally upstairs to the bedroom, where he throws her on the bed and prepares to rape her. Throughout this scene, the four youngest children huddle together as they listen with fear from the bedroom that they share. As the one space into which Jake does not readily travel and the site where Beth can go for comfort the day after the beating, this room functions as an oasis of calm within the household. Accordingly, its walls are infused with Grace's optimism: hanging on them are movie posters for *White Men Can't Jump* and *Lethal Weapon*, which bespeak an ideal of racial harmony Hollywood-style. Yet this last sanctum is also ultimately violated when Jake's drinking mate, Uncle Bully (Clifford Curtis), slips away from a party in full swing downstairs in order to rape Grace in her bed while the other children in the room are sleeping. The horror of this violation, in conjunction with the messages she receives about the seeming inevitability of a life led in service of men, leaves Grace hopeless and despairing enough to commit suicide.

Subsequent to Grace's tragic death, Beth makes it her top priority to "do right" by her dead daughter and, in turn, to ensure that her remaining children have a supportive living environment in which they can thrive. As a first step toward the realization of this dual goal, Beth decides to return to the family land from which she fled as an impetuous youth in order to bury Grace among her ancestors. Upon announcing her intention to do so, Beth encounters resistance from Jake. In the argument that ensues, the central problematic animating the last act of the film—how to conceive of home in the realm of the unhomely—comes to a head with the following exchange:

BETH: I want us to take Grace back home . . . to the *marae*.[36]
JAKE: This is her fucking home.
BETH: No, it's not. This was never her home, never.
JAKE: And that fucking place is? Fucking Maoris who think they're better than the rest of us? I hate them, bastards living in the fucking past.
BETH: It's our past too, Jake.

JAKE: What's that supposed to mean?

BETH: I want Grace to be with her people. We should have gone back a long
time ago.

In the first three lines of dialogue quoted above, "home" is mentioned as
many times, yet with each iteration, the word accrues an additional meaning
that both contests and complements other meanings already in circulation;
as such, it emerges as a slippery signifier, an exemplary site of Derridean
différance. While the "home" named by Jake is of the most literal variety,
it is set off against those invoked by Beth, the first of which is her familial
homeland and the second of which is an ideal defined apart from the violence and violation, aggression and battle lines, scarcity and sadness to
which the Heke household has been playing host for so many years.

Given the fact that *Once Were Warriors* takes as its subject members of
New Zealand's Aboriginal population, this destabilization of home is highly
significant, for it allows the film to negotiate successfully the challenge of
asserting a people's connection with a place without reducing them to that
connection. As a result, *Once Were Warriors* is able to forge a middle ground
between two contradictory tendencies in contemporary discourse, both of
which were discussed in the introduction: that on the part of many postcolonial theorists to reject essentialism *tout court* and that evident in certain
strands of Indigenous writing to make land the linchpin of identity. Because
Once Were Warriors seizes upon Grace's death to stage a return to the family *marae* and thus an appeal to tradition on Beth's part (which parallels
ones made by Nig and Boogie, as I discuss later), it bears some resemblance
to those texts discussed by Chadwick Allen, which define identity in and
through a "blood/land/memory complex." For this reason, certain critics
have argued that the film offers anachronistic answers to contemporary
quandaries by suggesting that contemporary Maori must choose between
pursuing a course of self-destruction and cultural alienation, as Jake has,
or living in the (fucking) past, along with the relatives for whom Jake has
such scorn. Yet to make such an accusation is to ignore the fact that Beth's
homecoming is not an end unto itself, even though Beth's lament that she
"should have gone back a long time ago" seems to suggest otherwise. Rather,
it functions as a prelude to the personal journey that Beth has embarked
upon by the conclusion of the film. In short, to invoke Paul Gilroy, Tamahori's interest in roots in no way precludes one in routes; by extension, he
refuses to relegate tradition exclusively to the past or the pastoral.[37]

Despite the fact that Beth cut off contact with her relatives after marrying Jake, it is clear from the way she muses nostalgically about her lost

childhood during a rare family outing earlier in the film that the separation from them was not absolute and, moreover, that her family land continues to hold sway over her both emotionally and spiritually. With her resolution to return home after so many years of absence, Beth reestablishes a connection to her past, which is represented visually when a dissolve links Beth's face with that of the traditional wooden carving that crowns the roof of the structure in which Grace is laid out on the day of her funeral. While this connection is indeed a significant event in its own right, it serves additionally to fortify Beth so she can ultimately return to South Auckland and resume a life there independent of Jake. Thus, it is not only the film's inspired opening but also its resolution that takes place in an urban context that makes literal the diaspora space—that is, a "site where the native is as much a diasporian as the diasporian is the native"—that Avtar Brah charts in theory.[38] As a result, the significance of "home" extends beyond the borders of the *marae* as the first home named in the above exchange between Jake and Beth is supplemented by the second. It is actually, however, the third of these "homes," one defined less by geography than affect and one rooted in a hypothetical future rather than an idealized and distant or brutal and recent past, that the film ultimately attempts to envision. Yet insofar as its realization depends upon a reversal of the effects of unhomeliness—that is, a reinscription of the boundary between private and public—such a home proves elusive despite the film's will to closure.

Tamahori readily admits that to end the film with Beth discovering what happened to Grace upon reading her journal and Jake beating the life out of Bully when confronted with the incriminating evidence was to resort to "just pure melodrama" in order to satisfy a spectatorial need for catharsis.[39] Nevertheless, it could be argued that Beth's triumphant exit is the most profoundly melodramatic moment of the narrative. For even though *Once Were Warriors* ends with a sense of victory as Beth walks away from Jake and makes the definitive pronouncement, "We're going home," the rest of the film calls into question the feasibility of such a swift and successful resolution. This type of conclusion might be commonplace in Hollywood films like those advertised on Grace's walls, which pose individualized solutions to social problems; and in the case of a film set in a legitimately postcolonial context, it might ring less false (although not entirely true, given the effects of neocolonialism). In light of the reality of a settler society, however, the designation "home" bespeaks a yearning more than a certainty. Thus, even when Tamahori does narrow the film's aperture in order to achieve narrative closure, he cannot adequately resolve the various social issues that the film has raised in order to do so convincingly. Having already embraced an unhomely aesthetic by staging a variety of intricate invasions, particularly those associated with a culture of masculine bravado, *Once Were Warriors* makes clear, as does the term "Fourth World," to what extent unhomeliness is routine even for those populations that are "Native" to the nation in which they reside.

Stryker: "The native way of thinking ain't the way of the old"

While *Once Were Warriors* shares with *Powwow Highway* an investment in tradition as a source of strength and integrity, it nonetheless also constructs Maori culture as capable of, even eager for, change, thereby acknowledging, like *Smoke Signals*, the necessarily syncretic and dynamic nature of life in the Fourth World. Noam Gonick's *Stryker*, in comparison, takes this embrace of the transformative possibilities of adaptation to urban environs and formation of new social networks a step further by making them a source of creative productivity. This is not to say that city life in *Stryker* is free of conflict. On the contrary, the neighborhood at its center, namely the North End of Winnipeg, is as plagued by violence as the local spaces through which members of the Heke family move, since it is the setting for a turf war between two dueling gangs: the Indian Posse (IP) with Mama Ceece (Deena Fontaine), fresh off a stint in jail, at its head, and the largely Filipino Asian Bomb Squad (ABS), led by the biracial Omar (Ryan Black), who took advantage of Mama Ceece's recent absence by monopolizing the market in drug trafficking and sex work and thereby consolidating control of the North End. Yet the film derives vitality not from the frank depiction of that violence and its effects but rather from the performances of self and affiliation that it conditions. In other words, while the physical brutality and emotional devastation featured in *Once Were Warriors* are so acute and affective as to throw into question Beth's capacity to realize her domestic ideal, *Stryker* lays greater emphasis on the gains the members of the IP make than on the losses they sustain in an urban context. While Gonick's filmmaking track record (which includes the feature *Hey, Happy!* from 2001) as well as his inclusion of numerous "two-spirited" or transgendered characters in *Stryker* demonstrate his committed engagement with questions of gender and sexuality, it is this emphasis on the enriching, even utopian, possibilities of personal and social transformation that most subtly yet profoundly qualify Gonick's vision as queer in sensibility.

Like *Once Were Warriors*, *Stryker* immediately announces its defiance of traditionalist tropes while simultaneously raising the specter of a historical past that continues to shape the present. Yet while the former film realizes such ends with a camera movement that traces the disjuncture between idealized and actual and thereby slyly plays both with and on spectatorial expectations, the latter film does so in a more confrontational manner, harnessing the tremendous energy of a transnational artistic form, rap music, to comment on a past and present of racial oppression. Specifically, during the film's opening credits, four hundred years of history unroll in a sequence of archival images, ranging from woodcuts depicting contact during the earliest days of European settlement to photographs representing a wide variety of Native experiences from the past century and a half, including prairie living, residential education, and urban assimilation. Accompanying this sequence is a song by rap artist Hellnback (the first of many on the film's soundtrack), which typifies the genre of "res rap" by "[blending] the cultural heritage of traditional storytelling with the heavy stylistic influence of American hip hop."[40] Speaking to—indeed, back to—the history being presented visually in digest form, Hellnback sings:

> My reservation
> I'm feeling the pain
> The strain on my mental weighs heavy
> Genocide makes me live my Native life deadly
> I hope you get me
> If you don't let it marinate the mindset of my people
> We try to set that straight
> We never brought residential schools to this place
> We never brought alcoholic fluid to our tastes
> We were never gonna try to change you
> What you did to my descendents changed the elders' lives too
> And all the time you knew, now we feeling reserved
> Living disturbed, living the life we never deserved
> The Native way of thinking ain't the way of the old
> It's time to look towards the future, let our story unfold[41]

The future-tense story that does unfold from this point on is decidedly iconoclastic insofar as it, like Hellnback's music, derives from a reality that so often escapes representation—namely, an urban Indigeneity in Canada. It is precisely this reality that Bonita Lawrence foregrounds in *"Real" Indians and Others: Mixed Blood Urban Native Peoples and Indigenous Nationhood*, the result of a recent series of interviews that she conducted with thirty mixed-blood Indians living in Toronto. In a couple of significant ways, *Stryker* bears out the phenomena that Lawrence describes in her study, in the process linking rather than counterposing rural and city space, reserve and urban communities. For one, the film, like so many of Lawrence's participants, acknowledges that urban residence does not preclude ties to a reserve community by starting the film on the Brokenhead reserve, where the film's unnamed protagonist (who eventually comes to be called Stryker, the word for a gang member in training) sets fire to a church before fleeing to Winnipeg on the roof of a boxcar. Providing him common ground with select gang members and prostitutes whom he meets in the city, the reserve continues to exert a structuring influence on his identity in absentia despite the fact that he has no apparent intentions of returning and does not look to his reserve membership as a stamp of authenticity. Additionally, the film anticipates the response of one of Lawrence's subjects who "suggested that Native people had to rethink what was meant by 'Indian land'—that when Native people agreed to limit 'Indian land' to reserves, they were ignoring the fact that all the land had once been theirs."[42] Indeed, this is one of the most salient points made by Gonick; referring repeatedly to the streets of Winnipeg as "Native land," be it through IP graffiti or the defiant protests of Gloria (Joy Keeper), an older woman in the North End community, the film not only urbanizes Indigenous identity but also Indigenizes the city streets of Winnipeg.

At the same time that *Stryker* makes the city a site of annexation, it also makes no reference to a traditional notion of home, as either an actuality or an ideal, a lost past or a potential future. In other words, much as *Smoke Signals* takes for granted that which *Powwow Highway* laments (that is, the permeable boundaries of the reservation), *Stryker* regards as a fait accompli that which *Once Were Warriors* attempts to rectify, the interpenetration of public and private and the disorientation that it effects. As a result, it exists on the other side of the hope that Beth holds out for a home where her children can grow up in safety. In *Stryker*, the majority of the characters occupy liminal spaces that lack in both permanence and privacy, as exemplified by Cody's (Nick Oullette) makeshift shelter set up in an alley; the converted garage that functions as an ABS clubhouse; the abandoned warehouse where the members of the IP squat; and Omar's car, which serves as site for both business transactions and sexual encounters. Moreover, the two relatively traditional residences featured in the film are perversions of the Heke household, flawed and besieged as it is. The first is occupied by Talia (Dominique Rémy Root), a middle-aged woman of Eastern European descent who agrees to serve as foster mother to any Native boy whom the city sends her way so that she can take advantage of him sexually; and the second is home to a large community of Native transvestites and transsexuals who turn tricks and do drugs in order to survive. Finally, even the reservation, which serves as a point of departure for the film, is not constructed as a site of safety and authenticity, for it is precisely a vestige of colonial imposition, an abandoned church, that Stryker targets with his arson before leaving for Winnipeg.

Between rampant drug use and urban warfare, sexual abuse and insufficient shelter from the severe winter weather of Winnipeg, the characters featured in *Stryker* are suffering the "postcolonial" legacy of the events described in both song and image at the film's outset. Yet what distinguishes *Stryker* from *Once Were Warriors*, not to mention numerous other media images, is that it tempers its representation of such troubling phenomena with enthusiasm about that which is able to take shape in the wake of the breakdown of those boundaries that figure so centrally in Bhabha's discussion of the unhomely. In other words, just as Hellnback's soundtrack for the film looks toward the future without forgetting the past, the film is as invested, if not more, in those narrative elements that feature social fluidity and historical change—in short, the possibility of renewal through redefinition—as it is in those scenarios emphasizing suffering. The character that most incisively captures this dual investment and, in the process, embodies the emotional and political stakes of unhomeliness is the transgendered Daisy (Joseph Mesiano), who makes her home in the second of the two residences mentioned above.

While Daisy is complicit in an exploitative relationship with her pimp, Omar, willingly taking him up on occasional offers of drugs and affection only then to be subjected to physical abuse and demands for cash, she is also the heart of the film: she harbors hope for the possibility of an alternative to her current life by saving for the future, holding onto her dreams, and eventually making the changes necessary to ensure a different fate for herself. Yet even in the present, she is integral to the creation of a community that transcends the boundaries that typically fragment the North End. Not only does she refuse to take sides in the conflict between the IP and the ABS, but she also shows compassion for and solidarity with those who occupy a similarly neutral position, taking in Stryker (Kyle Henry) upon his arrival to Winnipeg and befriending Ruby (Nancy Sanderson), lover to both Omar and Mama Ceece, once they start working the same street corner. Moreover, her capacity for transformation gains expression through the home she shares with at least three other trannie prostitutes. With two makeup tables stationed in the living room, the arrangement of space foregrounds the performativity of their identities, which confound conventional Eurocentric gender categories. As if by example, the home inspires additional transformations as well, which are on full display during a raucous party that takes place there early in the film. Caught up in the atmosphere of libidinal abandon that the party incites, one ABS member comes to conclude that "a hole is a hole, especially in the North End," embracing a more fluid, if not feminist, understanding of sexuality. More generally and importantly, the party provides an opportunity for Filipinos and Indians to socialize in a variety of ways, temporarily rendering insignificant those racially defined boundaries across which street violence is typically waged.

Given Gonick's interest in creating a space, both geographic and textual, characterized by fluidity and thus capable of subverting established norms, it would seem that Omar would be a character of productive complexity due to the fact that he is part Asian and, as he tells Stryker, "part skinner" (that is, part Native). Yet instead the film comes, over the course of its duration, to render him a two-dimensional villain vis-à-vis Mama Ceece, even though the two gang leaders consistently behave in the same fashion by demanding compliance from their followers, verbally and physically asserting their power, and showing little to no sympathy to the plight of others. In so doing, *Stryker* exemplifies far better than *Once Were Warriors* the kind of aperture narrowing discussed by Jane Smith. That is, it eventually abandons a vantage that views its characters in relation to their past and present social location and falls back on a narrative strategy bound up with individual psychology and archetypal antinomies. The effects of this move are profound, for in providing no narrative pretext for Omar's relative demonization, the film not only fails to problematize or challenge the derogatory terms in which

The home as site of transformation in *Stryker*. (Wild Boars of Manitoba Inc.)

his identity is consistently figured by his enemies (for example, "half-breed" and "mongrel") but also shores up the historically sedimented associations between hybridity, pollution, and degeneracy that inform such labels. The means by which the film does so are on most blatant display in two scenes that take place late in the film and contribute to a series of actions that precipitate Mama Ceece's supplantation of Omar as the North End heavy. The first portrays Mama Ceece, surrounded by members of the IP, as she brutally assaults Cody and then leaves him for dead in punishment for his continued loyalty to Omar. The second surveys the aftermath of a fire that Stryker set in Talia's home; in it, Talia is hysterical on her front lawn as firefighters attempt to contain the damage while Omar, the only foster son who has remained loyal to Talia despite her predatory ways, rushes to her side in order to offer consolation. Formally, these scenes are strikingly similar insofar as both present their dramatic action in a single long shot. The effects of that mode of presentation, however, are quite divergent due to that which is thereby rendered remote and thus deprived of affective impact: Mama Ceece's murderous aggression on the one hand and Omar's capacity for compassion on the other. To be sure, *Stryker* contains a number of long shots that serve to locate its characters in their environs, but it typically uses this representational strategy in conjunction with a host of others, including close-ups and medium shots. To abandon such overtures of intimacy at this particular point in the film is evidence of a certain textual overdetermination, which lays the groundwork for an ending that consolidates the respective fates of Omar and Mama Ceece. Specifically, the film's last image of Omar has him on his knees, drenched in gasoline, and pleading with Stryker to light the match that will ensure his death. In contrast, Mama Ceece makes her final appearance within the context of an IP victory party, wherein the accompanying music of Hellnback and the blithe movements of the gang members as they dance, laugh, and socialize produce an atmosphere of levity and harmony heretofore unseen in the film.

Yet it is not only at Omar's expense that the film diminishes the impact of Mama Ceece's blows; rather, the film's capacity to posit an alternative to gang life and the street violence it conditions is also at stake. To be sure, Mama Ceece is a unique female character insofar as she speaks her desires and acts decisively when it comes to both love and war. For all her ferocity, however, she hardly qualifies as a (proto-)feminist figure, since her exceptionality serves only to fortify and perpetuate that which features so centrally in both *Stryker* and *Once Were Warriors*: a culture of masculine bravado wherein feelings of social impotence fuel a proclivity for violence in typical Fanon-esque fashion. As a result, she stands in stark contrast to

Beth from the latter film, who assumes a position outside of that culture when she critiques it, reproaching Jake for his actions and declaring her independence in a climactic fight: "Our people once were warriors, but not like you, Jake. They were people of *mana*, pride, people of spirit. If my spirit can survive living with you for eighteen years, then I can survive anything. Maybe you taught me that."[43] That the film too endorses this perspective is evident in the way this final confrontation is filmed: isolated against a black night sky, framed in a low-angle shot, backlit for a halo effect, and approached by a slowly tracking camera, Beth is empowered both visually and verbally until she takes leave of a diminished Jake ranting in her wake. Operating in concert with that critique is Tamahori's representation of alternate paradigms of Maori masculinity through the characters of Nig and Boogie. As is the case with Jake, the identities of these two characters take shape to a certain extent in and through their experience of violence, yet that violence is of a very different order since it is enacted in the service of building community, fueled less by rage than ritual, and respectful of the boundary between world and home. In short, Nig and Boogie both forge an affirmative connection to their ancestral past writ large by engaging in various ways with the warrior legacy invoked above and thereby emerging as its proper heirs. Nig does so by joining an urban Maori gang, which draws heavily upon the Maori warrior persona by incorporating into its identity certain cultural practices that attest to male strength, while Boogie is trained to fight and, more important, to think like a traditional warrior as part of his education at a state-run reformatory school.

In *Stryker*, in contrast, there is no outside to the world on display. The film does feature characters who take leave of that world, the most significant among them being Daisy, who boards a bus en route to Vancouver once she has decided to "save herself." Nonetheless, it never attempts to envision her journey, never mind her destination, preferring instead to foreground those acts of transformation that Winnipeg gang culture conditions, many of which are of a gender-bending nature: men performing as and/or transitioning into women, women exercising agency and wielding power in a male-dominated milieu. Indeed, it is significant that when Daisy leaves her Winnipeg home for the last time, she is shown to be leaving behind more than hardship, for she is dressed in male attire and stripped of her usual makeup and wig. In positioning gang culture as the locus of transformation, the film strikes an uneasy ideological bargain. On the one hand, it respectfully engages a social reality that often escapes notice and lends its characters both agency and gravitas by linking their turf war to the ongoing struggle for recognition of Native land title. On the other, however, it ultimately replicates the logic of gang culture in the process by reifying the cult of masculinity and the us-versus-them posture upon which that culture depends. Thus, by its conclusion, *Stryker* not only depicts but also partici-pates in the celebration of the IP's victory over the ABS, and the result is a vision of social change that is as limiting as it is romantic. In the end, it is left to Hellnback alone, as he sings over the closing credits, to express frus-tration with a present haunted by the past and thus to lay the groundwork for a future of social as well as individual change:

> I'm sorry for the stabbing and shooting that transpired.
> I'm sorry for those that chose the path where a fist bloodies a chick's nose
> I'm also sorry for the dealing and stealing, the lying and cheating,
> The priesting and cheating, the residential mistreating
> The drug addiction and alcoholism, colonialism
> The Natives that's locked up in prison
> On top of all that please
> Just take my hand
> I'm a lost soul born to man that didn't understand
> The main plan and path he was on
> I'm sorry my son, where the hell did we go wrong?[44]

4. Speech Acts

Toward a "Postcolonial" Poetics

Among the multiple prizes Niki Caro's *Whale Rider* won subsequent to its initial release in 2002, the audience awards from a wide array of prestigious international film festivals, including Sundance, San Francisco, Toronto, and Rotterdam, best captured categorically the cornerstone to the film's success. Dissenting critics who faulted the film for its sentimentality notwithstanding, myriad spectators around the world found themselves moved, inspired, and richly rewarded by Caro's story of an indomitable girl who defies her grandfather's prohibitions in order to assume her place as heir to his role as community leader. Most viewers likely had little, if any, knowledge of the Maori culture whose traditions are at stake throughout the film, so its widespread appeal is a testament to Caro's deft adaptation of Witi Ihimaera's novel[1]: as first a screenwriter and then a director, she fashioned a story replete with cultural particularity into one with seemingly universal resonance. While the rewards for this act of fashioning have been great, in terms of both receipts and recognition, it is the costs thereof that concern certain Maori critics who emphasize Caro's identity as Pakeha.

Both Tānia M. Ka'ai and Tracy Johnson, for example, critique the film on the grounds that Caro's status as a cultural outsider inevitably affects her capacity to capture the nuances of Maori experience. Ka'ai compiles a long list of items that Caro gets wrong in her version of Ihimaera's tale: among them, the traditional relationship between grandparent and grandchild; the logic behind a variety of cultural practices, including the gendering of select spaces and the recognition of future leaders; and the status of women in Maori culture at large as well as in Ngati Porou, the specific tribe at the story's center, which Ka'ai describes as "the most pro-female *iwi* of them all."[2] This final point is, for her, the most significant since it speaks directly to the primary lens through which Caro refracts her source material: that of a Eurocentric feminism ill-suited to address the role gender plays in Aotearoa. Echoing Ka'ai, Johnson also faults the film for its reductive equation of Maori tradition with patriarchal oppression but in the process lays stress on that which Caro omits rather than distorts: the pernicious role played by colonialism in the creation of the situation that protagonist Paikea (Keisha

Castle-Hughes) negotiates, one wherein the family unit has devolved into dysfunction, cultural integrity has been compromised, and gender roles have lost the fluidity they had in the precontact era.[3]

Defending the film against critiques such as these, Deborah Walker shifts focus from that which is lost in Caro's translation of the source material to that which is preserved: specifically, the spirit of Ihimaera's story. In the process, she argues that *Whale Rider* is not an instance of cultural appropriation but rather a response—and an exemplary one, at that—to "the need of every human being to represent the Other."[4] To support her dual claim, she cites a number of practices that Caro engaged in during the production of *Whale Rider* that testify to her concerted effort to recognize and redress the issues raised by her status as cultural outsider, including actively seeking feedback from Maori advisors during all stages of the process, filming on location in Whangara, where the bulk of the novel is set, and incorporating local community members into the cast and crew. By virtue of these practices, Walker argues, *Whale Rider* illustrates Emmanuel Levinas's face-to-face encounter as it is understood by Jeffrey Murray, for whom the defining criterion is a posture of supplication on the part of the (dominant) self confronting the (marginalized) other. In short, Walker answers critics like Ka'ai and Johnson not by denying their primary assumption—that the vantage of every filmmaker is necessarily limited by his or her own cultural identity, social location, intellectual formation, and life experience—but by laying stress on Caro's laudable attempts to surpass those limits through a respectful and receptive approach to the process of adaptation.

I begin this chapter by recounting these two positions not because I want to endorse one over the other; indeed, as just suggested, they differ in emphasis more than in argument. Rather, they are intriguing in that they approach the same issue—the politics of *Whale Rider*—from two distinct directions: on the one hand, Ka'ai and Johnson route their discussions of the film through those misapprehensions that are seemingly inevitable, yet nonetheless lamentable, for a cultural outsider like Caro, while Walker, on the other, seizes upon Caro's capacity to listen intently and thus engage successfully in a collaborative practice that renders permeable the line between inside(r) and outside(r). Yet what merits further discussion is that which both lies between these emphases on content and context and exceeds the individual filmmaker, no matter how myopic or well-intentioned he or she may be: that narrative paradigm that David Bordwell refers to as the straight corridor.[5] Indeed, whatever ideological imperatives Caro is arguably responding to, be they linked to a Eurocentric feminism and/or a commitment to biculturalism, they are necessarily implicated in narratological ones as well. Houston Wood illustrates as much when he notes the end to which the book's sense of community was attenuated and by which Paikea's family members were transformed when the story was adapted for the screen. By constructing Paikea's father as absentee, her grandfather as callous, and her uncle as ineffectual, Caro was able to cast Paikea in a role similar to that of the "poor orphan" seen in many Western narratives and thus to position her as a type—individuated, self-reliant, sympathetic—with widespread legibility.[6]

By no means a guarantee of (near-)universal accolades, but almost certainly a prerequisite for such, the straight corridor lends familiar form to even the most unfamiliar material. Combining an archetypal Western narrative structure with a self-effacing mode of narration, it is characterized by a series of features associated with classical Hollywood cinema, including an individual protagonist with psychological complexity, a goal-oriented story ordered by cause-and-effect logic, an ending that satisfies by way of closure (structure) and triumph (content), the use of continuity editing to make cuts invisible, and a cinematographic analysis of space and time that renders both coherent. While Walker does not specify, it is likely the extent to which *Whale Rider* conforms with this hegemonic paradigm that compels her to qualify her assessment of the film: "I would very much like to be able to see Caro's work also as an honouring of absolute Otherness, following directly from the major exponent of post-modern ethics, Emmanuel Levinas. However, I find myself reluctant to do so. For if ethnic Otherness is able to be comprehended, felt, represented by Caro in *Whale Rider*, it is very often through points of sameness. Levinas wisely distrusts the role of sameness for its tendency to reduce or totalise the Other into one's own terms. Nonetheless, it is through points of sameness that we negotiate, articulate and communicate with Otherness."[7] Ultimately, this passage functions as prelude to the main thrust of Walker's argument; as mentioned earlier, she goes on to appeal to Murray in order to characterize *Whale Rider* as a quintessentially ethical text. Yet the line of inquiry that Walker introduces only to foreclose is a pressing one. In *Whale Rider*, the points of sameness to which Walker refers are implicated in, perhaps even produced by, a narrative structure that comes from without rather than from within the Maori culture being represented. Thus, the argument could be made that rather than narrowing the gap between self and other so as to facilitate communication across it, Caro closes the gap, thereby erasing difference. John Mowitt, author of *Re-takes: Postcoloniality and Foreign Film Languages*, is one scholar who would likely take the latter position, for it is in perfect keeping with his trenchant formulation, "The straight corridor ushers, via the shortest route possible, foreignness from the cinema."[8]

The specific films that inspire Mowitt to make this declaration are those that have achieved recognition by the Academy of Motion Picture Arts and Sciences (AMPAS) since 1948, when the first Oscar for a foreign film was awarded. Indeed, it is his argument that AMPAS has over the years exerted a normalizing influence on world cinema by reserving its honors for those films that are reassuringly familiar in their form and only foreign in their dialogue—hence, the name the Oscar has gone by since 1956: the Foreign Language Film Award. Yet, in effect, Mowitt is making an argument with far more extensive implications, since the same thing that wins a film recognition from AMPAS also lends it commercial viability within an international marketplace dominated by Hollywood product, something that almost all feature films vie for. Against a straight corridor cinema, which not only conforms to a hegemonic norm but also thereby contributes to an understanding of film as story rather than as discourse, Mowitt counterposes a cinema of postcolonial poetics, which is bilingual, self-reflexive, and split in its enunciation. By laying great emphasis on this last term, Mowitt sets himself apart from most contemporary film theorists, for whom the question of enunciation is passé. For Mowitt, however, it is precisely through enunciation that the process of cultural differentiation, which involves relations of both exchange and conflict, plays itself out and, moreover, makes itself known in cinema.

In order to tailor the discourse of cinematic enunciation to his critical needs, Mowitt builds upon the theoretical tradition forged by the likes of Christian Metz, Raymond Bellour, and Daniel Dayan but refuses the ocular-centricism that tradition shares with the neoformalist work of its most vocal critics—namely, David Bordwell and Noël Carroll, for whom enunciation is tainted by its association with Grand Theory. In so doing, he is able to conceive of his project as an examination of the mutual interaction between language and film form rather than as an exercise in adapting paradigms derived from linguistics to an analysis of the means by which film communicates visually. Explaining the assumptions dictating the critical practice against which he defines his own, he writes: "Instead of language, whether as concept or metaphor, having any relation either to the design or the construction of [filmic narration], it is surrendered, as Derrida would doubtless insist, to the paradigm of speech and regarded as essentially irrelevant to any conception of the codes of cinema, but certainly irrelevant to any conception of the codes operating to stitch the dialogue into the soundtrack and to cement the soundtrack and the image track together."[9] Mowitt, in contrast, is fundamentally concerned with the way different grammatical structures shape film form and inflect reflexivity within those texts that are not dictated by the conventional—that is, Anglophone—codes of dominant cinema. Given their capacity to throw such operations into fresh relief, bilingual films, which mobilize multiple modalities of enunciation, are for Mowitt the richest in analytical possibility. Thus, he concludes his study with discussion of works by Jorge Sanjinés and Ousmane Sembene, two filmmakers whose careers dovetail with the theory and practice of Third Cinema.

Given the agenda of this chapter, an exploration of the relationship between Aboriginal identity and acts of cinematic narration, Mowitt's work is extremely compelling. Like him, I am less interested in dwelling on those films that make a bid for universal legibility by way of the straight corridor than in examining those that are more self-reflexive about the process of aesthetic and political (self-)representation. Thus, I follow his lead in foregrounding issues of (split) enunciation in relation to three texts that demand as much: Tracey Moffatt's *beDevil* (1993), Zacharias Kunuk's *Atanarjuat* (2001), and Sherman Alexie's *The Business of Fancydancing* (2002). Contributing to a cinema of "postcolonial" poetics, these films negotiate the connection between voice and vision to an end summarized well by Joanna Hearne: that of "relocating ethnographic practices and Hollywood discourses to Native nations through visual representation of storytelling as a social practice."[10] One thing that unites the three filmmakers named above and makes them particularly attentive to questions of narration both within and by their films is the fact that their cinematic storytelling is continuous with their work in other representational media: Moffatt is most widely known, both within and beyond her native Australia, for her photographic series, many of which share with her films a hyperrealist aesthetic and a narrative thrust; before taking on a feature-length project, Kunuk spent decades producing videos for broadcast television, first while working at the Inuit Broadcasting Corporation and then in affiliation with Igloolik Isuma Productions, which he cofounded in 1988; and Alexie is among the most prolific and well-read American Indian writers working today, with eleven volumes of poetry, four novels, three short story collections, and two screenplays under his belt.

Before proceeding with my three case studies, however, it is necessary to return to the line of inquiry that Walker introduced only to foreclose so as to note that I did the same by so quickly offering up Mowitt's position as a counter to hers. In truth, I do not think there is an automatic answer to the question of whether *Whale Rider*—or any movie by any type of director—can represent difference through points of sameness, nor do I subscribe to a schema so programmatic as to conceive of cinema in terms of two mutually exclusive categories: the politically compromised, straight corridor variety on the one hand and the subversive, self-reflexive, bilingual one on the other. To do so would entail ignoring those films about Indigenous peoples, some from Indigenous directors, that travel by way of the straight corridor but nonetheless extend its limits enough to accommodate a vision that has cultural specificity. A recent New Zealand film that speaks persuasively to this point is the 2006 release *Naming Number Two* (aka *No. 2*) by writer and director Toa Fraser, who has Fijian and British ancestry, lives in New Zealand, and also came to cinema by way of another medium first—in this case, theater.

Following a large cast of primarily Fijian characters over the course of a single day as they prepare for a family gathering, the film combines a focus on interpersonal dynamics, as is typical of family dramas, with the loose narrative structure of, say, a backstage musical: it starts with the setting of an ambitious goal, ends with the triumphant realization of that goal, and devotes the rest of its time to the required preparation process in all its fits and starts. With his casting choices, Fraser left himself vulnerable to critique: using African American actress Ruby Dee in the role of Nanna Maria, the Fijian matriarch at the film's center, and a whole roster of Polynesian, including Maori, actors for her various children and grandchildren, he forsook the opportunity to put Fijian actors on-screen and thereby chagrined those audience members with close ties to the material. Nonetheless, it is not this issue so much as the film's embrace of generic expectations that leads Houston Wood to describe it, along with two other recent features from New Zealand—*Samoan Wedding* (aka *Sione's Wedding*) (2006), by the non-Indigenous director Chris Graham, and *Eagle vs. Shark* (2007), by the Maori writer and director Taika Waititi (aka Cohen)—as "celebrations of assimilation."[11] Yet to designate *Naming Number Two* as such is to overstate its adherence to classical conventions (it does, after all, feature an episodic narrative and a group protagonist) and, more generally, to suggest that cultural intermixture must always happen on the terms of the dominant culture.[12] On the contrary, *Naming Number Two* is marked less by its conformity with some mainstream norm than by relations of active exchange and acts of knowing appropriation. Just as the inspiration for the feast day is Nanna's fantasy of a traditional Sicilian gathering—"they drink red wine, everybody sings, and there's always a priest"—the prototype for Fraser's film comes from beyond the community he is depicting; yet, in both cases a borrowed form is flexible enough to allow for protracted meditation on the highly relevant issues of community bonds, filial responsibility, and the combination of continuity and change that conditions the survival of cultural traditions over time.

Presiding over the feast is Nanna Maria, who uses it as an occasion to name her successor and thus enlist a younger generation in the responsibility of maintaining the family. Son of the most estranged member of the family and regarded by many as irresponsible, her grandson Soul (Taungaroa Emile) is not the obvious choice for the role. Over the course of the film, however, he proves himself to both Nanna and the audience to be extremely committed to the well-being of the family and, moreover, to understand what is necessary to keep a community vital: a refusal of insular thinking. Indeed, almost entirely on Soul's initiative, Nanna's injunction of "no outsiders," which applies to anyone outside the immediate family, gives way to an open-door policy, both literally and metaphorically. First of all, Soul breaks through Nanna's front door, which was boarded up twelve years earlier so as to bar entrance to a curse, and thereby dramatically rectifies a situation that is a source of familial discord, particularly within his father's generation. Second, he ensures the success of the feast by inviting a number of "outsiders," including his friends, extended family members, and even an Asian neighbor, with whom he had a near miss in his car and a subsequent altercation earlier in the day. The fact that Soul is played by Taungaroa Emile from *Once Were Warriors* only lends his position as Nanna's "No. 2" more resonance: Soul is a mature Boogie, capable, like his (grand)mothers before him, of ensuring the continuity of cultural tradition and convinced, like his directors, that doing so does not preclude building on some points of sameness, be they between self and other or between dominant cinema and its Indigenous counterpart.

In contradistinction to *Naming Number Two*, the films to which I turn my attention now are extremely self-reflexive in their use, or refusal, of dominant cinematic conventions and thereby demonstrably attentive to the process of cultural differentiation. Forging a productive tension between the local and global, the traditional and vanguard, the national and first national,[13] they constitute Fourth World variations on Mowitt's bilingual cinema; positioning themselves as liminal, they offer up new ways both to see and to hear as well.

beDevil: At the Limits of Representation

Midway through Tracey Moffatt's feature film *beDevil*, one of its leading players, an Aboriginal Australian named Ruby (Auriel Andrews), launches into an impromptu cooking lesson as she and a friend prepare a meal of wild pig and yabbies outside a dilapidated home where Ruby lived years ago. Although Ruby is already practiced at direct address by this point in the film, the manner in which she speaks to the camera changes slightly in this scene, as she seizes upon the opportunity to play the role of pedagogue and perform authority: she carefully enumerates the steps involved in the meal's preparation, she translates comments made by others present to the presumably Anglophone viewer, and, in a move both maternal and commanding, she even pauses to wipe dust off the camera lens with a tissue drawn from her blouse. It is only when Ruby is scolded by her friend for pouring the hollandaise sauce incorrectly that she reverts to a more offhanded speaking style, indignantly retorting, "You don't have to carry on, bloody Queen Victoria of bush cuisine!"

This scene exemplifies well an aspect of Moffatt's work (be it in photography, film, or video) that commentators often underscore: her postmodern tendency to work in, with, and between recognizable generic forms to parodic ends. Catherine Summerhayes's reading of it is a case in point insofar as she acknowledges Ruby's performance as both comedic and critical, laying stress on the latter: "Besides introducing humor, this form of direct address interrogates the way in which documentary film has been used as an 'objective' instrument of observation within anthropology."[14] Yet this sequence takes on other dimensions additionally when Moffatt's biracial identity is taken into consideration, for it resonates with Aboriginal storytelling practices as well as with the specifically televisual tradition of the cooking show and the general tradition of visual ethnography toward which Summerhayes gestures. In her work of comparative linguistics, Daniéle M. Klapproth concludes that storytelling in Australian Aboriginal communities is a fundamental site for the imparting and withholding of knowledge. Based on her analysis of the oral tradition of the Pitjantjatjara and Yankunytjatjara people of Central Australia, she notes, "Many storytellers give a great amount of detail in relation to incidents that (from an Anglo-Western point-of-view) are not directly relevant to the main storyline. This is particularly true with respect to information about food preparation (e.g., how a hunter may cut up, prepare and cook a kangaroo) and food distribution (e.g., who is given which part of the animal). This kind of information is, from an Aboriginal point of view, of course, highly relevant to what the storytelling act is all about, both because giving detailed information about particular aspects of daily life is a way of passing on important cultural knowledge, and because it is perceived as contributing to making the text a 'good story.'"[15] Given the narrative premise of *beDevil*, a tripartite investigation of ghosts and the multicultural communities they haunt, it is tempting to regard the film's culinary interlude as a digression. Yet in light of Klapproth's observations, it can also be read as a central event, one that has resonances both local and global and one that foregrounds the film's function as tutor text. As instructive as Ruby's comments about bush cuisine may be, however, the larger lesson to be learned from this scene—and, by extension, from the film as a whole—is one related to Mowitt's chief concern of cinematic enunciation. Indeed, Ruby's bid for discursive authority in conjunction with her explicit acknowledgment of the camera signals a two-tiered project that is fundamental to *beDevil*: that of laying bare the process of narration, as it is enacted both *within* and *by* the film.

Within the film, Moffatt draws attention to the speech act by featuring languages other than English on occasion and diversely accented varieties of English the rest of the time. The result is a text that exemplifies the multivocality that Hamid Naficy associates with accented cinema, one wherein a profusion of speaking styles gives voice to diverse social identities and discrepant versions of history.[16] At the center of the first section, titled "Mr. Chuck," is an encounter between Rick, a young Aboriginal boy, and the spirit of an American GI who haunts the swamp in which he drowned while stationed in Australia during World War II. Narrating this encounter in the present day are Rick as an adult (Jack Charles) and a local white woman named Shelley (Diana Davidson), who had taken young Rick under her wing after learning of the abuse he suffered at the hands of his family. The second section, "Choo Choo Choo Choo," has at its center a variety of supernatural phenomena, including an invisible train driven by a mute conductor and the ghost of a blind girl whom that same train had struck and killed. In this section, three narrators figure prominently: the aforementioned Ruby, who had multiple experiences with both the train and the girl when she was living in a house next to a set of train tracks; Mickey (Lex Foxcroft), an alcoholic white man who reports his take on the ghosts in a drunken slur; and Bob (Cecil Parkee), a Chinese Australian man who has converted an old train station into a local museum full of memorabilia from the past. Finally "Lovin' the Spin I'm In," the third section of the film, has a Greek couple, Dimitri (Lex Marinos) and Voula (Dina Panozzo), recounting to their son, Spiro (Riccardo Natoli), the story of a young Aboriginal couple to whom they used to rent the warehouse space next to their own living quarters. Having died a mysterious death twelve years earlier, the two lovers now haunt their former place of residence, appearing on occasion to Spiro and his family as well as to the current tenants of the warehouse.

In an astute reading of *beDevil*, Glen Masato Mimura demonstrates how the ghost stories therein function effectively as trope, allowing for the materialization of memories on the part of those Aboriginal Australians and Torres Strait Islanders who have suffered displacement at the hands of land developers spurred on by suburban sprawl and tourist trade. As a result, he concludes, Moffatt's film has a profound affinity with the ghosts at its center: it "critically haunts Australian and global cinema in their national and international contexts, lingering like a bad memory to phantasmatically repeat the ghostly histories and geographies that the mainstream cinemas seek to evict."[17] An additional way in which the spectral serves symbolic and, in turn, ideological purposes, however, is by dramatizing issues of presence and absence, seeing and telling. Indeed, the project in which both the film and its sprawling cast of eclectic characters are engaged is that of giving presence to an essentially intangible phenomenon, be it through the stories told about that phenomenon by people in the present bearing witness to the past or through the flashbacks wherein it assumes material form through specifically cinematic means (superimposition, dream sequence). That those doing the representing in and through *beDevil* are individuals typically denied discursive authority on the grounds of their alterity only lends this aspect of her work more gravitas.

In addition to explicitly thematizing the process of narration and thus the means by which (hi)stories are recounted and knowledge is produced, however, Moffatt also foregrounds her own act of narration throughout *beDevil*. The means she employs in order to realize this, the second tier of her project, are a wide variety of anti-illusionistic strategies, which are also on display in her much-discussed shorts *Nice Coloured Girls* (1987) and *Night Cries: A Rural Tragedy* (1989): the generation of a highly stylized mise-en-scène, a refusal of the conventions of continuity editing in favor of intellectual montage, and the staging of provocative juxtapositions between soundtrack and image track. In light of the representational strategies she employs, viewers must engage with Moffatt's films much as they would with her photographic series. As Cynthia Baron notes, "The mise-en-scène elements, sound-image combinations, and sequence-to-sequence combinations are so dense with meaning that they invite, require, and reward the kind of contemplation often reserved for one's leisurely or studied encounter with art gallery exhibitions."[18]

Yet within the context of a public screening, a leisurely encounter, if not a studied one, is difficult to achieve since the ability to pause or slow the film's flow is out of the spectator's control. As Christian Metz notes, it is those attributes that distinguish film from photography—movement, plurality, phonic sound, nonphonic sound, and musical sound—that "challeng[e] the powers of silence and immobility which belong to and define all photography, immersing film in a stream of temporality where nothing can be *kept*, nothing stopped."[19] Moreover, it is those attributes that also deprive film of "photographic authority," that quality which allows the photo to function as a fetish object, successfully arresting the spectator's gaze and proving a satisfying substitute for the reality it represents. Film, Metz contends, can lay claim to no such authority since it continuously points beyond the boundaries of its images to an offscreen space that is both signified and significant, even in its absence. As a result, film is instead "an extraordinary activator of fetishism [the process]. It endlessly mimes the primal displacement of the look between the seen absence and the presence nearby."[20] For this reason, specifically cinematic authority is a result of those techniques that produce a suturing effect, directing the spectator's attention away from the limits of the frame and all that they reveal: the circumscribed nature of the image and hence its status as produced rather than natural, spoken as well as speaking. Among the most salient of such techniques, according to Jean-Pierre Oudart and, in turn, Daniel Dayan, is shot–reverse shot editing. By making offscreen space present before its absence proves disconcerting, it constructs an all-enveloping illusion that evokes abundance rather than deprivation; by assigning its view of the world to an on-screen character, it constructs the film as "a product without a producer, a discourse without an origin" at the same time.[21]

Refusing to absorb the spectator in any thoroughgoing way, *beDevil* has little purchase on cinematic authority. Certainly, a viewer gets caught up in it by way of its temporal flow; moreover, as Vivian Sobchack observes, the stream of temporality that Metz identifies is precisely what endows film with the capacity to construct an inhabitable space, one that accommodates lived bodies and invites the spectator into the world on display.[22] Nonetheless, that same viewer will rarely find himself or herself stitched into the film, or the gaps in the film stitched over, through those devices that allow for, as Dayan puts it, possession of the image and, in turn, possession by the dominant ideology for which the film is a ventriloquist.[23] Interested in the frame of the image as much as in that which lies within it, Moffatt regularly plays both with and at the limits of visual representation. The result is images that not only call attention to their delimited nature and thus their fundamental lack but also link up to other images in a discontinuous manner. Preferring to forge associative and affective relationships rather than ones based on causality or chronology, Moffatt employs the conventions of continuity editing selectively, tending instead to create textual gaps by cutting regularly between multiple lines of action, characters, narrative modes, historical moments, and milieus. In sum, much like the narrative whole, which presents in succession three discrete ghost stories with only a thematic thread to tie them, each of the three segments composing *beDevil* is likewise fragmented.

The film's first section, "Mr. Chuck," functions as a primer on Moffatt's vision by laying bare the fragmentation on which her work depends. In it, Shelley and Rick serve as narrators, both addressing the camera directly as if participating in a documentary about the American GI who haunts their local swamp. While Rick's narration is typically limited to the visceral details of his ghostly encounter (the smell of the swamp, the feel of the GI's touch), Shelley speaks to a number of additional topics as well, including her relationship with Rick as a child. In a sequence dedicated to this matter, the film cuts back and forth between Shelley in the present and flashbacks of the events she describes: Rick's attempts to steal from her shop, her thwarting of those attempts, and their cultivation of a familiar relationship. During this sequence, Moffatt circumscribes the viewer's vantage in such a manner as to draw attention to the edges of the image and thus to the fact of (cinematic) enunciation; at the same time, she also signals a number of representational strategies that she will rely on frequently throughout *beDevil*. For example, during the flashback scenes, she depicts the discovery of Rick's thievery through a type of shadow play, and she represents Shelley by isolating details of her appearance: her manicured hands and coiffed hair, the neckline of her dress and a well-heeled foot tapping in disapproval. In the present, moreover, she offers up a shot of Shelley reacting in shock to some stimulus without a corresponding reverse shot.

As central as these visual strategies are to the self-reflexivity that marks *beDevil*, it is the film's manipulation of sound as well—the way voices get "stitched" into the soundtrack and "cemented" to the image track—that qualifies the text as an exemplar of "postcolonial" poetics. In other words, it is the intersection of an interest in multivocality and a self-reflexive form that allows the text, in Mowitt's words, to "give content to what might otherwise strike us as a blank or so-called purely formal process" and thereby "make the question of enunciation, the who-sent-this-from-where-and-to-whom, belong to the statements put in circulation by the film text."[24] Just as absence of some variety defines the visual strategies cited above—each is an index of, metonym for, or deflection from the subject at hand—it plays a significant role in the soundtrack as well, at least in this first section. A case in point is Shelley's selective narration in the sequence described above. At one point, she mouths her age—"seventy"—rather than speaking it aloud, thereby playfully drawing attention to her ability to refuse to speak and thus, at least potentially, to withhold information. On two other occasions, however, her falling silent has more serious repercussions. In the first of these, she concludes a suggestion that Rick suffered at the hands of his step-uncles in a decidedly incomplete and inconclusive manner: "I shouldn't say it, but I don't think his home life was . . ." Exemplifying the connection between sight and sound to which Mowitt refers, Shelley's silence dictates the occlusion of anything but hints of such abuse from the film's image track as well, thereby risking its invisibility within his-story at large. The second time she trails off is when she discusses her awareness of Rick's situation: "Yes, I knew what was going on. We on the island all knew. We could've helped that child. We could've . . ." In this instance, she implicates herself and her community in Rick's fate in an ambiguous manner, both performing her emotional investment and simultaneously raising the specter of, but still distancing herself from, unspeakable historical practices, such as state-mandated internment and adoption.

Rather than foregrounding the gaps within any one individual's speech, the second section of *beDevil*, "Choo Choo Choo Choo," concerns itself with the gaps between various people and their stories. "Mr. Chuck" prepares the ground for such a focus by laying bare the extent to which Shelley's social location and her speech acts mutually condition each other: as noted above, her narration is relatively wide-ranging, bespeaking those things in which she, more than Rick, has a vested interest, including not only her affection for Rick but also her association with the American soldier who died and her father's involvement in developing the island that she and Rick both call home. "Choo Choo Choo Choo," in comparison, offers up many more voices, all of which prove necessarily personal and partial. In addition to the three characters singled out to provide testimonials in direct address, as did Shelley and Rick before them, the entire surrounding community becomes complicit in the act of narration as well when random members are shown singing a song and performing a choreographed series of gestures inspired by local lore of the phantom train. Moreover, there is little overlap in the phenomena being described from these multiple points of view. Ruby begins her narration with mention of the ghost that eventually takes shape on-screen—a blind girl who walks the train tracks—but she subsequently broaches a wide variety of other mysterious phenomena as well; Bob relays the story that the townspeople pantomime, one involving a train conductor who hanged himself and his ghostly voyages; and, finally, the alcoholic Mickey describes a female spirit that visits him, but stresses that she is not the blind girl to whom Ruby refers. The sum result of this is a series of narrative fragments, both aural and visual, that never quite coheres. Rather than offering multiple perspectives on the same phenomenon, "Choo Choo Choo Choo" refracts the viewer's field of sight such that the acts of telling assume far greater dimension than the stories told.

When compared to the first two sections, the film's final one, "Lovin' the Spin I'm In," proves almost conventional in form. To be sure, Moffatt's touch is evident in the stylized mise-en-scène, the non-naturalistic use of dance to communicate certain interpersonal dynamics, and the refusal to reveal select sights to the viewer. Nonetheless, the fourth wall remains intact since no one speaks to or acknowledges the camera in any way, and both the segment's narrative and narration are relatively straightforward, with Voula alone recounting the story of the couple that haunts the area. Even its editing is more exemplary of a classical paradigm. In fact, "Lovin' the Spin I'm In" replicates the situation at the heart of *Rear Window* (Alfred Hitchcock, 1954), a film in which shot–reverse shot editing plays such a central structuring role that it exemplifies the workings of suture better than any other: Spiro's bedroom window looks out on the haunted warehouse, providing him with an unobstructed view of the tenants therein. In the scene in which Voula describes to her son the events that ended tragically years ago and led to the present hauntings, the two of them sit side-by-side, assuming the position of rear window voyeurs whose act of looking is intercut with the object of their gaze. In a later scene, Spiro even tracks his father's movement through the warehouse, as Jefferies (James Stewart) does with Thorwald (Raymond Burr), by watching him pass from one window to the next. Yet in light of the two segments that precede this final one, *beDevil* calls into question that which *Rear Window* shores up. When Jeffries's perspective is seemingly validated by the latter film's end, the fallibility of his vision (which is most clearly demonstrated when he falls asleep on the job) and the holes in his—and Hitchcock's—story (the identity of the woman with Thorwald that same night) come to matter little to the sutured spectator. In *beDevil*, however, it is the gaps—those events, ideas, and vantages that escape, even defy, description—that demand recognition and haunt the text, even in the section with the fewest visible seams. Necessarily circumscribed by her own social location, Voula's version of events is not the whole story. In making absence present, *beDevil* calls into question the completeness of a historical record and visual arts tradition that regularly marginalize certain voices. It thus exemplifies the poetics of cinematic "postcoloniality," giving expression to the concerns that animate this chapter: the stakes of narration, both aesthetic and political, both pleasurable and perilous.

Atanarjuat: At the Limits of Translation

Unlike *beDevil*, with its multivocal soundtrack and multicultural cast, *Atanarjuat* does not immediately appear to be a film whose enunciation is split, as per Mowitt's bilingual cinema, since the characters speak exclusively in Inuktitut and the story is set in a distant, precontact past when the only invasive forces to fear are supernatural in nature. Yet, as argued

Voula saying, as she and Spiro look out their (rear) window, "Let me tell you about Immelda."
(Women Make Movies/www.wmm.com)

by Monika Siebert, the film complicates this traditionalist vision with its closing credits, which stake out an alternate site from which to speak, one encompassed—and thus recognized—by the modern nation-state. During those credits, a series of images of the film's production features the cast and crew outfitted with select signifiers of mass consumer modernity, from rubber boots and nylon parkas to headphones and video cameras, such that the film demands to be re-read "not only as a project in representing an authentic indigenous past, but also (and more importantly) as the work of contemporary indigenous people making collective decisions about representing their past and present."[25] In other words, what the film's coda acknowledges is that despite the "categorically indigenist point of view" that seems to prevail throughout most of *Atanarjuat*, its makers—and thus the film itself—are positioned at the juncture of multiple cultural influences, sociopolitical contexts, and representational traditions.[26] This fact is further borne out by the film's production process, which was necessarily bilingual at every stage. As recounted by screenwriter Paul Apak Angilirq, who tragically died before the film was completed, the first step he took after consulting eight to ten Inuit elders in order to get their versions of Atanarjuat's legendary tale was to draft his own in English so he could approach a variety of public funding agencies, including Canada Council and eventually Telefilm. From that starting point, he and four collaborators (Zacharias Kunuk, Norman Cohn, Pauloosie Qulitalik, and Hervé Paniaq) spent three months drafting two screenplays, one in Inuktitut and one in English.[27] As a result, the film's subtitles were not, as is far more typical, an afterthought; *Atanarjuat* was always a text in translation and thus exemplary of what Abé Mark Nornes calls the "contradictory social formation of national cinema"—in this case, *first* national cinema—"and transnational traffic."[28]

Although thoroughly integrated into the production process, the translation in *Atanarjuat* is, however, not complete; thus, the film illustrates one of the strategies that Nornes associates with the abusive subtitling practice for which he advocates, one wherein the subtitler "uses textual and graphic abuse . . . to bring the fact of translation from its position of obscurity, to critique the imperial politics that ground corrupt practices while ultimately leading the viewer to the foreign original being reproduced in the darkness of the theater."[29] Specifically, Kunuk engages in what Sophie McCall calls partial translation in that he, on rare occasion, withholds the subtitled translation of phonic sound. While infrequent, these instances are nonetheless significant, as is indicated by the film's opening line, which explicitly acknowledges the possibility of an audience divided by members' access to particular knowledge. In it, an "up North stranger" named Tuurnguarjuat

(Abraham Ulayuruluk) tells the family whose story will subsequently take center stage, "I can only sing this song to someone who understands it." As the film progresses, it too only sings its song to those who understand it at select moments. Specifically, no translation is provided when Oki (Peter-Henry Arnatsiaq), Atanarjuat's antagonist, rapes Atuat (Sylvia Ivalu), his first wife; when Atuat interacts with her infant son; and when a song with special significance to the family is sung during the story's final moments. In a film that is generally quite forthright in its translation, these moments call attention to themselves, "highlight[ing] the space of cultural contact and difference in acts of textualizing orature and orality."[30]

Given the oblique presentation of certain information that is germane to the film's plot, including the relationships between various characters, the function of certain shamanistic rituals, and the codes dictating appropriate behavior, the strategy of partial translation could be regarded as the most literal instantiation of a more general tendency on the part of the film to leave the non-Inuit viewer, in the words of *Sight and Sound*'s Peter Matthews, "kayaking without a paddle." Predicting the experience of the typical southern spectator, Matthews continues, "One's response throughout is apt to be a mixture of fascination and frustration at an infinitely rich spectacle whose details remain inscrutable. *Atanarjuat* describes a whole world closed to the outsider, who is obliged to take up the role of an ethnographer cracking the alien codes."[31] In spite of this, however, those whose job it is to produce commentary, even about inscrutable material, quickly figured out an expedient way to make sense of the film, as amply demonstrated by Arnold Krupat. After surveying a wide array of southern reviews of the film, he concludes that "very positive responses," of which there are many, "are thoroughly dependent upon a translation of the film's difference into . . . familiar Western categories."[32] The most popular of those categories is a literary tradition embodied by Homer, Shakespeare, and even Victor Hugo, all authors with whom Kunuk shares an interest in the drama of rivalry, devotion, jealousy, murder, revenge, and lust.

Yet this tendency to engage with *Atanarjuat* by way of that which is familiar therein and thereby "[to translate] it into [one's] habitual interpretative comfort zones" is not limited to reviewers, for a similar trend is evident within more scholarly discussions of the film as well.[33] Specifically, many of the scholars who have published articles about *Atanarjuat*, including Michelle Raheja and Joanna Hearne as well as Siebert, discuss it in relation to ethnographic cinema. To be sure, the reasons they invoke a yardstick against which to measure *Atanarjuat* are distinct from those of the popular critics whom Krupat discusses. While the latter typically liken the film to the work of a Western master so as to underscore the universality of its themes, the former are more inclined to dwell on those moments of inter-textual reverberation that allow for critique of a Western paradigm; that is, they cite specific scenes in *Atanarjuat* that echo ones from an ethnographic classic—usually Robert Flaherty's *Nanook of the North* (1922), but also Edward Curtis's *In the Land of the War Canoes* (1914)—to the end of ironizing, rejoining, and/or correcting them. Moreover, the authors' grounds for doing so are absolutely sound since *Atanarjuat* is, in part, a pointedly countercin-ematic text. At the same time, however, to make the argument that Kunuk de-centers stereotypical representations of Inuit depends on a (re-)centering of those representations in the first place. In other words, insofar as these articles proceed from the assumption that "the South, though absent from the diegesis, makes its appearance at the level of form," they end up conceiv-ing of the film's difference in terms of the same, in the terms of dominant (or southern) cinema.[34] What thus remains to be explored adequately is the way the film not only obliges the non-Inuit spectator to take up the role of "an ethnographer cracking the alien codes" or even to reflect critically upon others' (for example, Curtis's and Flaherty's) assumption of that role but also creates the possibility for a different mode of engagement altogether. Director of photography Norman Cohn gestures toward such an alternative when he states the filmmakers' intentions with language that both echoes and radically diverges from that used by Matthews: "We wanted people to feel inside the action, looking out, rather than outside looking in. This lets people forget how far away they really are, and to identify with our story and characters as if they were just like us."[35]

In her essay "Outside In Inside Out," postcolonial theorist and filmmaker Trinh Minh-ha suggests that notions such as "partial translation" speak as much to the status of the critics who employ them as to the phenomenon they are describing. Specifically, she identifies that which "is often viewed by the outsiders as strategies of partial concealment and disclosure aimed at preserving secrets that should only be imparted to initiates" to be evidence of something else entirely to the cultural insider who is engaged in the act of (self-)representation at issue: that is, his or her use of "non-explicative, non-totalizing strategies that suspend meaning and resist closure."[36] For Trinh, ethnographic cinema has contributed greatly to the cultivation of this outsider vantage insofar as it takes as its agenda the extraction of informa-tion, a dual process that entails isolating the meaning of a behavior, ritual, action, or interaction from the context in which that meaning is not only produced but produced as proliferous and reifying that meaning as an object of exchange and mastery. In contradistinction to this paradigm, Trinh posits another one predicated on an embrace of the interval, a multiform concept that she develops across a series of essays and describes, in one instance, as "what persists between the meaning of something and its truth" and "a break without which meaning would be fixed and truth congealed."[37] In light of this notion of the cinematic (as) interval, the particular kind of insider experience created by *Atanarjuat* comes into focus: it is one that does not, perhaps, facilitate the cracking of codes but instead immerses the viewer in contexts in which meanings are inseparable from materiality, in which even the immaterial has texture.

In thinking through the means by which Kunuk manages to forge such a context, Laura U. Marks's recent work on cinema's capacity to reflect (on) the divergent ways that sensory experience is cultivated across different cultures is quite helpful. In *The Skin of the Film*, she routes this focus through an examination of intercultural cinema, that which "is not the property of any single culture, but mediates in at least two directions," for it is herein, she argues, that representation tends to be more mimetic than symbolic, privileging the indexical sign over the iconic one, the proximal senses (taste, touch, smell) over vision, and the embodied experience over its abstraction or transcendence.[38] In order to make her case, Marks proffers legion examples from work by exilic, diasporic, ethnic, and Indigenous filmmakers, including, significantly, three Isuma productions that preceded *Atanarjuat*: *Qaggig* (1989), *Nunaqpa* (1991), and *Saputi* (1994). The result is an extensive catalog of representational strategies that encourage what she calls haptic visuality, a mode of looking wherein "the eyes themselves function like organs of touch" such that they tend "to move over the surface of [their] object rather than to plunge into illusionistic depth, not to distinguish form so much as to discern texture."[39] Read against this catalog, *Atanarjuat* emerges as a largely mimetic text, since it displays so many of the traits Marks identifies elsewhere. First, the film draws much attention to the sensual component of Inuit culture by lingering in extensive takes on its favored materials, including fur, bone, ice, fire, and animal flesh. Second, it foregrounds narrative events that illuminate the feelings evoked and traces left by those materials; while the naked sprint that Atanarjuat (Natar Ungalaaq) makes across a great expanse of ice with Oki in pursuit is the most obvious of these, there are others as well, many of which revolve around the bodies of Atanarjuat's wives. Finally, it frequently engages in filming techniques that emphasize the surface of the digital video images over their illusionistic depth, such as shooting at close range, which focuses on figure to the exclusion of ground; shooting into the sun, which produces lens flares; and shooting in low-light situations, which reduces contrast.

Yet in addition to those aspects of *Atanarjuat* that Marks's work renders visible, I am also interested in that which escapes her view—indeed, any view—and that is the role of sound in Kunuk's work. Thus, taking my cue from Mowitt, I move away from an ocularcentric understanding of mimetic representation, which culminates in the notion of haptic *visuality*, toward one that attends to questions of voice, sound, and enunciation as well. In and through its bilingual enunciation, *Atanarjuat* demands as much.

As Nornes notes at the outset of his study, most viewers, including critics, do not think about subtitles except when they are so inadequate as to frustrate apprehension; at those moments, the act of translation draws attention to the poverty of the subtitles relative to the presumed fullness of the spoken language in the film. In the case of *Atanarjuat*, however, the subtitles speak to a poverty of another sort, that which results from understanding an utterance (in any language, whether spoken or transcribed) in terms of its meaning exclusively. In other words, *Atanarjuat* draws attention not to the possibility of misprision that always attends an act of translation but rather to the limits of the translation process itself. Of course, the way a line is spoken—that is, the speaker's intonation, accent, pitch, speed of delivery, and so forth—always colors the meaning of that line, but *Atanarjuat* underscores this point in dramatic form by showcasing the human voice as capable of enormous range, much of which is extralinguistic. To wit, the film is full of instances when the meaning of a voice is so bound up with its materiality that it lays bare the extent to which an utterance is always tied to the body that produces it, gives it texture, and sites it in space and time. A case in point is the prominent role played by wailing in the film: at many moments—upon sight of family members' dead bodies, when Atanarjuat is discovered missing—the speech acts of individuals are continuous with cries of distress. One such moment that is particularly noteworthy because of its sheer duration occurs during the aftermath that ensues once Atanarjuat's second wife, Puja (Lucy Tulugarjuk), and his brother, Amaqjuaq (Pakkak Innuksuk), are discovered having sex. As Puja attempts to explain herself twice—first to her family, whom she manipulates into exacting revenge, and then to the women she has betrayed, Atuat and Amaqjuaq's wife, Uluriaq (Neeve Irngaut)—her lines of dialogue are coupled with her relentless wailing, which conveys, indeed performs, her anguish more acutely than any line she speaks through it.

As noteworthy as those instances when the materiality of an utterance enhances its meaning, however, are those when meaning resides entirely in materiality, when subjects signify by way of sounding rather than by speaking. Again, *Atanarjuat* is replete with such instances, for featured prominently in the film are acts of crying, moaning, grunting, belching, giggling, panting, and, perhaps most important due to its cultural specificity, throat singing, all of which express much but without recourse to language. Moreover, the very force that sets the film in motion, the evil embodied by the "up North stranger," gains presence even in his absence through two chief means, both of which are oral: the sound of the stranger's laugh and a deep, guttural growl. While the latter of these is introduced at the start of the film, when the evil claims its first murder victim, only to recur at its end, just before the evil is ritualistically expunged, the former punctuates two scenes in between so as to denote the forces fueling the villainous Oki; specifically, the laugh is heard at the start of the punching match that culminates in Oki's loss of Atuat to Atanarjuat and in the midst of the murderous attack Oki makes on Amaqjuaq and Atanarjuat as they sleep.

By relying so consistently on vocal expression that problematizes translation, *Atanarjuat* emerges as another instantiation of cinematic pedagogy. In this case, however, the lesson to be learned by the film's end is related less to the partiality of perspective (which figures prominently in *beDevil*) than to the meaning of the material. Kunuk gradually encourages the non-Inuit spectator to embrace the mimetic and thus regard *Atanarjuat* "not as something that must be analyzed and deciphered in order to deliver forth its meaning but as something that means in itself."[40] The difference between these two attitudes is thrown into fresh relief by the story's conclusion. As mentioned earlier, the film's final scene features a song that goes untranslated on-screen but appears in the published screenplay as follows:

> Aii ya . . . ay yai yaa . . .
> I can't find my blanket . . . ayai yaa
> In the middle of the night,
> when we're sleeping . . . ai ya yaa
> Trying to make a song . . . ai ya yaa
> In the middle of the night
> When everybody's sleeping
> . . . ayaii yai yaa . . .[41]

Evaluated in light of the desire animating much ethnographic cinema—as Trinh puts it, "WE WANT TO KNOW WHAT THEY THINK AND HOW THEY FEEL"—the absence of any subtitled translation reads as an act of defiant withholding.[42] Yet within a cinema of the interval, it is translation rather than its refusal that entails significant loss. Given that a full third of the syllables that constitute the song are extralinguistic sounds whose rhythmic repetition lends it texture, distilling meaning by way of language alone is a way of writing the Inuit body right out of the frame.

The Business of Fancydancing: At the Limits of Selfhood

In an article dedicated to Sherman Alexie's sonnets, Carrie Etter demonstrates how the writer has taken liberties with the form so as to address the specificity of American Indian experience. In multiple poems from *The Business of Fancydancing* (1991) and *Old Shirts and New Skins* (1993), he supplants the traditional structure—three quatrains and one couplet—with three tercets and one quatrain and thereby rewrites the form's function as well: by refusing the concluding couplet, which typically provides closure, "each of the sonnets works against resolution, urging that every Indian dilemma resists the pat denouement of the English sonnet."[43] His critical rewriting is even more pointed, however, in those poems that are conventional in structure. In two works from *First Indian on the Moon* (1993), for example, he retains the couplet only to pervert it, forcing it to swerve away from its typical aim in order to "reflect on the preceding dilemma summarily without resolving it."[44] A decade later, Alexie brought the same two-pronged approach of refusing and perverting conventions to bear upon another representational form, narrative cinema, when he made his directorial debut with *The Business of Fancydancing*, the film. Illustrating Etter's point with a manifesto's fiery incision, Alexie explains the logic behind his approach in the preface to the film's published screenplay, a piece titled "What I've Learned as a Filmmaker": under an enumerated point called "Aristotle was not a Spokane Indian," he writes plainly, "Fuck resolutions, fuck closure, fuck the idea of story arc. Embrace the incomplete, embrace ambiguity, and embrace the magical and painful randomness of life."[45] (Ironically, though, Aristotle *is* a Spokane Indian in *The Business of Fancydancing*, for one of the film's main characters is named after the Greek thinker. Not content with only rejecting the father of three-act structure, Alexie must appropriate so as to transform him as well.)

Unabashedly experimental with form, *The Business of Fancydancing* functions as a kind of treatise on the incomplete, the ambiguous, and the random; nonetheless, all that experimentation ultimately serves rather than undercuts a narrative core, lending tremendous dimension to the interpersonal dynamics of the four main characters. At the film's center is Alexie's proxy, Seymour (Evan Adams), a gay or "two-spirited" poet living in Seattle who has achieved great success and fame in the literary world yet has done so at the expense of his ties to another world, that of the Spokane reservation, the childhood home that serves as both setting and subject for most of his work. The other three main characters all live in that latter world: Aristotle (Gene Tagaban) and Mouse (Swil Kanim), whom Seymour identifies as "the men I loved before I loved men," are his former best friends, and Agnes (Michelle St. John) is his half-Spokane, half-Jewish ex-girlfriend who moved to the reservation after university to take up a position as a schoolteacher. While very close, these three are divided in their estimation of Seymour. On the one hand, Aristotle and Mouse feel both betrayed by and resentful of his success since it has come, to their mind, at his community's expense. As Mouse notes, after reading aloud a poem wherein Seymour narrates an incident from Mouse's childhood in the first person, "It's like I'm not even alive, it's like I'm dead." Agnes, in contrast, proves Seymour's most vocal champion on the reservation by answering accusations of opportunistic appropriation with the following defense: "He's fighting the war, you know? He's telling everybody that we're still here. He does it for all of us. It's not just for him, even if it looks that way."

What occasions an exploration of these relationships as well as the personal and social history that informs them is a single event: Seymour's return to the reservation after many years of absence in order to attend Mouse's funeral. While Seymour's physical journey provides the film with its narrative backbone, footage thereof is presented only intermittently. The rest of the film is given over to a complex collage of material that fleshes out the many issues the journey raises. Included therein are the following: slice-of-life scenes depicting Seymour in the city with his partner, Steven (Kevin Phillip), or Agnes, Aristotle, and Mouse on the reservation; flashbacks to Seymour's years at university, which detail his relationship with Agnes, his coming out, and his showdown with Aristotle when the latter announces his intention to drop out of school and go home; segments of an interview wherein Seymour and, on one occasion, Aristotle occupy the hot seat opposite an antagonistic questioner; a series of readings and signings where Seymour performs his poems for fawning audiences; interludes of Mouse playing the violin and/or other characters dancing in various costumes, which serve to crystallize issues related to the performance of identity; and sequences wherein direct-address narration of stories is paired with visual illustration of the scenarios being described.

In contrast to the self-reflexively multivocal *beDevil* and the selectively translated *Atanarjuat*, *The Business of Fancydancing* is split in its enunciation due to this dizzying array of rhetorical strategies, all of which position the viewer differently vis-à-vis the text. In this regard, the film bears resemblance to much contemporary American Indian literature, which, according to Susan Berry Brill de Ramírez, is informed by not only a history of text-based literary culture but also a tradition of oral storytelling prac-tices. In order to distinguish these two legacies and the types of exchange they respectively foster, she employs two terms: on the one hand, conversive communication positions the listener (or reader) as an active participant in the storytelling process, a co-creator in an act of productive synergy, and on the other, discursive communication is monologic and thus dependent upon a distinction between the speaking subject and his or her objectified others, be they those whom are spoken to or spoken about. Partaking in both of these modes of communication by virtue of its dual inheritance, American Indian literature delineates the space between them; as Brill de Ramírez notes, "All Native writers, . . . whether they are Métis, mixedblood, or fullblood, raised on or off the reservation, straddle both discursive and conversive worlds to varying extents, writing in diverse styles that reflect a mixed convergence and divergence of orally based and textually informed realities and voices."[46]

Given my interest in *The Business of Fancydancing*, one aspect of this argument that is particularly noteworthy is its refusal of a discourse of (low-) technological determinism. Although Brill de Ramírez associates conversive communication with orality, she does not limit it to such since her ulti-mate goal is to identify those literary strategies that allow for an inclusive and mutual exchange between writer and reader. Alexie's use of the second person in certain poems from *First Indian on the Moon* is for her a case in point. When bringing the distinction between conversive and discursive to bear on cinema, it is tempting to graft it onto existing paradigms: given its emphasis on an actively engaged viewer, modernist cinema could be deemed conversive, while illusionistic cinema's tendency to produce a highly circum-scribed spectatorial position would seemingly align it with discursive com-munication. Yet to do this is to privilege certain aspects of Brill de Ramírez's terms (namely, activity and passivity) at the expense of others, including, for example, the "real transformational growth" she associates with conversive communication and the "dissipation of energy" that attends its discursive counterpart.[47] Indeed, one of the most important attributes of the oral tradi-tion—and, by extension, conversive communication in any medium—is the stock it puts in language as a means of creation, affirmation, and connection. As Joanne DiNova explains, Ferdinand de Saussure's notion of the arbitrary sign is incompatible with an Indigenous worldview, which regards signifier and signified, language and the reality it names as coming into being in and through each other and thus as fundamentally linked.[48] Insofar as an Indig-enous politics depends on seizing that productive potential, which is fostered in the context of dialogic exchange, strategies of deconstruction (at least, without a subsequent reconstruction) are counterproductive. For language to function politically, DiNova concludes, "the intersubjective element must consistently reach far beyond the strictly critical-narrative and must resist the temptation to collapse into solipsistic interrogations."[49]

In light of this emphasis on the intersubjective and co-creative, anti-illusionism is not a sufficient criterion for a conversive cinema. Rather, the most important issue at hand is the extent to which a film triangulates the relationship between author, subject, and audience along lines of empathy and inclusion. To wit, one of the most discursive components of *The Business of Fancydancing* is also one of its least naturalistic; perhaps even more surprising, however, is the fact that it is also one dedicated to a conversation. Filmed in a void—that is, an empty, blackened soundstage that is divested of the materiality of the diegetic world—the interview segments initially appear like clips from a *Charlie Rose* knockoff, yet their tone quickly qualifies them as something far more fantastic, namely, a confrontation between two sides of the interviewee, be it Seymour or Aristotle: his inner critic (embodied by the interviewer, played by Rebecca Carroll) and his public image (embodied by Seymour/Aristotle himself). Insofar as the former is aggressive and the latter evasive, the exchange is relentlessly hostile. Moreover, the camera, especially in the later segments, circles the characters repeatedly, as if to delineate the periphery of the action and thereby to mark the limit of the spectator's involvement. In short, the sum effect of these scenes due to their form and content is pervasive estrangement, a dissipation, to paraphrase Brill de Ramírez, of constructive energies. Nonetheless, they constitute only one end of a communication continuum that the film traverses over the course of its duration.

With its multiple modes of address, between which it moves continually, *Business* proves itself to be fundamentally concerned with questions of enunciation. One way Alexie tackles such questions is by exploring the medium through which he typically expresses himself, literature, in order to lay bare the cross-purposes it serves: to honor *and* debase, to remember *and* forget, to share *and* horde, and, most important for this discussion, to isolate *and* connect. Such multivalence is precisely what flourishes at the juncture between the conversive and discursive, the juncture where Seymour, like Alexie, positions his work. First of all, Seymour's poems have an oral life both prior and subsequent to their publication on the page. His writing process, as depicted multiple times throughout the film, is not a silently introspective one, for integral to the act of composition is the sounding out of lines in an attempt to establish a resonant rhythm. In one scene in particular, the link between this process and a traditional variety of musical performance is made explicit: Seymour is writing in bed when Aristotle joins him to lend assistance, first by chanting along and then by additionally drumming out a rhythm with Seymour's pencil and pad. Furthermore, once composed, the poems take the shape of spoken texts when performed, be it in the context of a reading for which there is a diegetic audience or in a sequence wherein the film viewer is being directly addressed. As evinced by differences between these two contexts, however, even oral performances can vary in their conversive potential. That is to say, the two types of contexts featured in *The Business of Fancydancing*—those within the film and the film itself—make explicit the different possibilities for the same expressive form and, moreover, demonstrate that the juncture of conversive and discursive communication relates but is not reducible to that of oral and written culture.

In those scenes wherein Seymour reads or speaks in front of a diegetic audience, particularly the three that are dedicated to a book launch that culminates in a book signing, there is an emphasis on his status as solitary artist and performing personality. Not only does he prove a confident speaker capable of taking in gullible fans with fanciful yarns, but the cinematography underscores his exceptional status by either isolating him in shots that are then intercut with reaction shots of his appreciative audience or centering him in a frame that is otherwise crowded with bodies jockeying for his attention. In short, these scenes establish Seymour's stardom even more than his artistry, his image even more than his substance. In comparison, those sequences wherein the film ruptures the diegetic frame and offers up a story in a less mediated fashion emerge as sites for dialogic discourse and creative collaboration. The most compelling of these is one dedicated to a game that Aristotle, Mouse, Seymour, and Seymour's sister played regularly as children: against Grandmother's wishes, they would climb her tree to gorge themselves on green apples and then drop to the ground in the hopes of luring her into a footrace across the yard. Contributing to the narration of this story are at least four people: Seymour and Aristotle, who, in alternation, tell the story directly to the camera from their position on an empty soundstage; director of photography and editor Holly Taylor, who supplements footage of the storytellers with poetic images illustrating the action being described; and Alexie, whose role as the voice behind Seymour's voice is amplified in those moments when the film divests itself of illusionism. While it is possible to read the contrast between these two types of performance as a comment on issues of medium specificity (as in, cinema is an inherently more collaborative medium than literature), to do so would entail ignoring one of Alexie's larger projects, which is thinking through the relationship between the individual Indigenous artist—*any* individual Indigenous artist—and community. Instead, what this contrast lays bare are the possibilities of a co-creative relationship as well as those factors, like the cult of celebrity, that work against their realization.

In addition to the context of enunciation, Alexie is also interested in the content thereof; thus, another one of his larger projects is experimenting with the way American Indians are represented. Although *The Business of Fancydancing* is, in many ways, organized around Mouse's absence, it is through the articulation of his presence that such experimentation proves most productive. Specifically, Alexie uses Mouse not only to explore the extremes of conversive and discursive communication but also to lay bare the connection between these modes of communication and the figuration of Indian identity in visual culture and popular discourse. The one thing, other than his violin, that Mouse gets associated with over the course of the film is his video camera, which mediates not only his interactions with other characters but also the viewer's interactions with the diegetic world since footage from that camera is incorporated into the fabric of *The Business of Fancydancing* on multiple occasions. One such occasion is the film's first scene, which is made up entirely of continuous footage shot by Mouse. In it, Aristotle and Seymour are introduced immediately after their graduation from Wellpinit High School. Dressed in cap and gown and adorned with sashes announcing their shared "valedictorian" honors, the two mug for the camera and talk excitedly about St. Jerome the Second University, where they will be roommates and "buddies forever." Despite his position as camera operator, Mouse establishes his embodied presence in multiple ways. He commands the situation vocally by telling his friends to "get together" and asking them about their future plans; his hand enters the frame as he points to their sashes and jokes, "They spelled 'dick' wrong"; and he turns the camera on himself after revealing that he got his GED in order to conclude facetiously, "I'm gonna work in the uranium mines." Some subsequent scenes, including one wherein Aristotle demonstrates "how to huff gas," are like this one insofar as they consist exclusively of footage that Mouse shoots. Others, in contrast, combine Mouse's footage with material shot, like the majority of the film, on digital video and from an "objective" or outsider's vantage. Presented in this manner is Mouse's encounter with Agnes upon her arrival at the reservation and the scenario discussed above, wherein Mouse and Aristotle accuse Seymour of stealing their memories and, indeed, their very lives.

For two main reasons, these scenes serve to establish an intimate rapport between the viewer and Mouse, which mirrors the dynamic that exists between Mouse and the people he films. First, he is an insouciant presence in them, providing commentary with cheeky wit and animated delivery. Second, and even more significant, as evinced in the film's opening scene, he is a full participant in the situations he records; not only does he actively engage with the other people he films, reaching out to them both verbally and physically from behind the camera, but he also turns the camera on himself regularly. As a result, the point of view that the spectator necessarily adopts is thoroughly fleshed out: it is identified with a single body, a particular voice, and a specific subject position, all of which are enveloped by the social context caught on camera. In short, the viewer's identification with Mouse is doubled, but not in the way supposed by Teresa de Lauretis when she coins the term "double identification." Within her gendered model of cinematic spectatorship, identification is doubled by virtue of being split—a female viewer identifies with the male gaze and the female image simultaneously—but the moments in Mouse's footage wherein he both looks and is looked at produce a double identification that is compounded such that Mouse is, at least temporarily, the viewer's only point of reference.

In sharp contrast to these scenes are two wherein Mouse is figured as both object and abject. In the first, he and Aristotle are shown sharing a drink. From the number of empty beer cans that surround them and the lumbering nature of Mouse's movements, there can be no doubt they are on a binge, but the severity of that binge becomes all too evident when Mouse adds rubbing alcohol to his beverage. The second begins with a title frame that reads "How to make a bathroom cleaner sandwich" and then presents a tightly framed, strung out Mouse as he sprays bathroom cleaner onto a piece of white bread, folds it in half, takes a bite, and experiences its effects. Given the silent desperation on display in these scenes, they bear a striking resemblance to a poem from *First Indian on the Moon* that Brill de Ramírez discusses, one wherein Alexie narrates the ignoble death of a drunk Indian man who drowns in a puddle. While Brill de Ramírez's reason for invoking the poem is to discuss the means by which Alexie's use of language lends the situation pathos and the man subjectivity, she first lays emphasis on that which these two scenes from *The Business of Fancydancing* offer up in stark form: a reification of a most wretched stereotype. As she concludes, "If dominant discourse is that of affluent, white America, Indian America has few other options beyond that of objectified others passing out and drowning in mud puddles"—or, for that matter, eating bathroom cleaner sandwiches.[50]

In his poem, Alexie manages to humanize the drowned man in part by stressing a connection between himself, the speaking subject, and the man, the object of dominant discourse: "An *Indian* man drowned *here* on *my* reservation" (Brill de Ramírez's emphasis).[51] In *The Business of Fancydancing*, he makes a connection similar in sort with his treatment of Mouse. Certainly by setting scenes of dire self-destruction against ones of compelling charisma, Alexie lends dimension to what would otherwise be a mere stereotype, but even more effective in his humanization of Mouse is the inclusion of a single scene wherein these dual representations converge. At the start of the scene, Aristotle is driving down a long stretch of empty road while Mouse rides shotgun, chattering away and filming the situation. Upon spotting a white man whose car has run out of gas, they stop their truck, get out, and begin talking to him. Prompted by the man's observation that they are Indian, Mouse starts to toy with him, identifying himself and Aristotle as Mohawks—"We build skyscrapers for a living. We beat the crap out of gravity fifty-two weeks out of the year, man"—and then suggesting that the man has mistaken them for Sacajawea. Aristotle, in contrast, responds to the situation violently, cutting the verbal play short by beating the man up over Mouse's emphatic protests. When he is done, he commands Mouse to strike a blow as well, but Mouse resists out of fear for his hands. Eventually swayed, he lays his camera down on the ground and kicks the man twice before they flee the scene in a state of exhilaration. As is typical for scenes wherein Mouse is filming, portions of his resulting footage are intercut into material that approaches the situation from an external vantage. Upon exiting the truck, these portions change in their preferred subject matter: the prior ones feature Mouse more often than not, while the subsequent ones are intently focused on Aristotle and the white man. Yet it is with the last two shots taken from Mouse's camera and integrated into the scene that the most substantial change occurs. These shots are taken from footage recorded by the camera as it lies on the ground, unmanned, and they feature the white man's violated body, first as Mouse prepares to kick him and then once he is left alone.

While the positions of speaking subject and objectified other are mutually exclusive (yet connected) in the poem invoked above, in this scene Mouse occupies them both insofar as he starts out as a thoroughly engaging point of double identification only to transform into a stereotypical Indian whose rage can find no outlet other than arbitrary violence. What connects these two positions and thus humanizes the latter, however, is that which explains—not justifies or excuses, but explains—this transformation: that is, the series of events, both present and past, spoken and unspeakable, that make sense of a reservation reality that is, in Seymour's words, "equal parts magic and loss." In giving itself over to such events, *The Business of Fancydancing* takes as its mandate a process that is imperative for any peoples who have been reduced to static images and entrenched stereotypes: in the words of Joanne Hearne, that of "forg[ing] a collective identity based on narrative as well as on image."[52] What Alexie, Moffat, and Kunuk all make clear is the extent to which that process entails a redefinition of narrative itself—along the lines of the absent as well as the present, the material as well as the meaningful, and the collective as well as the individual.

AFTERWORD

In light of the material discussed at the close of the last chapter, scenarios of banal yet brutal abuse to both self and other, the title of this book could easily be read as a threat or, at least, a warning: Unsettling sights inside; read at your own risk! Yet I prefer, in this brief coda, to dwell on the ways in which the title also works as a promise, speaking to the capacity of certain contemporary films to unsettle something other than their viewers: that is, those representational conventions that have historically served to shore up, to quote Fatimah Tobing Rony again, "the episteme of the Ethnographic."[1] Such public acts of unsettling have tremendous potency; I do not think it far-fetched to suggest that films like *Rabbit-Proof Fence* and *Beneath Clouds* helped, in some way, to prepare the ground for Prime Minister Kevin Rudd's apology to Australia's Aboriginal peoples in February 2008, or that filmmakers as diverse as Alanis Obomsawin and Noam Gonick have contributed to widespread awareness of the residential school system in Canada for which Prime Minister Steven Harper apologized four months later. At the same time, I don't want to overstate my case. After all, no film prevented Canada or Australia—or for that matter, the United States or New Zealand—from being among the four countries to vote against the otherwise widely supported UN Declaration on the Rights of Indigenous People in 2007. Clearly, the ties that bind the four countries with which this book has been concerned endure, taking shape in initiatives both embraced and opposed.

Nonetheless, there are some grounds for cautious optimism, especially in relation to contemporary commercial cinema, where Indigenous people are steadily making inroads in a variety of capacities. As remarked at the outset of this volume, a strictly Fourth Cinema is an elusive ideal, but the extent to which certain collaborative ventures, dependent on varying degrees of input from a diversity of participants, have happened on the terms of the Aboriginal parties involved therein points to a horizon of aesthetic and political possibility defined by reciprocity and respect, if not complete autonomy. For this reason the aforementioned *Ten Canoes* and *The Journals of Knud Rasmussen* as well as the more recent *Before Tomorrow* (2008), which features an Inuit woman and her grandson fighting for survival on the cusp of contact with white culture, are interesting films with which to close, for they exemplify cross-cultural exchange at its most thoroughgoing. All were made by a Native/non-Native directorial team: respectively, Peter Djigirr and Rolf de Heer, Zacharias Kunuk and Norman Cohn, and Madeline Piujuq Ivalu and Marie-Hélène Cousineau. All have successfully engaged a global as well as a local audience through both their textual operations (subtitles and/or voice-over narration) and their circulation (chiefly via the film festival circuit). Finally, all, in an act of pointed appropriation, have worked extensively with source material produced by non-Aboriginal people, thereby re-functioning aspects of white-authored contact narratives in the service of stories both of and from an Aboriginal perspective. In the case of *Before Tomorrow*, that material is a short story by Danish writer Jørn Riel, while in that of *Ten Canoes* and *The Journals of Knud Rasmussen*, it is various anthropological documents: namely, photographs taken by Donald Thomson in the 1930s on the one hand and writings and drawings produced by Rasmussen in the 1920s on the other.

By virtue of these three commonalities, *Ten Canoes*, *The Journals of Knud Rasmussen*, and *Before Tomorrow* all site themselves at the center of the "field of intersubjectivity" by which Marcia Langton defines Aboriginality, "rema[king] over and over again" the terms of a fraught yet urgent discussion.[2] In so doing, they, like so many of the texts taken up in this book, are unsettling sights, both aesthetic and political, to productive ends. What remains to be seen is exactly how developments in film culture continue to dovetail with changes in other arenas as well. That Australia just reversed its position on the UN declaration mentioned above, spurring New Zealand to announce its intentions to reconsider the matter as well, suggests that there is a paradigm shift under way, one that is largely rhetorical at present, but provides the requisite rationale for substantial policy changes as well.[3] As index, if not incentive, for such a shift, the cinema of Aboriginality promises to persist as a vital, and vitally important, aspect of public culture on the scale of the local, the national, and the international alike.

Filmography

Note: Rental and/or purchase information is included only for those films that are not widely available on DVD.

Atanarjuat (aka *Atanarjuat: The Fast Runner* and *The Fast Runner*; 2001)
Director: Zacharias Kunuk
Production companies: Aboriginal Peoples Television Network, Canadian Film or Video Production Tax Credit, Canadian Government, Canadian Television (CTV), Canadian Television and Cable Production Fund License Program, Channel 24 Igloolik, Igloolik Isuma Productions Inc., National Film Board of Canada, Telefilms Equity Investment Program, Vision Television
Language: Inuktitut
Contact for rental or purchase: While *Atanarjuat* is widely available currently, an array of supporting materials is also available on the Isuma (http://www.isuma.ca) and IsumaTV (http://www.isuma.tv) Web sites.

beDevil (1993)
Director: Tracey Moffatt
Production company: Anthony Buckley Productions Pty. Ltd.
Language: English
Contact for rental or purchase: Women Make Movies (http://www.wmm.com/index. asp), Ronin Films (http://www.roninfilms.com.au/)

Before Tomorrow (2008)
Directors: Marie-Hélène Cousineau, Madeline Piujuq Ivalu
Production companies: Igloolik Isuma Productions Inc., Kunuk Cohn Productions, Alliance Atlantis, Alliance Vivafilm, Telefilm Canada, Société de développement des entreprises culturelles (SODEC), The Nunavut Film Commission, National Indigenous Television (NITV)
Language: Inuktitut
Contact for rental or purchase: While *Before Tomorrow* is widely available currently, an array of supporting materials can be found on the Isuma (http://www.isuma. ca) and IsumaTV (http://www.isuma.tv) Web sites.

Beneath Clouds (2002)
Director: Ivan Sen
Production companies: Australian Film Finance Corporation (AFFC), Autumn Films Pty. Ltd., Axiom Films
Language: English
Contact for purchase: Ronin Films (http://www.roninfilms.com.au/)

Black and White (2002)
Director: Craig Lahiff
Production companies: Duo Art Productions, Scala Productions
Language: English

Black Robe (1991)
Director: Bruce Beresford
Production companies: Alliance Communications Corporation, First Choice,
    Goldwyn Pictures Corporation, Rogers Telefund–Rogers Communications,
    Samson Productions, Téléfilm Canada
Languages: English, Cree, Mohawk, Algonquin, Latin

The Business of Fancydancing (2002)
Director: Sherman Alexie
Production company: FallsApart Productions
Language: English
Contact for rental or purchase: *The Business of Fancydancing* home page (http://
    www.fallsapart.com/fancydancing/)

The Chant of Jimmie Blacksmith (1978)
Director: Fred Schepisi
Production companies: The Film House, Victorian Film
Language: English

Dances with Wolves (1990)
Director: Kevin Costner
Production Companies: Tig Productions, Majestic Films International
Languages: English, Sioux, Pawnee

Dead Man (1995)
Director: Jim Jarmusch
Production companies: Pandora Filmproduktion, JVC Entertainment Networks,
    Newmarket Capital Group, 12 Gauge Productions
Language: English

Deep Inside Clint Star (1999)
Director: Clint Alberta
Production company: National Film Board of Canada
Language: English

The Fringe Dwellers (1986)
Director: Bruce Beresford
Production company: Fringe Dwellers Productions
Language: English
Contact for purchase: Umbrella Entertainment (http://www.umbrellaent.com.au/)

Indian Summer: The Oka Crisis (2006)
Director: Gil Cardinal
Production company: Ciné Télé Action International
Language: English
Contact for purchase: Ciné Télé Action (http://www.cineteleaction.com/en/pages/
OKA.html)

Jedda (1955)
Director: Charles Chauvel
Production company: Charles Chauvel Productions
Language: English
Contact for purchase: National Film and Sound Archive (http://www.nfsa.gov.au/)

The Journals of Knud Rasmussen (2006)
Directors: Zacharias Kunuk, Norman Cohn
Production companies: Barok Film A/S, Igloolik Isuma Productions Inc., Kunuk
Cohn Productions
Languages: English, Inuktitut, Danish
Contact for rental or purchase: While *The Journals of Knud Rasmussen* is widely
available currently, an array of supporting materials can be found on the Isuma
(http://www.isuma.ca) and IsumaTV (http://www.isuma.tv) Web sites.

Kanehsatake: 270 Years of Resistance (1993)
Director: Alanis Obomsawin
Production company: National Film Board of Canada
Language: English
Contact for purchase: National Film Board of Canada (http://www.nfb.ca/)

The Last of the Mohicans (1992)
Director: Michael Mann
Production company: Morgan Creek Productions
Languages: English, French, Mohawk

Map of the Human Heart (1993)
Director: Vincent Ward
Production companies: Australian Film Finance Corporation (AFFC), Les Films
Ariane, Map Films, PolyGram Filmed Entertainment, Sunrise Pictures Company,
Vincent Ward Films, Working Title Films
Language: English

Naming Number Two (aka *No. 2*; 2006)
Director: Toa Fraser
Production company: Numero Films Ltd.
Language: English
Contact for rental or purchase: Cyan Pictures (http://www.cyanpictures.com), Aro
Video (http://www.arovideo.co.nz)

The New World (2005)
Director: Terrence Malick
Production companies: New Line Cinema, Sunflower Productions, Sarah Green
  Film Corp., First Foot Films, The Virginia Company LLC
Languages: English, Algonquin

Nice Coloured Girls (1987)
Director: Tracey Moffatt
Production companies: Women's Film Fund, The Australian Film Commission
Language: English
Contact for rental or purchase: Women Make Movies (http://www.wmm.com/
  index.asp), Ronin Films (http://www.roninfilms.com.au/)

Night Cries: A Rural Tragedy (1989)
Director: Tracey Moffatt
Production company: The Australian Film Commission
Language: English
Contact for rental or purchase: Women Make Movies (http://www.wmm.com/
  index.asp)

Once Were Warriors (1994)
Director: Lee Tamahori
Production companies: Communicado Productions, New Zealand Film Commis-
  sion, New Zealand On Air
Languages: English, Maori

The Piano (1993)
Director: Jane Campion
Production companies: The Australia Film Commission, CiBy 2000, Jan Chapman
  Productions, New South Wales Television and Film Office
Languages: English, British Sign Language, Maori

Powwow Highway (1989)
Director: Jonathan Wacks
Production company: HandMade Films
Language: English

The Proposition (2005)
Director: John Hillcoat
Production companies: Surefire Films, UK Film Council, Autonomous, Jackie O
  Productions, Pictures in Paradise, Pacific Film and Television Commission,
  Film Consortium
Language: English

Rabbit-Proof Fence (2002)
Director: Phillip Noyce
Production companies: The Australian Film Commission, Australian Film Finance Corporation (AFFC), HanWay Films, Lotteries Commission of Western Australia, Olsen Levy, Rumbalara Films, ScreenWest, Showtime Australia
Language: Wangajunka, English

River Queen (2005)
Director: Vincent Ward
Production companies: Silverscreen Films, The Film Consortium, Endgame Entertainment, Invicta Capital, New Zealand Film Commission, New Zealand Film Production Fund, UK Film Council
Languages: English, Maori

Rosalie's Journey (2003)
Director: Warwick Thornton
Production company: CAAMA Productions
Language: Arrernte
Contact for purchase: Central Australian Aboriginal Media Association (http://caama.com.au/)

Smoke Signals (1998)
Director: Chris Eyre
Production companies: ShadowCatcher Entertainment, Welb Film Pursuits Ltd.
Language: English

Stryker (2004)
Director: Noam Gonick
Production company: Wild Boars of Manitoba Inc.
Language: English

Ten Canoes (2006)
Director: Rolf de Heer
Co-director: Peter Djigirr
Production companies: Adelaide Film Festival, Fandango Australia, Special Broadcasting Service, Vertigo Productions Pty. Ltd.
Languages: Yolngu Matha, English

Utu (1983)
Director: Geoff Murphy
Production companies: Glitteron, The Pickmen Film Corporation
Language: English

Walkabout (1971)
Director: Nicolas Roeg
Production company: Si Litvinoff Film Production
Language: English

Whale Rider (2002)
Director: Niki Caro
Production companies: ApolloMedia, New Zealand Film Commission, New
    Zealand Film Production Fund, New Zealand On Air, Pandora Filmproduktion,
    South Pacific Pictures
Languages: English, Maori

Yellow Fella (2005)
Director: Ivan Sen
Production companies: CAAMA Productions, The Indigenous Branch of the
    Australian Film Commission, Australian Film Finance Corporation (AFFC),
    SBS Independent
Language: English
Contact for purchase: Central Australian Aboriginal Media Association (http://
    caama.com.au/), Ronin Films (http://www.roninfilms.com.au/)

NOTES

Preface

1. Barclay, "Celebrating Fourth Cinema," 7, 9.

2. Ibid., 11.

3. Granted, when compared to Toronto's ImagineNATIVE festival, which offered in 2006, as it does annually, five full days of programming related to Indigenous filmmaking and media arts, TIFF hardly emerges as a bastion for Fourth Cinema. Yet, given the festival's recent reputation as, in Rebecca Winters Keegan's words, "the most influential film festival" in the world, its inclusion of *The Journals of Knud Rasmussen* and *Ten Canoes* is highly significant since it brought tremendous visibility to films that might otherwise go unnoticed, particularly by spectators who do not regularly patronize ImagineNATIVE or other festivals that share its mission. Keegan qtd. in Kopun, "Toronto's Film Festival Rivals Cannes."

4. Siebert, "*Atanarjuat* and the Ideological Work of Contemporary Indigenous Filmmaking," 544.

5. For example, Glauber Rocha, "An Esthetic of Hunger" (1965), and Fernando Solanas and Octavio Getino, "Towards a Third Cinema: Notes and Experiences for the Development of a Cinema of Liberation in the Third World" (1969), both of which are reprinted in Michael Martin's anthology *New Latin American Cinema: Theory, Practices and Transcontinental Articulations*.

6. Guneratne, "Introduction," 20.

7. Langton, "Aboriginal Art and Film," 99–100.

8. Given Barclay's stress on the capitalization of "Indigenous," I should speak to my own approach to lowercase versus uppercase letters. Throughout this book, I typically capitalize the terms "Native," "Indigenous," and "Aboriginal" (as well as any variations on them), so as to acknowledge respectfully the specificity of these identities. I will make exceptions to this rule on the following occasions: when I am using these words in a different manner (for example, "flora that is indigenous/native to the area"), when I am quoting an author who does not capitalize, and when I am speaking specifically of "the native" as a stereotype that prevails within Western representational regimes.

9. Rony, *Third Eye*, 197.

10. Ginsburg, "Culture/Media," 6.

Introduction: The Cinema of Aboriginality as Transnational Phenomenon

1. See Gunning, "Aesthetic of Astonishment" and "Cinema of Attractions."

2. Stam and Spence, "Colonialism, Racism, and Representation," 4.

3. In *American Anatomies: Theorizing Race and Gender*, Robyn Wiegman discusses the process by which race has come to be "constituted as a visual phenomenon, with all the political and ideological force that the seemingly naturalness of the body as the

locus of difference can claim" (22). Building upon Michel Foucault's *The Order of Things*, Wiegman examines how the rise of the discipline of natural history in the seventeenth century served not only to align vision with scientific authority but also to set the stage for the emergence of a racial taxonomy based on corporeality. Wiegman traces the origins of contemporary constructions of racial difference back to naturalist François Bernier, who was the first to classify people according to their skin color (in conjunction, occasionally, with attributes such as hair, nose shape, and stature) rather than by their geographical origin. While Bernier's system of classification was deliberately constructed to be nonhierarchical and divested of any assumptions regarding people's innate worth, its emphasis on the differences, as opposed to the similarities, between human beings and its inscription of whiteness as norm made it available for racist appropriation, especially by those positing the "natural order" of slavery. In the nineteenth century, biologist George Cuvier initiated such appropriation with his pioneering work in the fields of physiognomy, phrenology, and craniology, wherein he posited a correlation between the size and shape of one's brain and/or skull, one's intelligence, and one's position on an evolutionary continuum.

4. In making this assertion, Rony draws upon the work of historian of anthropology George W. Stocking Jr. See Rony, *Third Eye*, 7.

5. Stam and Shohat, *Unthinking Eurocentricism*, 1–2.

6. Griffiths, *Wondrous Difference*, xxix.

7. Among the films Cooper and Schoedsack collaborated on before *King Kong* were *Grass: A Nation's Battle for Life* (1925) and *Chang: A Drama of the Wilderness* (1927), which showcased life among the Bakhtiari of Iran and the Siamese, respectively.

8. McClintock, *Imperial Leather*, 30.

9. *Beur* is a term for someone of North African descent who was born in and/or lives in France.

10. Ezra and Rowden, *Transnational Cinema*, 7.

11. Naficy, *Accented Cinema*, 11.

12. Ibid., 134.

13. Pearson, *Politics of Ethnicity in Settler Societies*, 13.

14. Naficy, *Accented Cinema*, 15.

15. Ibid., 11.

16. Ibid., 14.

17. Although "Native American" has proven a popular term in recent years, especially among non-Native academics, throughout this book I follow the lead of Indigenous writers and activists, including, for example, Russell Means and Sherman Alexie, who have stated their overwhelming preference for the term "American Indian" or simply "Indian." When addressing the Canadian context, I typically opt for either "Native" or "First Nations person," as is common practice.

18. The same argument could be made for the terms "Native Canadian," "Aboriginal Australian," and even "Maori," which means, simply, "native, indigenous, ordinary" as opposed to those who are different or "Pakeha." See Briggs, *English-Maori*.

19. Naficy, *Accented Cinema*, 13.

20. Peters, "Exile, Nomadism, and Diaspora," 18.

21. Brah, *Cartographies of Diaspora*, 191.

22. Ibid., 192–93.

23. Ibid., 209.

24. Churchill, *Acts of Rebellion*, 141.

25. Ibid.

26. George Manuel and Michael Posluns, *Fourth World*, 5.

27. Ibid., 7.

28. Van Meijl, "Indigenous People in a Fourth World Perspective," 33.

29. That publication was Lieuwe Pietersen's *Taalsociologie*, which is discussed in Maddock, *Identity, Land and Liberty*, 5.

30. Griggs, "Excerpt from CWIS Occasional Paper #18."

31. Maaka and Fleras, *Politics of Indigeneity*, 53.

32. Allen, *Blood Narrative*, 220.

33. Ibid., 199.

34. DiNova, *Spiraling Webs of Relation*, 66.

35. Ibid., 118.

36. Michaels, *Bad Aboriginal Art*, 113–14.

37. For Worth and Adair, in particular, this approach leads to a number of specious claims. Relying upon a vague notion of film as a language without ever referencing the then burgeoning field of cine-semiotics or demonstrating the analytical rigor exemplified by that field, they assume a facile relationship between how one sees and how one represents the world.

38. Turner, "Defiant Images," 12.

39. Ibid.

40. Stasiulis and Yuval-Davis, "Introduction," 3.

41. Pearson, *Politics of Ethnicity in Settler Societies*, 8–9.

42. MacKenzie, "National Identity, Canadian Cinema, and Multiculturalism."

43. For an interesting discussion of ethnic intermarriage in New Zealand that frequently draws comparisons between New Zealand on the one hand and Australia, Canada, and the United States on the other, see Callister, Didham, and Potter, "Ethnic Intermarriage in New Zealand."

44. Denoon, "Understanding Settler Societies," 518.

45. Stasiulis and Yuval-Davis, "Introduction," 17.

46. It was Laura Mulvey who, quite famously, declared in her landmark essay "Visual Pleasure and Narrative Cinema" that sadism demands a story.

47. Bloom, "Beyond the Western Frontier," 197. According to Ella Shohat and Robert Stam's calculations, Westerns constituted a full quarter of Hollywood's output between the years 1926 and 1967. Stam and Shohat, *Unthinking Eurocentricism*, 114–15.

48. G. Lewis, *Australian Movies and the American Dream*, 8.

49. Mowitt, *Re-takes*, 13.

50. Ezra and Rowden, *Transnational Cinema*, 2.

51. For Canadians, Australians, and New Zealanders, the stakes of the question of how to position one's cinema vis-à-vis Hollywood have only gotten higher. Given the recent tendency on the part of American companies to outsource so many of its production tasks to foreign crews and postproduction teams, many of which can be hired at less expense than their counterparts in the United States, the threat of not only eclipse but also subsumption is profound.

52. White, *Cinema of Canada*, 4.

Part One: Making Contact, Producing Difference

1. Roeg and Agutter, "Commentary."
2. Chow, *Primitive Passions*, 22.
3. Ibid.

1. Birth Pangs: Constructing the Proto-national Hero

1. *Dances with Wolves* was a huge success on a couple of different fronts. Namely, it grossed $184.2 million domestically and $424.2 million internationally, and it won seven Oscars in 1991, including the much coveted Best Picture and Best Director pair.
2. Canby, "Soldier at One with the Sioux."
3. James, "Jesuits vs. Indians, with No Villains."
4. Rafferty, "True Believers," 120.
5. Ibid., 120–21.
6. Churchill, *Fantasies of the Master Race*, 234.
7. Thomas, "*Black Robe* Draws Fire from U.S. Natives."
8. Qtd. in ibid.
9. Churchill, *Fantasies of the Master Race*, 245.
10. Edward D. Castillo, Review of *Dances with Wolves*, *Film Quarterly* 44, no. 4 (1991): 18.
11. This set of terms is employed by Michael Hilger in *From Savage to Nobleman*.
12. While Robert Baird makes this statement in relation to *Little Big Man* (Arthur Penn, 1970) and *Dances with Wolves*, it can easily be extended to myriad other films. "'Going Indian,'" 160.
13. The version of *Dance with Wolves* released theatrically runs 181 minutes. A 234-minute version, however, was released briefly in select foreign markets and subsequently aired in November 1993 on ABC. One of the main things that distinguishes this longer cut is the fact that it creates a degree of moral ambiguity around the Sioux people by including, among other things, a scene in which the tribe engages in a raucous celebration after killing a group of white buffalo hunters for no reason other than revenge.
14. Lake, "Argumentation and Self," 81.
15. This phrase is Robert Baird's.
16. Woolf, *Room of One's Own*, 35.
17. Hoffman, "Whose Home on the Range?" 48.
18. Freebury, "*Black Robe*," 123.
19. Evans, "Beyond the Frontier," 152.
20. Ibid.
21. Routt, "More Australian than Aristotelian."
22. As only fragments of *The Story of the Kelly Gang* remain (approximately nine minutes' worth), it is impossible to prove this claim definitively. Based on supporting documents, however, the film is believed to have had a running time of 65 to 70 minutes.
23. Routt, "More Australian than Aristotelian."
24. Bhabha, "Of Mimicry and Man," 126.
25. Ibid.
26. In "Signs Taken for Wonders: Questions of Ambivalence and Authority under a Tree outside Delhi, May 1817," Bhabha discusses further the simultaneous supposition of identity and difference between colonizer and colonized, citing it as a source

of ambivalence in colonial discourse. As he explains in the context of that article, the colonizer explains his or her ability to understand, anticipate, and voice the material and political needs of the colonized by positing their hypothetical sameness while at the same time appealing to their trenchant difference (i.e., the superiority of the colonizer, the inferiority of the colonized) in order to justify the unequal distribution of material wealth and political power. Bhabha articulates this point in a most succinct manner when he writes, "The 'part' (which must be the colonialist foreign body) must be representative of the 'whole' (conquered country), but the right of representation is based on its radical difference" (172).

27. Bhabha, "Of Mimicry and Man," 132.

28. T. Lewis, "Behind the Scenes."

29. Interview with John Hillcoat and Nick Cave.

30. Jeffords, "Big Switch," 197.

31. Shohat, "Gender and Culture of Empire," 63.

32. Kaplan, *Looking for the Other*, 45.

33. Twain first lampooned Cooper's work in the July 1895 issue of *North American Review* and then followed up his attack with an essay edited by Bernard De Voto and titled "Fenimore Cooper's Further Literary Offences." Although Twain is the most famous, he is by no means the only detractor of Cooper's work, for his sentiments have been echoed by many critics in recent history. J. Walker, "Deconstructing an American Myth," 170–86.

34. J. Walker, "Deconstructing an American Myth," 171.

35. Brantlinger, "Forgetting Genocide," 18.

36. A series of articles published in *Screen* soon after the film's release laid the groundwork for the ongoing discussion of this issue. In a special section devoted to *The Piano*, both Stella Bruzzi and Sue Gillett argue for the film's subversive and empowering potential. Bruzzi suggests that in subjectifying Ada's gaze and rendering Stewart's gaze impotent, Campion supplants scopophilia with a sexual economy organized around touch, while Gillett actually adopts Ada's voice in the process of arguing that the film allows for the circulation of an active female desire. In response to these articles, Suzy Gordon contends that attempts to positivize Ada's sexuality lead to a glossing over of the film's violence. In contrast, she highlights instances of Ada's abnegation and employs the concept of auto-eroticism to explore the masochistic implications of asking the spectator to identify with a character at moments of desubjectification (such as her attempted suicide) and via a voice that is unrepresentable (Ada's mind's voice). Bruzzi, "Tempestuous Petticoats"; Gillett, "Lips and Fingers"; Gordon, "'I Clipped Your Wing, That's All.'"

37. The issue of whether the end justifies the means is one that has been much debated within the critical literature surrounding *The Piano*.

38. It is important to note that Campion includes a second ending in addition to the one just described and thereby creates ambivalence around the "happily ever after" finality of conventional romance. Rather than concluding with a shot of Ada and Baines in Nelson, the film ends with a final shot of Ada tied to her piano underwater and floating above it peacefully as she says via voice-over, "At night I think of my piano in its ocean grave. And sometimes of myself floating above it. Down there everything is so still that it lulls me asleep. It is a weird lullaby and so it is. It is mine. There is a silence where hath been no sound. There is a silence where no sound may be in the cold grave under the deep, deep sea." In this final shot, Ada envisions herself not in

the context of a conventional heterosexual pairing but in a place outside of a phallogo-centric social order, thereby presenting a visual coda to the film that problematizes the narrative resolution proposed a shot earlier and calls into question the extent to which Ada's triumphantly normal life in Nelson can rectify the sexual extortion, emotional devastation, and physical violence that have preceded it. She lays claim to the result-ing lullaby by speaking the same words she used earlier in the film in reference to the piano: "It is mine." The fact that she cannot, however, in this case be dispossessed of what she claims as hers suggests that despite its fantastic nature, this hypothetical set-ting, however "weird" or macabre, offers a theoretical refuge from patriarchal law and raises the question of what conditions would allow for women to define their place in the world not relationally but rather autonomously.

39. In doing this, *The Proposition* partakes of a well-established tradition in Austra-lian cinema, which can be traced not only diachronically back to the first bushranger tales, especially those detailing the exploits of the Kelly gang, but also synchronically across genres. A case in point is *Black and White* (Craig Lahiff, 2002), a courtroom drama based on historical events that occurred in South Australia in the late 1950s. Lending the film so much of its dramatic resonance is the way it stacks its opposing sides: on the one hand are the Irish lawyer, David O'Sullivan (Robert Carlyle), and his white female associate, Helen Devaney (Kerry Fox), who have been enlisted to defend Max Stuart (David Ngoombujarra), an Aboriginal man accused of raping and murdering a nine-year-old girl; on the other is the elitist and racist prosecutor (Roderic Chamberlain) whom Devaney at one point describes as "more British than the British."

40. Butler, "Imitation and Gender Insubordination," 314.

41. Jeffords, *Big Switch*, 205.

42. Root, *Cannibal Culture*, 70.

43. Ibid., 42.

44. Corliss, "Dashing Daniel," 66; Kempley, "*The Last of the Mohicans*."

45. Means, "Acting against Racism."

46. Maslin, "Hunks Help to Sell History."

47. Van Lent, "'Her Beautiful Savage,'" 211.

48. Ibid., 216.

49. Marubbio, "Celebrating with *The Last of the Mohicans*," 146.

50. While discussion of this first scene figures prominently in much of the critical literature surrounding *The Last of the Mohicans*, there is no writer who scrutinizes it more closely than Gary Edgerton. In "'A Breed Apart': Hollywood, Racial Stereotyping, and the Promise of Revisionism in *The Last of the Mohicans*," Edgerton argues that the film marginalizes Chingachgook and Uncas and provides as proof a plot segmentation of the first and last scenes.

51. Lehman, *Running Scared*, 16.

52. Bourassa, "Tracking the Dialectic," 728.

53. Dyer, *White*, 146.

54. Brantlinger, "Forgetting Genocide," 25.

55. Dyson, "Return of the Repressed?" 267.

56. According to Dyson, "'Pakeha' is a Maori word, highly contested in translation, referring to those with European ancestry or, more generally, 'outsiders'" ("Return of the Repressed?" 268–69).

57. Neill, "Land without a Past," 145.

58. Dyson, "Return of the Repressed?" 268.

59. Ibid., 273.

60. Jacobs, "Playing Jane Campion's *Piano*," 759.

61. Reid, "Few Black Keys and Maori Tattoos," 115, 113.

62. For a thorough discussion of the various meanings ascribed to, issues raised by, and stakes involved in filmic representations of the male body in general and the penis more specifically, see Lehman, *Running Scared*.

63. Jacobs, "Playing Jane Campion's *Piano*," 761.

64. This argument is most fully developed in Spivak's "Can the Subaltern Speak?" 66–111.

65. Chow, "Where Have All the Natives Gone?" 126.

2. Swan Songs: Speaking the Aboriginal Subject

1. Landry and MacLean, "Subaltern Talk," 289.

2. Spivak, "Questions of Multi-culturalism," 59–60.

3. Collins and Davis, *Australian Cinema after Mabo*, 9.

4. To describe *Dead Man* in such a manner may seem a stretch given the fact that it is the white William Blake (Johnny Depp) rather than his American Indian traveling companion, Nobody (Gary Farmer), who serves as the film's point of focalization; indeed, not only does the film's structure privilege William's journey, foregrounding his experience at every significant turn (the beginning, the end, and those moments in the journey when he and Nobody part company), but its form serves to align the spectator with William by providing a number of point-of-view shots from his perspective. Nonetheless, I would concur with those critics who argue that Nobody is as important as William—if not more—for a number of diverse reasons, including his activity in comparison to his partner's passivity and Farmer's charismatic performance, which serves to produce, in Jonathan Rosenbaum's words, "the most fully realised character in Jarmusch's work" (*Dead Man* 57). On these grounds, the film qualifies for inclusion in the grouping I posit.

5. Spivak, "Three Women's Texts and a Critique of Imperialism," 272.

6. "Shifting the center" is a central theme in Margaret L. Andersen and Patricia Hill Collins's edited volume *Race, Class, and Gender: An Anthology*.

7. Spivak, "Can the Subaltern Speak?" 93.

8. Ibid., 104.

9. Gittings, *Canadian National Cinema*, 212.

10. Russell, *Narrative Mortality*, 7, 2, and 3, respectively.

11. Hibbin, review of *Utu*.

12. Harris, "American Film Genres and Non-American Films," 50.

13. Ibid., 51.

14. Blythe, *Naming the Other*, 248.

15. Ibid., 234.

16. In contrast to Blythe, Harris argues, "this representation of the Maoris contributes to an assertion of a New Zealand national identity mainly by putting the New Zealand–born whites in the position of colonizers in place of the British" ("American Film Genres," 52).

17. Both Murphy and Ward began making films in the late 1970s but came to prominence with their feature-length films from the early 1980s. Murphy's road movie *Good-*

bye Pork Pie (1981) was one of the first local productions to attract a large and enthusiastic following among New Zealand audiences, while Ward's *Vigil* (1984) not only enjoyed local success but also screened in competition at the Cannes Film Festival.

18. Wainright, "Australia North," 30.

19. Ibid., 31.

20. Russell, *Narrative Mortality*, 7, 6.

21. This shot of Avik on the ice echoes another shot that comes much earlier in the film and constructs in a quite pointed manner Avik's powerlessness and mandated compliance to the norms of white culture. In it, an eleven-year-old Avik lies on his bed in the sanatorium, encased in a white body cast that is intended to facilitate his recovery by literally immobilizing him.

22. Russell, *Narrative Mortality*, 23, 25.

23. Pribram, *Cinema and Culture*, 122.

24. Rosenbaum, *Dead Man*, 57.

25. Ibid.

26. Russell, *Narrative Mortality*, 140.

27. Jones, "Acts of God," 25.

28. Hall, "Now You Are a Killer of White Men," 8.

29. Ibid., 8.

30. Nieland, "Graphic Violence," 191.

31. Ibid., 192.

32. Rosenbaum, *Dead Man*, 61.

33. Spivak, "Can the Subaltern Speak?" 75.

34. Sterritt, "Film, Philosophy, and Terrence Malick's *The New World*," B12.

35. See the epilogue in Kracauer, *Theory of Film*.

36. Moreton, "*The Chant of Jimmie Blacksmith*."

37. Cunningham, "Charles Chauvel," under "Jedda," http://wwwmcc.murdoch.edu. au/ReadingRoom/1.1/Cunningham.html.

38. Jennings, *Sites of Difference*, 37.

39. Cunningham, "Charles Chauvel."

40. Rattigan, *Images of Australia*, 88.

41. Rony, *Third Eye*, 49.

42. Lydon, *Eye Contact*, 25.

43. Wynne-Davies, "Rhythm of Difference," 76.

44. Spivak, "Can the Subaltern Speak?" 102.

Part Two: Mapping the Fourth World

1. Churchill, *Fantasies of the Master Race*, 246.

2. Qtd. in Anne Brewster, *Literary Formations*, 3.

3. This is not to say that there are no Indigenous versions of the contact scenario. Tracey Moffatt's *Nice Coloured Girls* (1987) and Zacharias Kunuk and Norman Cohn's *The Journals of Knud Rasmussen* prove otherwise.

4. Leuthold, *Indigenous Aesthetics*, 5.

3. Land Claims: Dramas of Deterritorialization

1. R. Lewis, *Alanis Obomsawin*, xii.

2. Ibid., 93.

3. Bhabha, "World and the Home," 445.

4. Ibid.

5. Ibid., 447–48.

6. Ibid., 450.

7. Steven Cohan and Ina Rae Hark identify *On the Road* as a turning point in the history of the road movie. While prior to its publication, women quite frequently had a place on the road (usually alongside a male companion with whom they were or became romantically involved), after its publication the road movie became a much more gendered genre. Cohan and Hark, *Road Movie Book*, 6.

8. For an interesting discussion of the ways that films like *Thelma and Louise*, *Leaving Normal* (Edward Zwick, 1992), and *Boys on the Side* (Herbert Ross, 1994) serve not only to re-gender the road movie but also to create a new subgenre of women's film, see Shari Roberts, "Western Meets Eastwood," 45–69.

9. Anderson, "Driving the Red Road," 147.

10. Ibid., 150.

11. Langen and Shanley, "Culture Isn't Buckskin Shoes."

12. Eric Gary Anderson explains one of his reasons for designating *Powwow Highway* a cult film thus: "Screening a scene from the film with fifty Pawnee high school students, I was struck by the 'cult' qualities of their response: they anticipated lines of dialog and particular shots, and they publicly shared their inside knowledge of the film" ("Driving the Red Road," 150, n. 1).

13. In an interview with Ray Pride, Eyre remarked, "Anything that the film does is political, I think, because it's about Indians, y'know? And that in itself hasn't been done by Indians" (Pride, review of *Smoke Signals*).

14. Because Alexie worked in such close collaboration with Eyre throughout the duration of the production and was as visible as Eyre, if not more so, in the publicity surrounding the film both prior to and following its release, it is necessary to identify both men as the principle creators of *Smoke Signals*.

15. Ebert, review of *Smoke Signals*.

16. West and West, "Sending Cinematic *Smoke Signals*," 31.

17. Ibid., 37.

18. While the film makes no mention of Suzy's family, the published screenplay contains a scene in which Suzy reveals to Victor that both of her parents are dead. See Alexie, *Smoke Signals*, 78–80.

19. Shannon Louise Roberts, "Spatial Dispersion of Native Americans in Urban Areas."

20. Awad, "Aboriginal Affairs," 54.

21. See, for example, the following articles in Susan Lobo and Kurt Peters's *American Indians and the Urban Experience*: Susan Lobo, "Is Urban a Person or a Place?"; Terry Straus and Debra Valentino, "Retribalization in Urban Indian Communities"; and Angela A. Gonzalez, "Urban (Trans)Formations."

22. "QuickStats about Māori: Location / Te Wāhi"; "Aboriginal Peoples of Canada"; "Australia's Aboriginal and Torres Straits Islander Peoples."

23. Miller, "Telling the Indian Urban," 29.

24. Qtd. in Brunette, "In New Zealand, This Film Beats Jurassic Park," sec. 2:13.

25. Qtd. in Sklar, "Social Realism with Style," 27.

26. Patterson, "Warrior Woman," 72.

27. Thompson, "*Once Were Warriors*," 232.

28. With a premiere at the 1993 Cannes Film Festival and theatrical release in Europe and North America in the fall of that year, *The Piano* preceded *Once Were Warriors* by at least fifteen months. Both *Heavenly Creatures* and *Once Were Warriors* made their debut at the Toronto International Film Festival in 1994, but the former beat the latter into widespread distribution, typically hitting theaters a couple of months earlier.

29. Alleva, "Way Down Under," 16.

30. Pihama, "Repositioning Maori Representation," 191.

31. Lorde coined this term in her chapter "Age, Race, Class, and Sex: Women Redefining Difference," where she defines it as "white, thin, male, young, heterosexual, Christian, and financially secure" (116). In *Sister Outsider*, 114–23.

32. Pihama, "Repositioning Maori Representation," 192. In this instance, *tupuna* can be translated as "ancestors."

33. Smith, "Knocked Around in New Zealand," 387.

34. Ibid., 391.

35. Ibid.

36. A *marae* is a facility used for community gatherings among Maori.

37. Responding to his critics, Tamahori has explained himself in the following manner: "I was never offering up such a naïve and simplistic solution as to say that something as simple as a return to one's cultural and spiritual roots will be the salvation of one's problems in an alienated urban culture. . . . Of course, it's not an answer in itself and can't be because, for a start, it doesn't offer any tangible solutions to economic problems." See Sklar, "Social Realism with Style," 26.

38. Brah, *Cartographies of Diaspora*, 209.

39. Sklar, "Social Realism with Style," 27.

40. Young, "Res Publica."

41. Song lyrics reprinted courtesy of Arbor Records.

42. Lawrence, *"Real" Indians and Others*, 204.

43. *Mana* can be translated as "status."

44. Song lyrics reprinted courtesy of Arbor Records.

4. Speech Acts: Toward a "Postcolonial" Poetics

1. Ihimaera's novel *The Whale Rider* was first published in 1987 by Reed Books in Auckland. The English-language edition that is readily available in North America was published in 2003 by Harcourt Paperbacks.

2. Ka'ai, "*Te Kauae Mārō o Muri-ranga-whenua*," 6.

3. Johnson, "Deconstructing the Pakeha Gaze."

4. Walker, "Representing the Self, Representing the Other," 104.

5. Bordwell, *Narration in the Fiction Film*.

6. Wood, *Native Features*, 16.

7. Walker, "Representing the Self, Representing the Other," 109.

8. Mowitt, *Re-takes*, 63.

9. Ibid., 63–64.

10. Hearne, "Telling and Retelling in the 'Ink of Light,'" 326.

11. Wood, *Native Features*, 172.

12. Given whom Fraser claims to be most influenced by, his deviation from classical form on these counts is not surprising: "My biggest inspirations in terms of film are

Robert Altman, Scorsese, Coppola. People who aren't really keen necessarily on that traditional three act structure, but are really into milieu and people and specific settings." Qtd. in Bisley, "Interrogation of Toa Fraser."

13. While the term "First Nations" is specific to Canada, where it has, since the 1970s, replaced "Indian bands" in popular discourse, I use the term "first national" in a more inclusive manner to evoke the communal ties shared by the First Peoples in any given state.

14. Summerhayes, "Haunting Secrets," 20.

15. Klapproth, *Narrative as Social Practice*, 313.

16. Naficy, *Accented Cinema*.

17. Mimura, "Black Memories," 122.

18. Baron, "Films by Tracey Moffatt," 153.

19. Metz, "Photography and Fetish," 83.

20. Ibid., 87.

21. Dayan, "Tutor-Code of Classical Cinema," 224.

22. Sobchack, *Carnal Thoughts*, 144.

23. Dayan, "Tutor-Code of Classical Cinema," 223–24.

24. Mowitt, *Re-takes*, 89–90.

25. Siebert, "*Atanarjuat* and the Ideological Work of Contemporary Indigenous Filmmaking," 538.

26. Ibid., 534. Those involved in the production of the film frequently used interviews to acknowledge this position as well. A typical instance of such is the following comment, made by Norman Cohn during a conversation with Cynthia Fuchs: "And Zac [Kunuk]: he wakes up in the morning, goes into the office, checks his email, puts on his parka, starts his skidoo, drives out onto the ice and catches a seal. What world is he in? I can't even fathom it. For me, the equivalent is flying back and forth, which is always very weird, like 'Beam me up, Scotty,' like Star Trek travel. But he was born into this world, 9 years old before he got off of that land. And now here we are, in DC, in Paris. And he's completely fluent, in both worlds. To think about 'bilinguality' in essential cultural terms, it creates a kind of intelligence that most people never have a chance to experience." Fuchs, "Interview with Zacharias Kunuk and Norman Cohn."

27. The film's production process is discussed in detail in the companion book: Angilirq et al., *Atanarjuat*.

28. Nornes, *Cinema Babel*, 10.

29. Ibid., 176–77.

30. McCall, "'I Can Only Sing This Song to Someone Who Understands It,'" 27.

31. Matthews, "*Atanarjuat: The Fast Runner*," 36. In contradistinction to the film, the extratextual materials surrounding it are extremely forthcoming. With the companion book and the *Isuma Inuit Studies Reader*, both edited by Gillian Robinson and published by Isuma after the film's release, as well as the *Atanarjuat* Web site, which serves as an archive for interviews, production notes, reviews, plot point synopses, and explanations of Inuit cultural practices, the filmmakers have seemingly pursued a goal of making the film as transparent as possible to its non-Inuit viewers.

32. Krupat, "*Atanarjuat, the Fast Runner* and Its Audiences," 617.

33. Ibid., 610.

34. Siebert, "*Atanarjuat* and the Ideological Work of Contemporary Indigenous Filmmaking," 538.

35. Qtd. in Gunderson, "Zacharias Kunuk," 51.

36. Trinh, *When the Moon Waxes Red*, 74.

37. Ibid., 30.

38. Marks, *Skin of the Film*, 6.

39. Ibid., 162.

40. Ibid., 145.

41. Angilirq et al., *Atanarjuat*, 193.

42. Trinh, *When the Moon Waxes Red*, 59–60; emphasis in original.

43. Etter, "Dialectic to Dialogic," 144.

44. Ibid., 147.

45. Alexie, *Business of Fancydancing*, 7–8.

46. Brill de Ramírez, *Contemporary American Indian Literatures and the Oral Tradition*, 161.

47. Ibid., 156.

48. DiNova, *Spiraling Webs of Relation*, 52.

49. Ibid., 147.

50. Brill de Ramírez, *Contemporary American Indian Literatures and the Oral Tradition*, 192.

51. Ibid., 193.

52. Hearne, "Telling and Retelling in the 'Ink of Light,'" 320.

Afterword

1. Rony, *Third Eye*, 197.

2. Langton's full definition of Aboriginality, already reproduced in the preface, is "a field of intersubjectivity in that it is remade over and over again in a process of dialogue, of imagination, of representation and interpretation." See Langton, "Aboriginal Art and Film," 99–100.

3. Australia announced its endorsement of the declaration on April 3, 2009, four months before this book went to press. On July 30, 2009, Simon Power, New Zealand's minister of justice, stated, "The Prime Minister has indicated that he would like to see New Zealand move to support the declaration, provided that we can protect the unique and advanced framework that has been developed for the resolution of issues related to indigenous issues." See "Order Paper and Questions."

BIBLIOGRAPHY

"Aboriginal Peoples of Canada." *Statistics Canada* 2001 Census. http://www12.statcan. ca/english/census01/Products/Analytic/companion/abor/canada.cfm#6 (accessed August 25, 2009).

Aleiss, Angela. *Making the White Man's Indian: Native Americans and Hollywood Movies.* Westport, CT: Praeger, 2005.

Alemany-Galway, Mary. *A Postmodern Cinema: The Voice of the Other in Canadian Film.* Lanham, MD: Scarecrow Press, 2002.

Alexie, Sherman. *The Business of Fancydancing: The Screenplay.* Brooklyn: Hanging Loose Press, 2003.

———. *Smoke Signals: A Screenplay.* New York: Hyperion, 1998.

Allen, Chadwick. *Blood Narrative: Indigenous Identity in American Indian and Maori Literary and Activist Texts.* Durham, NC: Duke University Press, 2002.

Alleva, Richard. "Way Down Under." *Commonweal* 122, no. 12 (1995): 16–17.

Andersen, Margaret L., and Patricia Hill Collins, eds. *Race, Class, and Gender: An Anthology.* Belmont, CA: Wadsworth Publishing, 2006.

Anderson, Eric Gary. "Driving the Red Road: *Powwow Highway* (1989)." In *Hollywood's Indian: The Portrayal of the Native American in Film,* edited by Peter C. Rollins and John E. O'Connor, 137–52. Lexington: University Press of Kentucky, 1999.

Angilirq, Paul Apak, Zacharias Kunuk, Hervé Paniaq, Pauloosie Qulitalik, Norman Cohn, and Bernard Saladin D'Anglure. *Atanarjuat, The Fast Runner.* Edited by Gillian Robinson. Toronto: Coach House; Igloolik: Isuma, 2002.

"Australia's Aboriginal and Torres Straits Islander Peoples." *Australian Government: Department of Foreign Affairs and Trade.* http://www.dfat.gov.au/facts/indg_ overview.html (accessed May 28, 2008; site now discontinued).

Awad, Michael. "Aboriginal Affairs." *Canadian Architect* 49, no. 5 (May 2004): 53–54.

Baird, Robert. "'Going Indian': *Dances with Wolves* (1990)." In *Hollywood's Indian: The Portrayal of the Native American in Film,* edited by Peter C. Rollins and John E. O'Connor, 153–69. Lexington: University Press of Kentucky, 1998.

Barclay, Barry. "Celebrating Fourth Cinema." *Illusions* 35 (2003): 7–11.

Baron, Cynthia. "Films by Tracey Moffatt: Reclaiming First Australians' Rights, Celebrating Women's Rites." *Women's Studies Quarterly* 30, no. 1–2 (Spring 2002): 151–77.

Bataille, Gretchen M., and Charles L. P. Silet, eds. *The Pretend Indians: Images of Native Americans in the Movies.* Ames: Iowa State University Press, 1980.

Baudry, Jean-Louis. "Ideological Effects of the Basic Cinematic Apparatus." In *Film Theory and Criticism: Introductory Readings,* edited by Gerald Mast, Marshall Cohen, and Leo Braudy, 302–12. New York: Oxford University Press, 1992.

Beard, William, and Jerry White, eds. *North of Everything: English Canadian Cinema since 1980.* Edmonton: University of Alberta Press, 2002.

Bhabha, Homi. "Of Mimicry and Man: The Ambivalence of Colonial Discourse." *October* 28 (Spring 1984): 125–33.

———. "Signs Taken for Wonders: Questions of Ambivalence and Authority under a Tree outside Delhi, May 1817." In *"Race," Writing, and Difference*, edited by Henry Louis Gates Jr., 163–84. Chicago: University of Chicago Press, 1985.

———. "The World and the Home." In *Dangerous Liaisons: Gender, Nation, and Postcolonial Perspectives*, edited by Anne McClintock, Aamir Mufti, and Ella Shohat, 445–55. Minneapolis: University of Minnesota Press, 1997.

Bird, S. Elizabeth, ed. *Dressing in Feathers: The Construction of the Indian in American Popular Culture*. Boulder, CO: Westview Press, 1996.

Bisley, Catherine. "The Interrogation of Toa Fraser: All about Collaboration." *Lumière Reader*, August 30, 2007. http://www.lumiere.net.nz/reader/item/1284 (accessed August 25, 2009).

Bloom, Peter. "Beyond the Western Frontier: Reappropriations of the 'Good Badman' in France, the French Colonies, and Contemporary Algeria." In *Westerns: Films through History*, edited by Janet Walker, 197–218. New York: Routledge, 2001.

Blythe, Martin. *Naming the Other: Images of the Maori in New Zealand Film and Television*. Metuchen, NJ: Scarecrow Press, 1994.

Bordwell, David. *Narration in the Fiction Film*. Madison: University of Wisconsin Press, 1985.

Bourassa, Alan. "Tracking the Dialectic: Theodor Adorno and Michael Mann's *The Last of the Mohicans*." *Canadian Review of Comparative Literature* 23, no. 3 (September 1996): 725–37.

Brah, Avtar. *Cartographies of Diaspora: Contesting Identities*. New York: Routledge, 1996.

Brantlinger, Patrick. "Forgetting Genocide: Or, the Last of *The Last of the Mohicans*." *Cultural Studies* 12, no. 1 (1998): 15–30.

Brewster, Anne. *Literary Formations: Post-colonialism, Nationalism, Globalism*. Victoria: Melbourne University Press, 1995.

Briggs, B. *English-Maori: Maori-English Dictionary*. Auckland: University Press, 1990.

Brill de Ramírez, Susan Berry. *Contemporary American Indian Literatures and the Oral Tradition*. Tucson: University of Arizona Press, 1999.

Brunette, Peter. "In New Zealand, This Film Beats Jurassic Park." *New York Times*, February 19, 1995.

Bruzzi, Stella. "Tempestuous Petticoats: Costume and Desire in *The Piano*." *Screen* 36, no. 3 (Autumn 1995): 257–66.

Butler, Judith. "Imitation and Gender Insubordination." In *The Lesbian and Gay Studies Reader*, edited by Henry Abelove, Michèle Aina Barale, and David M. Halpern, 307–20. New York: Routledge, 1993.

Callister, Paul, Robert Didham, and Deborah Potter. "Ethnic Intermarriage in New Zealand." Working paper, *Statistics New Zealand*, 2005. http://www.stats.govt.nz/NR/rdonlyres/14E5BF11-60CF-4F97-BB3B-CD76BAEAC6CE/0/EthnicIntermarriageinNZ.pdf (accessed January 3, 2007; no longer available).

Canby, Vincent. "A Soldier at One with the Sioux." Review of *Dances with Wolves*, directed by Kevin Costner. *New York Times*, November 9, 1990.

Castillo, Edward D. Review of *Dances with Wolves*, directed by Kevin Costner. *Film Quarterly* 44, no. 4 (1991): 18.

Chow, Rey. *Primitive Passions: Visuality, Sexuality, Ethnography, and Contemporary Chinese Cinema.* New York: Columbia University Press, 1995.

———. "Where Have All the Natives Gone?" In *Displacements: Cultural Identities in Question,* edited by Angelika Bammer, 125–51. Bloomington: University of Indiana Press, 1994.

Churchill, Ward. *Acts of Rebellion: The Ward Churchill Reader.* New York: Routledge, 2003.

———. *Fantasies of the Master Race: Literature, Cinema and the Colonization of American Indians.* Monroe, ME: Common Courage Press, 1992.

Cohan, Steven, and Ina Rae Hark, eds. *The Road Movie Book.* New York: Routledge, 1997.

Collins, Felicity, and Therese Davis. *Australian Cinema after Mabo.* New York: Cambridge University Press, 2004.

Corliss, Richard Corliss. "Dashing Daniel." *Time,* November 9, 1990.

Cresswell, Tim, and Deborah Dixon. *Engaging Film: Geographies of Mobility and Identity.* New York: Rowman and Littlefield, 2002.

Cunningham, Stuart. "Charles Chauvel: The Last Decade." *Continuum* 1, no. 1 (1987): 26–46.

Cutter, Martha J. *Lost and Found in Translation.* Chapel Hill: University of North Carolina Press, 2005.

Dayan, Daniel. "The Tutor-Code of Classical Cinema." In *The Film Studies Reader,* edited by Joanne Hollows, Peter Hutchings, and Mark Jancovich, 219–26. New York: Oxford University Press, 2000.

Denoon, Donald. "Understanding Settler Societies." *Historical Studies* 18, no. 73 (October 1979): 511–27.

DiNova, Joanne R. *Spiraling Webs of Relation: Movements toward an Indigenist Criticism.* New York: Routledge, 2005.

Dyer, Richard. *White.* New York: Routledge, 1997.

Dyson, Lynda. "The Return of the Repressed? Whiteness, Femininity, and Colonialism." *Screen* 36, no. 3 (Autumn 1995): 267–76.

Ebert, Roger. Review of *Smoke Signals,* directed by Chris Eyre. *Chicago Sun Times,* July 1998. http://rogerebert.suntimes.com/apps/pbcs.dll/article?AID=/19980703/REVIEWS/807030303/1023 (accessed August 25, 2009).

Edgerton, Gary. "'A Breed Apart': Hollywood, Racial Stereotyping, and the Promise of Revisionism in *The Last of the Mohicans.*" *Journal of American Culture* 17, no. 1 (Summer 1994): 1–20.

Etter, Carrie. "Dialectic to Dialogic: Negotiating Bicultural Heritage in Sherman Alexie's Sonnets." In *Telling the Stories: Essays on American Indian Literatures and Cultures,* edited by Elizabeth Hoffman Nelson and Malcolm A. Nelson, 143–51. New York: Peter Lang, 2001.

Evans, Julia. "Beyond the Frontier: Possibilities and Precariousness along Australia's Southern Coast." In *Colonial Frontiers: Indigenous-European Encounters in Settler Societies,* edited by Lynette Russell, 151–72. New York: Manchester University Press, 2001.

Ezra, Elizabeth, and Terry Rowden. *Transnational Cinema: A Film Reader.* New York: Routledge, 2006.

Francis, Daniel. *The Imaginary Indian: The Image of the Indian in Canadian Culture.* Vancouver: Arsenal Pulp Press, 1992.

Freebury, Jane. "*Black Robe*: Ideological Cloak and Dagger?" *Australian-Canadian Studies* 10, no. 1 (1992): 119–26.

Fuchs, Cynthia. "Interview with Zacharias Kunuk and Norman Cohn, Director and Producer of *Atanarjuat, the Fast Runner*." *PopMatters*, June 20, 2002. http://www.popmatters.com/film/interviews/kunuk-zacharias.shtml (accessed August 25, 2009).

Gillett, Sue. "Lips and Fingers: Jane Campion's *The Piano*." *Screen* 36, no. 3 (Autumn 1995): 277–87.

Ginsburg, Faye. "Culture/Media: A (Mild) Polemic." *Anthropology Today* 10, no. 2 (April 1994): 5–15.

Gittings, Christopher E. *Canadian National Cinema*. New York: Routledge, 2002.

Gonzalez, Angela A. "Urban (Trans)Formations: Changes in the Meaning and Use of American Indian Identity." In *American Indians and the Urban Experience*, edited by Susan Lobo and Kurt Peters, 169–85. New York: AltaMira Press, 2001.

Gordon, Suzy. "'I Clipped Your Wing, That's All': Auto-eroticism and the Female Spectator in *The Piano* Debate." *Screen* 37, no. 2 (Summer 1996): 193–205.

Griffiths, Alison. *Wondrous Difference: Cinema, Anthropology, and Turn-of-the-Century Visual Culture*. New York: Columbia University Press, 2002.

Griggs, Richard. "An Excerpt from CWIS Occasional Paper #18, The Meaning of 'Nation' and 'State' in the Fourth World." *Center for World Indigenous Studies*. http://cwis.org/fourthw.htm (accessed August 25, 2009).

Gunderson, Sonia. "Zacharias Kunuk: Running Fast to Preserve Inuit Culture." *Inuit Art Quarterly* 19, no. 3–4 (Winter 2004): 48–52.

Guneratne, Anthony R. "Introduction: Rethinking Third Cinema." In *Rethinking Third Cinema*, edited by Anthony R. Guneratne and Wimai Dissanayake, 1–28. New York: Routledge, 2003.

Gunning, Tom. "An Aesthetic of Astonishment: Early Film and the (In)Credulous Spectator." In *Viewing Positions: Ways of Seeing Film*, edited by Linda Williams, 114–33. New Brunswick, NJ: Rutgers University Press, 1995.

———. "The Cinema of Attractions: Early Film, Its Spectator and the Avant-Garde." In *Early Film: Space, Frame, Narrative*, edited by Thomas Elsaesser and Adam Barker, 56–62. London: British Film Institute, 1989.

Hall, Mary Katherine. "Now You Are a Killer of White Men: Jim Jarmusch's *Dead Man* and Traditions of Revisionism in the Western." *Journal of Film and Video* 52, no. 4 (Winter 2001): 3–14.

Harris, Kenneth Marc. "American Film Genres and Non-American Films: A Case Study of *Utu*." *Cinema Journal* 29, no. 2 (Winter 1990): 36–59.

Hearne, Joanna. "Telling and Retelling in the 'Ink of Light': Documentary Cinema, Oral Narratives, and Indigenous Identity." *Screen* 47, no. 3 (Autumn 2006): 307–26.

Hibbin, Sally. Review of *Utu*, directed by Geoff Murphy. *Film and Filming* (1985), qtd. in "*Utu*: Reviews and Notes," *Wellington Film Society*. http://www.filmsociety.wellington.net.nz/db/ screeningdetail.php?id=310 (accessed August 25, 2009).

Hilger, Michael. *From Savage to Nobleman: Images of Native Americans in Film*. Lanham, MD: Scarecrow Press, 1995.

Hoffman, Donald. "Whose Home on the Range? Finding Room for Native Americans, African Americans, and Latino Americans in the Revisionist Westerns." *MELUS* 22, no. 2 (Summer 1997): 45–59.

Howard, Bradley Reed. *Indigenous People and the State: The Struggle for Native Rights.* DeKalb: Northern Illinois University Press, 2003.

Ihimaera, Witi. *The Whale Rider.* Orlando, FL: Harcourt Paperbacks, 2003.

Interview with John Hillcoat and Nick Cave. *Uncut.* N.d. http://www.uncut.co.uk/film/uncut/special_features/8722 (accessed August 25, 2009).

Jacobs, Carol. "Playing Jane Campion's *Piano*: Politically." *MLN* 109 (1994): 757–85.

James, Caryn. "Jesuits vs. Indians, with No Villains." *New York Times,* November 24, 1991.

Janiewski, Dolores. "Gendering, Racializing and Classifying: Settler Colonization in the United States, 1590–1990." In *Unsettling Settler Societies: Articulations of Gender, Race, Ethnicity and Class,* edited by Daiva Stasiulis and Nira Yuval-Davis, 132–60. Thousand Oaks, CA: Sage Publications, 1995.

Jeffords, Susan. "The Big Switch: Hollywood Masculinity in the Nineties." In *Film Theory Goes to the Movies,* edited by Jim Collins, Hilary Radner, and Ava Preacher Collins, 196–208. New York: Routledge, 1993.

Jennings, Karen. *Sites of Difference: Cinematic Representations of Aboriginality and Gender.* South Melbourne, Vic.: Australian Film Institute, 1993.

Johnson, Tracy. "Deconstructing the Pakeha Gaze." *Aotearoa Independent Media Centre,* February 23, 2004. http://indymedia.org.nz/newswire/display/15571/index.php (accessed August 25, 2009).

Jones, Kent. "Acts of God." *Film Comment* 42, no. 2 (March–April 2006): 24–28.

Ka'ai, Tānia M. "*Te Kauae Mārō o Muri-ranga-whenua* (The Jawbone of Muri-ranga-whenua): Globalising Local Indigenous Culture—Māori Leadership, Gender and Cultural Knowledge Transmission as Represented in the Film *Whale Rider*." Special issue, *Portal Journal of Multidisciplinary International Studies* 2, no. 2 (July 2005): 1–15.

Kaplan, E. Ann. *Looking for the Other: Feminism, Film, and the Imperial Gaze.* New York: Routledge, 1997.

Kempley, Rita. "*The Last of the Mohicans.*" *Washington Post,* September 25, 1992.

Kilpatrick, Jacquelyn. *Celluloid Indians: Native Americans and Film.* Lincoln: University of Nebraska Press, 1999.

King, John, Ana M. López, and Manuel Alvarado, eds. *Mediating Two Worlds: Cinematic Encounters in the Americas.* London: BFI, 1993.

Klapproth, Daniéle M. *Narrative as Social Practice: Anglo-Western and Australian Aboriginal Oral Traditions.* New York: Mouton de Gruyter, 2004.

Kopun, Francine. "Toronto's Film Festival Rivals Cannes." *Toronto Star,* September 6, 2007. http://www.thestar.com/Special/FilmFest/article/253723 (accessed August 25, 2009).

Kracauer, Siegfried. *Theory of Film.* Princeton, NJ: Princeton University Press, 1999.

Krupat, Arnold. "*Atanarjuat, the Fast Runner* and Its Audiences." *Critical Inquiry* 33 (Spring 2007): 606–31.

Lake, Randall A. "Argumentation and Self: The Enactment of Identity in *Dances with Wolves*." *Argument and Advocacy* 34, no. 2 (Fall 1997): 66–89.

Landry, Donna, and Gerald MacLean. "Subaltern Talk: Interview with the Editors (1993–94)." In *The Spivak Reader: Selected Works of Gayatri Chakravorty Spivak,* edited by Donna Landry and Gerald McLean, 287–308. New York: Routledge, 1996.

Langen, Toby, and Kathryn Shanley. "Culture Isn't Buckskin Shoes: A Conversation around *Powwow Highway*." *Studies in American Indian Literatures* 3, no. 3 (1991): 23–29.

Langton, Marcia. "Aboriginal Art and Film: The Politics of Representation." *Race and Class* 35, no. 4 (1994): 89–106.

Lawrence, Bonita. *"Real" Indians and Others: Mixed Blood Urban Native Peoples and Indigenous Nationhood*. Lincoln: University of Nebraska Press, 2004.

Lehman, Peter. *Running Scared: Masculinity and the Representation of the Male Body*. Philadelphia: Temple University Press, 1993.

Leuthold, Steven. *Indigenous Aesthetics: Native Art, Media, and Identity*. Austin: University of Texas Press, 1998.

Lewis, Glen. *Australian Movies and the American Dream*. New York: Praeger, 1987.

Lewis, Randolph. *Alanis Obomsawin: The Vision of a Native Filmmaker*. Lincoln: University of Nebraska Press, 2006.

Lewis, Tom E. "Behind the Scenes: Characters." *The Proposition*, DVD. Directed by John Hillcoat, 2005. Toronto: Capri Releasing and Maple Pictures, 2006.

Lobo, Susan. "Is Urban a Person or a Place? Characteristics of Urban Indian Country." In *American Indians and the Urban Experience*, edited by Susan Lobo and Kurt Peters, 73–84. New York: AltaMira Press, 2001.

Lobo, Susan, and Kurt Peters, eds. *American Indians and the Urban Experience*. New York: AltaMira Press, 2001.

Lorde, Audre. *Sister Outsider: Essays and Speeches*. Trumansburg, NY: Crossing Press, 1984.

Lydon, Jane. *Eye Contact: Photographing Indigenous Australians*. Durham, NC: Duke University Press, 2005.

Maaka, Roger, and Augie Fleras. *The Politics of Indigeneity: Challenging the State in Canada and Aotearoa New Zealand*. Dunedin, New Zealand: University of Otago Press, 2005.

MacKenzie, Scott. "National Identity, Canadian Cinema, and Multiculturalism." *Canadian Aesthetics Journal/Revue canadienne d'esthétique* 4 (1999). http://www.uqtr.uquebec.ca/AE/vol_4/scott.htm (accessed August 25, 2009).

Maddock, Kenneth, ed. *Identity, Land and Liberty: Studies in the Fourth World*. Nijmegen, Holland: Centre for Pacific Studies, Katholieke Universiteit Nijmegen, Instituut voor Culturele en Sociale Antropologie, 1991.

Manuel, George, and Michael Posluns. *The Fourth World: An Indian Reality*. Don Mills, ON: Collier-Macmillan Canada, 1974.

Marks, Laura U. *The Skin of the Film: Intercultural Cinema, Embodiment, and the Senses*. Durham, NC: Duke University Press, 2000.

Martin, Michael, ed. *New Latin American Cinema: Theory, Practices and Transcontinental Articulations*. New York: Columbia University Press, 1995.

Marubbio, M. Elise. "Celebrating with *The Last of the Mohicans*: The Columbus Quintenary and Neocolonialism in Hollywood Film." *Journal of American and Comparative Cultures* 25, no. 1–2 (Spring–Summer 2002): 139–54.

Maslin, Janet. "Hunks Help to Sell History." *New York Times*, October 18, 1992.

Matthews, Peter. "*Atanarjuat: The Fast Runner*." *Sight and Sound* 12, no. 3 (March 2002): 35–36.

McCall, Sophie. "'I Can Only Sing This Song to Someone Who Understands It': Community Filmmaking and the Politics of Partial Translation in *Atanarjuat, The Fast Runner.*" *Essays on Canadian Writing* 83 (Fall 2004): 19–46.

McClintock, Anne. *Imperial Leather: Race, Gender, and Sexuality in the Colonial Context.* New York: Routledge, 1995.

Means, Russell. "Acting against Racism." *EW.com*, October 23, 1992. http://www.ew.com/ew/article/0,,312084,00.html (accessed August 25, 2009).

Metz, Christian. "Photography and Fetish." *October* 34 (Autumn 1985): 81–90.

———. "Story/Discourse (A Note on Two Kinds of Voyeurism)." In *Movies and Methods*, vol. 2, edited by Bill Nichols, 543–49. Berkeley: University of California Press, 1985.

Michaels, Eric. *Bad Aboriginal Art: Tradition, Media, and Technological Horizons.* Minneapolis: University of Minnesota Press, 1994.

Miller, Carol. "Telling the Indian Urban: Representations in American Indian Fiction." In *American Indians and the Urban Experience*, edited by Susan Lobo and Kurt Peters, 29–45. New York: AltaMira Press, 2001.

Mimura, Glen Masato. "Black Memories: Allegorizing the Colonial Encounter in Tracey Moffatt's *beDevil* (1993)." *Quarterly Review of Film and Video* 20 (2003): 111–23.

Mita, Merata. "The Soul and the Image." In *Film in Aotearoa New Zealand*, edited by Jonathan Dennis and Jan Bieringa, 36–54. Wellington: Victoria University Press, 1996.

Moreton, Romaine. "*The Chant of Jimmie Blacksmith.*" *Australian Screen*, 2007–8. http://australianscreen.com.au/titles/chant-jimmie-blacksmith/ (accessed August 25, 2009).

Mowitt, John. *Re-takes: Postcoloniality and Foreign Film Languages.* Minneapolis: University of Minnesota Press, 2005.

Mulvey, Laura. "Visual Pleasure and Narrative Cinema." In *Issues in Feminist Film Criticism*, edited by Patricia Erens, 28–40. Bloomington: Indiana University Press, 1991.

Naficy, Hamid. *An Accented Cinema: Exilic and Diasporic Filmmaking.* Princeton, NJ: Princeton University Press, 2001.

———, ed. *Home, Exile, Homeland: Film, Media, and the Politics of Place.* New York: Routledge, 1999.

Neill, Anna. "A Land without a Past: Dreamtime and Nation in *The Piano.*" In *Piano Lessons: Approaches to "The Piano,"* edited by Felicity Coombs and Suzanne Gemmell, 136–47. London: John Libbey, 1999.

Nieland, Justus. "Graphic Violence: Native Americans and the Western Archive in *Dead Man.*" Special issue, *CR: The New Centennial Review* 2, no. 1 (2001): 169–201.

Nornes, Abé Mark. *Cinema Babel: Translating Global Cinema.* Minneapolis: University of Minnesota Press, 2007.

Oksiloff, Assenka. *Picturing the Primitive: Visual Culture, Ethnography, and Early German Cinema.* New York: Palgrave, 2001.

"Order Paper and Questions: Questions for Oral Answer: 8. Declaration on the Rights of Indigenous Peoples—Recognition of Maori Rights." *New Zealand Parliament/Pāremata Aotearoa*, July 30, 2009. http://www.parliament.nz/en-NZ/

PB/Business/QOA/a/5/0/49HansQ_20090730_00000008-8-Declaration-on-the-Rights-of-Indigenous.htm (accessed August 25, 2009).

O'Regan, Tom. *Australian National Cinema*. New York: Routledge, 1996.

Patterson, Alex. "Warrior Woman." *Village Voice*, February 28, 1995.

Pearson, David. *The Politics of Ethnicity in Settler Societies: States of Unease*. New York: Palgrave, 2001.

Peters, John Durham. "Exile, Nomadism, and Diaspora: The Stakes of Mobility in the Western Canon." In *Home, Exile, Homeland: Film, Media, and the Politics of Place*, edited by Hamid Naficy, 17–41. New York: Routledge, 1999.

Pietersen, Lieuwe. *Taalsociologie*. Groningen, Holland: Tjeenk Willink, 1976.

Pihama, Leonie. "Repositioning Maori Representation: Contextualizing *Once Were Warriors*." In *Film in Aotearoa New Zealand*, edited by Jonathan Dennis and Jan Bieringa, 191–94. Wellington: Victoria University Press, 1996.

Pribram, Deidre. *Cinema and Culture: Independent Film in the United States, 1980–2001*. New York: Peter Lang, 2002.

Pride, Ray. Review of *Smoke Signals*, directed by Chris Eyre. *New City Net*, July 6, 1998. Film Vault Web site. http://filmvault.com/filmvault/chicago/s/smokesignals1.html (accessed August 25, 2009).

"QuickStats about Māori: Location/Te Wāhi." *Statistics New Zealand* 2006 Census. http://www.stats.govt.nz/Census/2006CensusHomePage/QuickStats/quickstats-about-a-subject/maori/location-te-wahi.aspx (accessed November 29, 2009).

Rafferty, Terrence. "True Believers." Review of *Black Robe*, directed by Bruce Beresford, and *Homicide*, directed by David Mamet. *New Yorker*, November 18, 1991.

Rattigan, Neil. *Images of Australia: 100 Films of the New Australian Cinema*. Dallas: Southern Methodist University Press, 1991.

Reid, Mark A. "A Few Black Keys and Maori Tattoos: Re-reading Jane Campion's *The Piano* in PostNegritude Time." *Quarterly Review of Film and Video* 17, no. 2 (2000): 107–16.

Roberts, Shannon Louise. "The Spatial Dispersion of Native Americans in Urban Areas: Why Native Americans Diverge from Traditional Ethnic Patterns of Clustering and Segregation." Master's thesis, Columbia University, 2004. Web site affiliated with Columbia University's Urban Planning Program (accessed May 28, 2008; site now discontinued).

Roberts, Shari. "Western Meets Eastwood: Genre and Gender on the Road." In *The Road Movie Book*, edited by Steven Cohan and Ina Rae Hark, 45–69. New York: Routledge, 1997.

Robinson, Gillian, ed. *Isuma Inuit Studies Reader*. Montreal: Isuma Distribution International, 2004.

Roeg, Nicolas, and Jenny Agutter. "Commentary." *Walkabout*, DVD. Directed by Nicolas Roeg, 1971. New York: Criterion Collection DVD, 1998.

Rollins, Peter C., and John E. O'Connor, eds. *Hollywood's Indian: The Portrayal of the Native American in Film*. Lexington: University Press of Kentucky, 1998.

Rony, Fatimah Tobing. *The Third Eye: Race, Cinema, and Ethnographic Spectacle*. Durham, NC: Duke University Press, 1996.

Root, Deborah. *Cannibal Culture: Art, Appropriation, and the Commodification of Difference*. Boulder, CO: Westview Press, 1996.

Rosenbaum, Jonathan. *Dead Man*. London: BFI Publishing, 2000.

Routt, William D. "More Australian than Aristotelian: The Australian Bushranger Film, 1904–1914." *Senses of Cinema* 18 (January–February 2002). http://www.archive.sensesofcinema.com/contents/01/18/oz_western.html (accessed August 25, 2009).

Rushing, W. Jackson, III, ed. *Native American Art in the Twentieth Century*. New York: Routledge, 1999.

Russell, Catherine. *Narrative Mortality: Death, Closure, and New Wave Cinemas*. Minneapolis: University of Minnesota Press, 1995.

Shohat, Ella. "Gender and Culture of Empire: Toward a Feminist Ethnography of the Cinema." *Quarterly Review of Film and Video* 13, no. 1–3 (1991): 45–84.

Siebert, Monika. "*Atanarjuat* and the Ideological Work of Contemporary Indigenous Filmmaking." *Public Culture* 18, no. 3 (2006): 531–50.

Singer, Beverly. *Wiping the War Paint off the Lens: Native American Film and Video*. Minneapolis: University of Minnesota Press, 2001.

Sissons, Jeffrey. "Maori Tribalism and Post-settler Nationhood in New Zealand." *Oceania* 75, no. 1 (2004): 19–31.

Sklar, Robert. "Social Realism with Style." *Cineaste* 21, no. 3 (July 1995): 25–27.

Smith, Amanda, and Thomas Loe. "Mythic Descent in *Dances with Wolves*." *Literature/Film Quarterly* 20, no. 3 (1992): 199–204.

Smith, Jane. "Knocked Around in New Zealand: Postcolonialism Goes to the Movies." In *Mythologies of Violence in Postmodern Media*, edited by Christopher Sharrett, 381–96. Detroit: Wayne State University Press, 1999.

Sobchack, Vivian. *Carnal Thoughts: Embodiment and Moving Image Culture*. Berkeley: University of California Press, 2004.

Spivak, Gayatri Chakravorty. "Can the Subaltern Speak?" In *Colonial Discourse and Postcolonial Theory: A Reader*, edited by Patrick Williams and Laura Chrisman, 66–111. New York: Columbia University Press, 1994.

———. "Questions of Multi-culturalism." Interview by Sneja Gunew. In *The Post-Colonial Critic: Interviews, Strategies, Dialogues*, edited by Sarah Harasym, 59–66. New York: Routledge, 1990.

———. "Three Women's Texts and a Critique of Imperialism." In *"Race," Writing, and Difference*, edited by Henry Louis Gates Jr., 262–80. Chicago: University of Chicago Press, 1985.

Stam, Robert, and Ella Shohat. *Unthinking Eurocentrism: Multiculturalism and the Media*. New York: Routledge, 1994.

Stam, Robert, and Louise Spence. "Colonialism, Racism, and Representation." *Screen* 24, no. 2 (March–April 1983): 2–20.

Stasiulis, Daiva, and Nira Yuval-Davis. "Introduction: Beyond Dichotomies—Gender, Race, Ethnicity, and Class in Settler Societies." In *Unsettling Settler Societies: Articulations of Gender, Race, Ethnicity and Class*, edited by Daiva Stasiulis and Nira Yuval-Davis, 1–38. Thousand Oaks, CA: Sage Publications, 1995.

Sterritt, David. "Film, Philosophy, and Terrence Malick's *The New World*." *Chronicle of Higher Education*, January 6, 2006.

Stewart-Harawira, Makere. *The New Imperial Order: Indigenous Responses to Colonialism*. New York: Zed Books, 2005.

Straus, Terry, and Debra Valentino. "Retribalization in Urban Indian Communities." In *American Indians and the Urban Experience*, edited by Susan Lobo and Kurt Peters, 85–94. New York: AltaMira Press, 2001.

Summerhayes, Catherine. "Haunting Secrets: Tracey Moffatt's *beDevil*." *Film Quarterly* 58, no. 1 (Fall 2004): 14–24.

Thomas, Bob. "*Black Robe* Draws Fire from U.S. Natives." *Globe and Mail,* December 21, 1991.

Thompson, Kirsten Moana. "*Once Were Warriors*: New Zealand's First Indigenous Blockbuster." In *Movie Blockbusters*, edited by Julian Stringer, 230–41. New York: Routledge, 2003.

Trinh Minh-ha. *When the Moon Waxes Red: Representation, Gender, and Cultural Politics.* New York: Routledge, 1991.

Turner, Terence. "Defiant Images: The Kayapo Appropriation of Video." *Anthropology Today* 8, no. 6 (December 1992): 5–16.

Twain, Mark. "Fenimore Cooper's Further Literary Offences." *New England Quarterly* 19 (September 1946): 291–301.

———. "Fenimore Cooper's Literary Offences." *North American Review* 161 (July 1895): 1–12.

Van Lent, Peter. "'Her Beautiful Savage': The Current Sexual Image of the Native American Male." In *Dressing in Feathers: The Construction of the Indian in American Popular Culture*, edited by S. Elizabeth Bird, 211–27. Boulder, CO: Westview Press, 1996.

Van Meijl, Toon. "Indigenous People in a Fourth World Perspective: Some Theoretical Reflections Illustrated with Examples from the New Zealand Maori." In *Identity, Land and Liberty: Studies in the Fourth World*, edited by Kenneth Maddock, 19–48. Nijmegen, Holland: Centre for Pacific Studies, Katholieke Universiteit Nijmegen, Instituut voor Culturele en Sociale Antropologie, 1991.

Wainright, J. A. "Australia North: The Gaze from Above/Down Under in *Map of the Human Heart*." *Australian-Canadian Studies* 12, no. 2 (1994): 29–38.

Walker, Deborah. "Representing the Self, Representing the Other: Ethics and Ethnicity in Contemporary Cinema of Aotearoa." *International Yearbook of Aesthetics* 10 (2006): 104–11.

Walker, Jeffrey. "Deconstructing an American Myth: *The Last of the Mohicans* (1992)." In *Hollywood's Indian: The Portrayal of the Native American in Film*, edited by Peter C. Rollins and John E. O'Connor, 170–86. Lexington: University Press of Kentucky, 1998.

West, Dennis, and Joan M. West. "Sending Cinematic Smoke Signals: An Interview with Sherman Alexie." *Cineaste* 23, no. 4 (1998): 28–32.

White, Jerry, ed. *The Cinema of Canada.* London: Wallflower Press, 2006.

Wiegman, Robyn. *American Anatomies: Theorizing Race and Gender.* Durham, NC: Duke University Press, 1995.

Wolski, Nathan. "All's Not Quiet on the Western Front—Rethinking Resistance and Frontiers in Aboriginal Historiography." In *Colonial Frontiers: Indigenous-European Encounters in Settler Societies*, edited by Lynette Russell, 216–36. New York: Manchester University Press, 2001.

Wood, Houston. *Native Features: Indigenous Films from around the World.* New York: Continuum, 2008.

Woolf, Virginia. *A Room of One's Own.* New York: Harvest/Harcourt Brace Jovanovich, 1989.

Worth, Sol, and John Adair. *Through Navajo Eyes: An Exploration in Film Communication and Anthropology*. Bloomington: University of Indiana Press, 1972.

Wynne-Davies, Marion. "The Rhythm of Difference: The Language of Silence in *The Chant of Jimmie Blacksmith* and *The Piano*." In *Post-Colonial Literatures: Expanding the Canon*, edited by Deborah L. Madsen, 58–71. London: Pluto Press, 1999.

Young, Jeremy. "Res Publica: Indigenous Res Rappers Like Hellnback and War Party Blend Storytelling and Hip Hop, Rhyming about Community, Impoverishment, and Social Deprivation." *McGill Daily*, November 13, 2006. http://www.mcgill-daily.com/view.php?aid=5594 (accessed August 25, 2009).

INDEX

Page numbers in italics denote illustrations.

Castillo, Edward, 37

Celluloid Indians: Native Americans and Film (Kilpatrick), 17

Chant of Jimmie Blacksmith, The (Keneally), 52, 108

Chant of Jimmie Blacksmith, The (Schepisi), 52, 79, 102–4, 108, 186

Chauvel, Charles, 79, 102–4, 105, 187

Chow, Rey, 31, 32, 33, 73–74

Churchill, Ward, 10–11, 35–36, 111, 114

cinema: accented, 6–9, 159; classical vs. new wave, 81, 89; as collaborative medium, xiii, 176–77, 181–82; cult, 199n12; ethnographic, 3–4, 21, 105–6, 167–69, 171, 181; first national, 166, 201n13; Fourth, xi–xv, 181, 191n3; independent, 23–24, 90–91; intercultural, 169–70; of the interval, 169–71; material flows, 2–3, 6–7; as part of natural world, 98; of postcolonial poetics, 154, 155, 162, 164; Third, xiv, 155. *See also* transnational cinema

Cinema of Canada, The (White), 25

cinematography: in *Atanarjuat*, 169; in *beDevil*, 162; in *Business of Fancydancing*, 177–79; in *Dead Man*, 95–97; in *Last of the Mohicans*, 64–66; in *Map of the Human Heart*, 87–89; in *New World*, 95–97; in *Once Were Warriors*, 149; in *Powwow Highway*, 121, 123, 124–25; in *Stryker*, 148

City Slickers (Underwood), 55

Cohn, Norman, xii–xiii, 27, 166, 168, 182, 187, 201n26

Collins, Felicity, 77–78

Collins, Patricia Hill, 79

colonial discourse: ambivalence of, 47, 194–95n26; production of the other in, 4, 9, 31, 47, 48–49, 73–74, 78–79, 94, 106, 107, 178

colonialism: anthropology and, 3; cinema and, xv, 1–5, 17–18, 20–22, 55, 68; British, 18, 46, 60–61; French, 19; frontier concept, 43–44; legacy of, 7–9, 111–12, 151–52 (*see also* deterritorialization); mimicry/mockery of, 47, 50–51, 52, 69–73, 74; omission of, from films, 134,

151–52; settler, 18–20; violence and, 47–48; women's position in, 55, 58–59

Conistan Story, 15

contact narratives, 21–22, 25–26, 29–33; Aboriginality as sign in, 61–75; contemporary, 32–33, 43–45; frontier culture in, 43–44; interest of Aboriginal filmmakers in, 114, 198n3; vanishing Natives in, 37, 43–44, 57, 67–69, 80–81, 84, 94, 111. *See also individual films*

conversive communication, 174–75, 177

Cooper, James Fenimore, 56, 67

Cooper, Merian, 4, 192n7

Costner, Kevin, xvi, 34–40, 111

costuming, 37, 70

Coeur d'Alene reservation, 119, 127–28

Cousineau, Marie-Hélène, 182

Craig, Molly, 76–77

credit sequences, 47–48, 53, 166

Crocodile Dundee (Faiman), 51

"Culture/Media: A (Mild) Polemic" (Ginsburg), xv–xvi

Cunningham, Stuart, 103–4

Curtis, Edward, 168

Dances with Wolves (Costner), xvi, 34–40, 43–44, 81, 129, 186; archival imperative fueling, 37, 111; characterization of tribes in, 37–38, 62–63; critical responses to, 35–36, 38–39, 43; Eurocentrism in, 39–40; two versions of, 194n13

Daves, Delmer, 39

Davis, Therese, 77–78

Dayan, Daniel, 154, 161

Day-Lewis, Daniel, 63–64, 67

Days of Heaven (Malick), 97

Dead Man (Jarmusch), 25, 78, 91–92, 93–97, 95, 102, 186, 197n4; relationship to Western genre, 91–92, 93–94

death: of Aboriginal characters, 43, 80–85, 88–89, 92 (*see also* contact narratives: vanishing Natives in); *sati*, 79–80

decolonization, 5, 32

deconstruction, 174–75; of identity, 9, 26–27, 61, 91

Deep inside Clint Star (Alberta), 117, 186

defamiliarization, 51, 70–71, 98–99

Corinn Columpar is an associate professor of cinema studies and English at the University of Toronto, where she teaches courses on film theory, various countercinematic traditions (especially Aboriginal, feminist, and "independent"), women's cultural production, and corporeality and representation. Her work has appeared in a wide variety of anthologies and journals, including *Women's Studies Quarterly*, *refractory*, and *Quarterly Review of Film and Video*, and she is a coeditor of the collection *There She Goes: Feminist Filmmaking and Beyond* (2009).